CW01500924

"I am fascinated by the story—certainly a very wonderful one of courage and determination—showing us what amazing people of all ages the Congolese are! Well done to the author, Joe Diamany, a real shining light bringing such a clear narrative to us, the readers."

Dr Rosa A Hubbard-Ford DPsych (Prof),
Harley St, London

WATER

A Life-saving Investment

JOE DIAMANY

To the victims!

CONTENTS

1. Introduction 1

2. Partners 7

3. In the Congo 23

4. The Victims 73

5. Bureaucracy 127

6. Ground-breaking 163

7. Courage 209

8. Success Stories 319

9. Next 411

10. Afterword 421

1

INTRODUCTION

As I write this introduction, in August of 2021, the world has been dealing with the Covid-19 pandemic for a year and a half. Life has been difficult in new ways for most of us, but we have also seen the wonders that can be achieved when we work together on a shared problem. It is my hope that, in writing this book, I will inspire people to join hands to overcome life's challenges, and in particular, the calamity of being without drinkable water in the Democratic Republic of the Congo (herein *the Congo*) and across the planet. It is inexcusable that, in this modern-day, many suffer and die for not having access to clean water.

To address this subject, I feel I should introduce myself. My name is Joe Diamany. I was born and bred in the Congo. My father (Raphaël) lost both his parents whilst a toddler but went on to be a lawyer widely respected by all who knew him. He instilled in me a great respect for the law and the institutions. My mother (Marie-Jeanne) was given into marriage at age 14, by her sister who had brought her up, but she never let her difficult start in life hold her back. She stayed home with seven children and was very active in our neighbourhood, eventually becoming a family and marriage counsellor, helping families in crisis, many of whom went on to be lifelong friends of the family. My parents taught me the need to share and live in harmony with others—lessons I have carried throughout my life.

I qualified as a teacher at 20 and got my first job at a private school not too far from my family home. I was brought in to cover maternity leave, being warned that the class I would take was the unruliest of the entire establishment. Entering the classroom, I was hardly surprised this should be so as I counted 74 children crammed in a room not even big enough for the government's regulated limit of 30. But within a week, the headmaster noticed a huge improvement in the behaviour of *my* kids and did not hesitate to ask how this had come about.

"I treated them like adults," I replied.

Having newly graduated, Jean-Jacques Rousseau's concepts and those of other pedagogy and developmental psychology thinkers were still fresh in my head. Hence, I first removed from the classroom the metre-long stick that was used to discipline the children. My training taught me to educate a child without the use of force.

A month after the end of my contract, both the headmaster and the owner visited Mum.

"You have brought up a nice young man," the former said.

Mum was chuffed.

So, when he asked her for permission to employ me permanently, she granted it. In this, he demonstrated that he understood the tradition of the respect to be paid to parents, for he and the law of the land considered me not fully an adult until 21. In taking up this employment, I insisted that my class be no larger than 30 pupils.

"What are you going to do with the extra 44?" the owner asked.

I worked with the school, the parents, and a local property developer to arrange for extra buildings on the same street to triple the number of classrooms because the other initial 11 were like mine in size. Through this undertaking, I got a sense of what can be achieved when a community comes together to problem-solve.

Brimming with confidence after this experience, I went on to further my studies in the United Kingdom, taking business and finance instead. I later joined various Euro-Asian consortiums, frequently travelling to four continents, including 16 Chinese cities and Hong Kong, for a good 12 years. My role was to establish and maintain long-term mineral supply contracts, overseeing transactional operations at the Jin Mao Tower and later at the China Diamond Exchange Centre, both in Shanghai's Pudong New Area. These deals involved millions of dollars a year but not a single million mine.

In this trade, China Customs acknowledged me as the first person to ever bring in a consignment straight from the Congo. All other Congolese minerals were transited by other countries, where they were given new certificates of origin, causing the Congo to be on the losing side as new, truthful, and more profitable valuations were generated.

Because of helping a struggling minerals processing factory in a Shandong province town save employment, the locals, making me one of theirs, granted me a piece of land in a nearby village to build myself a house and live in their midst.

I keep close ties with the Congo and always long to find a way to improve things there. This book is the story of how I made a portion of this dream happen with the right partners.

2

PARTNERS

Laura

In May of 1994, I attended *Uni* in London while also working as a translator and interpreter for government agencies and various businesses in the area. Always juggling the work that paid my bills and the learning I knew would improve my future, I often missed classes or attended half-days. One such afternoon, I hurried into class a tad late and headed for a place at the back. However, one of my fellow students moved her bag, clearing the chair beside her for me. I was reluctant, but with everyone watching, I had little choice but to take the seat.

Laura was an attractive girl and the only other African in the class, so it would have been natural for us to strike up a friendship, but I was shy and had so far avoided her. This was made easier because I rarely had time to mingle with others due to work obligations. She had, on this day, obviously decided to take matters into her own hands.

Teaching was Mohammed, an Egyptian who had come to the UK 25 years previously. He had a unique flair for presentation, and we were all hooked on his lecture as he was covering *Global Customers' Cultural Differences*. He told of a hotel chain that lost a lot of business in the Maghreb after its European hostesses, on a working holiday programme, appeared in swimsuits as part of the entertainment. Guests were offended by what they considered immodest dressing—a practice that went against their religion. This *faux pas* cost the company huge amounts of money and three years to rebuild its reputation, a situation which could have been avoided had they paid more attention to the cultural needs of their customers.

Mohammed had us discuss culture clashes. It led to me sharing an embarrassing incident of my own. Once, when staying the weekend with my then-girlfriend and her family, I had attempted to feed her with a fork with them present, only for her to respond:

"Not in this house!"

Her family was very religious and considered this an inappropriate level of affection. My colleagues all found my story hilarious, but back then, I was mortified and spent the rest of the weekend desperate to leave. On the other hand, she never understood why she would not be free to sunbathe in her bikini in front of my family if I ever took her to visit the Congo. There, swimwear was nothing but underwear, although, in all fairness, the lack of swimming pools and beaches made it unlikely that people would adopt this attire.

The class was further divided, with the all-Brits throwing arrows in the direction of those with non-UK-born families, who in turn staunchly fought their corner.

"But I have also seen the reverse," I said.

I took them to Swaziland (now Eswatini), where females danced with nothing covering their chests in front of children and male adults.

"I attended an international school near Mbabane for a year," Laura interrupted.

"Waterford?"

"How do you know that?"

"Seven months and 16 days of my life down the road in Manzini," I answered.

"Wow! I lived there with my maternal uncle and his family. He was a diplomat."

Everyone looked on, stunned by the coincidence. The discussion moved on to how images, word choice, greetings, expressing gratitude, addressing customers by their first names or surnames, and dress code, among other things, impacted especially international corporations.

With the class going quiet, Laura told me about herself. She was born in Montreal and lived there until age 10, when her dad, Elie, returned to his native Gabon to take over his family's business, and her mum decided not to go. Her new husband relocated them to San Francisco. With a rich father, she was afforded a life filled with travels, which gave her a love of cultures.

At the end of Mohammed's hour, she grabbed my wrist before I could dash out, inviting me out for a city-walkabout that Saturday, which was two days away. I considered putting her off. I could have spent that time working and getting ahead on my bills. But I decided to join her. Unbeknown to us, it was the beginning of a close friendship that would never end.

The Call

Laura moved to Hong Kong for her Master of Business Administration after London and married her high school sweetheart, Alex, from Sacramento, whom I had met twice in London when he visited her. They had two children. She wrote me long letters at least twice a year, filling me in on her life. But in early 2007, I received a life-changing call from her.

"It is time for you and me to work together, Joe!"

She had learnt a lot in East Asia and made vital connections. By the time of this call, she was a co-proprietor in three factories, with annual profits of $2 million plus. On the other hand, I had nothing to show for my time but a computer full of business plans and an handful of less-rewarding contracts.

The project I had been counting on for a year had abruptly ended the night before. A Mexican consortium and I had partnered to establish a budget airline in the Congo. I had approached them because of being sick and tired of the aviation fatalities there. The airplanes that operated there were nicknamed *cercueils volants* (flying coffins) because of their lack of maintenance. Of over 150 airlines registered, less than 10 were in service, none owning more than five aircraft, and zero under 40 years old. They were in such a poor state that not even one had permission to fly over the European Union airspace. Through a Chicago-based broker, I had secured four 1984 B732 Adv beauties that were coming out of service, but the Authority's refusal to issue one extra licence saw all the hard work go to waste.

"Let go, Joe!" Laura said. "The paint has peeled off the wall, and you know it."

She had farming and food processing in mind. The Congo had the fourth largest population in Africa and vast arable land, yet children died of malnutrition and hunger.

"I have a modest $5 million budget," she added. "Fear not!"

Forty percent of this sum was Elie's participation. He likewise favoured my country ahead of his because, despite having similar problems, the population on his side was 20 times lesser. He knew they could return to help Gabon comfortably if they could achieve a healthier return on their investment in the Congo.

She asked that I find people with social development at heart and the expertise to help my nation do better for itself, and I looked no further than my long-standing friends.

Tino

A nine-hour transit at the Madrid airport, travelling home from a holiday in Palma, Spain, in August 1996, found me negotiating with a rather hard floor for some sleep. A fellow traveller offered the use of his sleeping bag.

"My name is Tino," he said. "Short for Faustino."

"Joe! Short for Joseph."

He burst into laughter, knowing I had caught his joke.

"Best folded in two, inwardly and top to bottom," he advised. "I doubt the inside is still hygienic for another person."

Before this act of kindness, Tino had his head buried in a book. He went back to it while I napped for about an hour. Waking up, I took the second seat to his right, leaving a space between us so I would not be tempted to peek at what he was reading.

I took a book out of my own carry-on luggage. The bookmark was where I had highlighted a passage on the difficulties of facing the unknown regularly, if not all the time, as an entrepreneur. He noticed and asked about my interest in the subject. I told him of my desire to set up one day. We shared a dream. But he worried that he had no idea how to start, and I lifted his spirits, admitting that neither did I nor anybody until they had made it.

His openness allowed me into his past, while my verbosity was his ticket into my future. We spent the next five hours bonding. He had left Peru for the first time at age 20 for Uni. His dad believed that the best education would give his son a competitive advantage in life. Through farming, he paid for his four-year degree in Michigan yearly—an enormous sacrifice that saw the whole family go without some necessities.

When I met him, a former Uni friend had gotten him work with a water drilling company in Andalusia, but he failed to secure a work permit within three months of being on the job. This trip would be a holiday, for the cash-in-hand wages only helped break even from what he had spent to get there. He had no faith in life back home. I brushed off his pessimism that good fortune could come from anywhere. Besides, the grim truth of the Congo was no better than in his country. But I needed to learn more about where he was coming from.

Water accessibility in Peru was dreadful, and Tino grew up affected. He considered learning to tackle this shortage in the future. Therefore, he left his village near Cusco after high school to work for a drilling firm around Lima. Two years slipped by before he could recognise that this job was stealing his youth. He wracked his brain and handed in a notice to face the next chapter of his life with courage. His savings sufficed only to get him back to his family. With good health, nothing else mattered. His parents had let him go away to grow up rather than for money-making. Quitting Lima was a sign that he would always choose for himself, wisely. At home, his dad presented him with a bag of banknotes.

"What is this for, Dad?"

"Tell me your next move, Son."

Tino was off to study Geo-Sciences in Michigan. After his bachelor's, he managed only a few weeks home before dashing off to Spain. But he would get back to Peru this time to good fortune. He got employed as a government geological researcher, then as a deputy commissioner for the water department.

I called when he was wondering whether his decade-long dream of coming to the Congo with me was best forgotten. "*Mañana*" had come out of my mouth at parting in Madrid, whereas I had meant to say *gracias* for the bag and company. But he had all this long taken it that I had foreseen our working together *tomorrow* no matter when that was going to be.

Günter and Jan

In March of 1997, I left the hotel in Nairobi at noon to avoid late check-out penalties. My flight to Zurich was not until midnight. But I dismissed the temptation of one last tour of the city. I did not want to board the plane smelling bad from sweating. Besides, the blistering heat caused me to drink a lot, and I feared the lack of public toilets. Hence, soon after showering, I headed to the airport, where the check-in agent laughed at my insistence on a window seat, not on the wing or near the lavatories.

"How does the wifey cope with such a demanding hubby?" she jokingly asked.

Arriving early was not a good idea either, as I found it very tiring sitting in a crowded lounge for hours, with less air circulating. Leaving for the washroom, or to stretch the legs, meant coming back to stand up unless fancying the floor. Jomo Kenyatta was a major international hub that had since outgrown the capacity it was designed for, and the thick brick walls did the cooling system no justice at all. The only place dispensing free water was the basin in the restroom. No wonder water was more expensive there than beer. I bought a litre bottle every two hours between three o'clock and an hour before boarding time because the heat caused excruciating thirst.

Once in the air, I pressed my face against the windowpane until the lady on my left patted me on the shoulder.

"So, is home Nairobi or Zurich?"

"Neither!" I replied. "But rather 70 miles north of London."

Kenya was a quick nine-day trip amid a rigid graduate programme and temping work. I was on an errand for a friend's brother to check out a coffee processing plant beyond Nairobi he wanted to invest in, despite my inexperience. He was very generous in retaining me for this assignment. Katarina was going home to Switzerland for three months. She also referred to Kenya as home and spoke Swahili with a local accent.

"I came to Kenya on vacation within a year of becoming a widow," she told me. "It was my first time in Africa, and I met a local. We were both 46, with him only a month my senior. Abhu was a divorcee with six children."

She returned home at the end of her month-long holiday. They kept in touch through letters. Soon, they did not mind the cost of international calls.

"I came back and married him."

She had been making this journey for the previous 21 years.

"Is it not a long time without him?" I asked.

"It is," she conceded. "But he would not come. He does not trust anyone with his farm. I wish he would do it just for me. I ask every year, giving him six months to plan."

Her three children had loved him the moment they saw his pictures. They wanted her to rebuild her life as soon as possible, even if it meant relocating, saying their dad was gone, so she was doing no wrong. They only insisted she finish it if it was no longer working.

She travelled back to Switzerland each year to be with her children and eight grandchildren, now aged nine to 17. I was able to work out that she was 67. But Africa must have been good for her, as she looked 15 years younger. However, I wondered how long she would still have the strength for these trips. Her family had been visiting her and Abhu every three years and loved it.

Before parting, she wrote me her contact on the back of her boarding pass and took mine. Then hugged me as though she had always known me. I rushed to my gate.

* * *

I had barely unpacked when Katarina called. Her family wanted to see me before she went back to Africa. When I arrived two months later, Günter (her son-in-law), Jan (her son), and their wives turned the visit into theirs. They made me go back more over the years, and she was pleased to see them adopting me.

As a mechanical engineer, Günter could design, help make, and fix just about anything under the sun. He had worked for a German automobile manufacturer. After graduating with an electro-mechanical degree, Jan headed to India for a job at a drilling equipment manufacturing company. They loved what they did, but the thought of retiring with little in the bank rendered them restless. They were respectively 55 and 47 and considering consulting in Africa when I came knocking. Günter was coming to us also with the experience acquired from a young age working on his family farm. They were ready for stellar attainment, whatever we would throw at them.

Alvin and Amy

These were the American husband and wife from my time translating while a student. They worked for Mr. Cohen's clients on water projects in West Africa, and I had met them twice in London. We became friends thanks to interpreting all day once a month during their transcontinental telephone conferencing sessions.

They were happy to come out of retirement because they loved taking up development projects from scratch. Money was no longer their pursuit in life. Among what they could bring to the table were contacts with corporates, financiers, manufacturers, and researchers. Their understanding of the culture and expectation on the continent, although not uniform everywhere, was paramount. They accepted to take the direction of our fact-finding mission to the Congo because of their track record of succeeding where many had failed.

Themba

I visited Cape Town in June 1993. As much as I enjoyed the downtown area, I yearned to experience life in the township. Up north, Soweto and other parts of the country had taught me how liberating forgiving was, but I still had room for more soul-enlarging stories of the type I had been hearing. A new-development three-bed house became available in Khayelitsha after unsuccessful attempts in both Langa and Nyanga. I could not wait to make new acquaintances, and there was no better place to start than the local football club. I stood by the roadside with a tracksuit and a sports bag strap over my shoulder. Soon, someone hit the brakes and drove me to the pitch, mistaking me for a professional and hoping to become friends.

"Oh, Zaire!" exclaimed the coach. "That is a great football nation on this continent."

He threw me in at the deep end. It was their last competitive training before the weekend game in three days. A ball rolled out in my direction. I went past it to pick it up with both feet wrapped around it tightly from behind and flipped it up and over my head. I caught up with it coming down, a metre in front of me, at knee level, and slightly to my right, my only striking foot.

Bang!

The crossbar, some 20 metres away, was left rattling. I had unintentionally lobbed the guy who had miskicked it to me, while the goalkeeper plunged only to say he tried. Those distracted turned to the leather bouncing twice on the goal line before leaning inwardly to sit in the back of the net. The lucky ones to have witnessed it all clapped their hands frenetically, chanting my name as though I was that good.

"I am Themba," said a spectator at the end of the game. "They better sign you!"

He offered me a lift home, where I found no water out of the tap. I slept in my sweat from training the rest of that week.

* * *

The lads found it funny that I spoke not their Bantu languages and that even my English accent differed from theirs.

"How did you get into South Africa?" one of them asked.

"I flew into Johannesburg."

"Really! Do you hold a passport?"

Apartheid had made it extremely difficult for a black person to have one in the past. Things were changing, but most from the townships still limited themselves to a *pass* that served as proof of identification. Learning that I had travelled a bit, they emptied their questions on me, giving me no time to discover what racial segregation had left in them.

The next morning, Themba called to take me to Mitchells Plain for some bonding. I was about to leave with just a t-shirt because it was sunny and hot, but he insisted on bringing my trench coat. The weather changed several times over the day. As we talked, he shared with me that the country needed to work on its electricity and water systems once Apartheid was overcome. But, until then, he decided to further his own education. To that end, it was important to steer away from the negative influence he had grown up under. He left for Johannesburg to undertake a degree in engineering.

Upon graduating, he worked for the government for two years until restructuring did away with his position. He took loans from friends to study water drilling, subsequently finding a job with one of the college's partner companies. His new role took him to Malawi, Mozambique, and Tanzania. Soon, he was second-in-command on this project, but at the cost of seeing his family only one week every four months. When I called to discuss the chances of him joining us, he was more than ready, and I hoped his skills and experience would be needed.

3

IN THE CONGO

Exploring

Laura organised an exploratory trip to Kinshasa for the formed team, providing us with flights, a quality hotel, food, beverages, insurance cover, and paying for the time away. She intended to give employment to over 100 people, producing beans, cassava, Congo Goober, corn, rice, and a variety of potatoes found there, all of which grew without much care. The locals mastered the necessary techniques to help with their cultivation. Yet there was an alarming shortage of these items in the domestic market.

It bothered her that a people with so much cultivable land imported staple foods from nations with little room or less favourable climates. Despite being aware that other countries made money off the Congo, no leader showed any inclination to regain control. Therefore, in the spirit of doing more than was needed, we added to our plan edible fruits and vegetables that grew quickly and were harvestable at least twice a year.

Laura's choice of the Congo resulted from the leadership's media-published outcry for foreign investment to fight hunger and malnutrition. The country had been struggling with these two scourges for four decades, not to mention the interminable unemployment curse that went back to who remembers when. An unnamed war imposed there had also claimed millions of lives since 1994, if not earlier, and deepened these problems. All this happened under the nose of the World's Leaders. Nevertheless, the

Congolese continued to hope for a bright future, if not for themselves, then for their descendants. They were far from stooping down to their enemies, visible and invisible.

I could not have opposed Laura's choice to go into agriculture had she asked for my honest opinion, knowing that she was primarily investing in what this population needed enormously. The naturally fertile soil came second in her plans. She was prepared to import seeds if necessary because she was warned of the difficulty of finding rich ones locally.

In terms of commercialisation, not only was there a market to be served but also the opportunity to provide domestically produced foods at a reduced price, so many could benefit regardless of their revenue. Otherwise, they would still be enriching the many international parties involved in the value chain of what was coming to them, thus unintentionally exacerbating unemployment. There was nothing as belittling as seeing millions of tonnes of foodstuffs that could have been cultivated locally arriving from abroad. Imported foods had become a shopping preference out of necessity and not a choice the Congolese had made.

The statistics she had put her hands on were astounding. They were obtained through her US-based advisors who had contacts in the Congo and with some international development institutions. Her eyes were on what was promising to be an incredible return on investment. Although only projections at this stage, the numbers were hard for any well-advised investor to resist. They were far above any she had been presented with anywhere else.

To come up with a proposal that would take full advantage of this opportunity, making sure to be socially oriented, we planned to spend a week meeting people informally to get a less biased picture of the situation. This was intended to help us avoid any external influences in our decision-making. But our course would change abruptly because of what we discovered.

Water!

It was early evening when we came off the plane, down onto the tarmac, and on one of the buses lined up due to no jet bridge at Kinshasa's Ndjili airport. Nothing had changed since the country's independence in 1960. Hence, a city of 15 million people still operated with the facilities built for 300,000.

Entering the modest terminal building, we headed straight to the only stand in view, this side of the immigration. It sold only bottled water. The vendor had purposefully picked his spot and obtained permission from the RVA (*Régie des Voies Ariennes*)—the National Airport Authority—gaining an advantage over the competition we knew not of at this point.

He was allowed this positioning because of how humid and dehydrating it was for many coming to the Congo for the first time or those who had not been in a while. Having drinking water when it was needed helped calm down the impatient travellers who were sweating buckets and complaining about how long stamping their passports was taking. The weather was too hot for the time of the day—half past seven—and like in other African airports known to me, the air-con gave us an unfriendly welcome.

Because only one carousel was on, we retrieved our luggage two hours after landing. We were without a suitcase each. It seemed unreal for the same to happen to everyone in my team. Even with only two arrivals that evening, the collection area was chaotic with humans. Jan asked if this was a secondary airport in the capital, seeing how we were in through one door, from the apron, and literally out the other side of the terminal. It pained me to advise that this was all we had. He found it hard to believe. The Swiss Congolese diaspora he knew of were eloquent and always well-dressed, so he had formed himself the impression of a chic life in the Congo. I felt obliged to explain that those ran not the country.

As for our missing suitcases, the airline's representatives told us that the flight had found itself with too much load, so they would arrive the next day. We heard of bags that had gone missing for good and compensation that did not come close to the amounts claimed. These transporters expected people to present receipts for every item, including those clothes worn for a couple of years already.

We spent another hour registering with the clerk, who wrote at a snail's pace, faster only than the immigration officer now behind us. Three metres from there, a man matched our luggage tags to the ones on the back of our boarding passes. He and his colleagues were preventing theft, mostly by the overwhelming non-passengers. They kindly produced their credentials when we questioned their powers, for they were in plain clothes.

Customs declaration was next, with us dragging our luggage on the floor due to no trolley in sight. We had made a mistake buying suitcases with no wheels. We lined up for inspection. Most of the oversized bags were getting opened wide, and their contents spilled out as hands clad in latex gloves rifled through. Two agents waved us through the moment we got behind the last person in the only 30-metre long queue, wherein people almost stood on the heels of those ahead of them, telling how badly they wanted out of there. However, that did not speed up the process.

The officer standing aside wished us a pleasant stay as we passed, and we obliged. It seemed that they trusted we had no commercial goods nor posed a threat to the state. As much as I wanted everyone treated equally, security should not be taken lightly. The lads were doing their best with what they had. The lack of sniffer dogs and metal detectors left them with no alternative than going through as many bags as possible.

We all noticed outside that drinking water presented an incredible potential for business, seeing that pretty much everyone had a sachet or a bottle in their hand, if not at their mouth. Children and youth carried containers thereof on their heads, most of it warm. Sixteen years away, I was returning to a world I struggled to recognise. Selling water in this manner appeared innovative. Although not impressive nor big to get me excited where development was concerned, it pulled at my heartstrings. In front of me were people who had spotted a gap and were filling it the best they could—hopefully, making a profit. The whole thing confirmed in my head that my people refused to surrender to life's hardship.

Harm

On our first morning in the country, we headed out of the urban area, passing through the *Communes* (boroughs) of Barumbu and Limeté. Kinshasa is divided into 24 administrative communes. Near Ndjili Airport, we branched off to the right and slowly drove for about six kilometres. We were in the middle of Mikondo, and our exuberance to see the end thereof faded with finding out that we were not yet even through a quarter of this conurbation after we had covered a further eight kilometres.

Leaving the asphalted roads incurred penalties with the car hire company. We did not mind as we could not achieve much staying in the luxury of tarred ones. However, it was difficult to negotiate with the thick, deep, and slippery mud, not to forget the large puddles resulting from days of rain, some coming up to the bottom of the doors of our vehicles.

Along there, we painfully contemplated many women and girls carrying large basins. Teenage boys also battled with yellow or white plastic jerrycans seemingly too heavy to lift with one hand. These were extremely awkward to transport, as evidenced by the poor posture of those on duty. They were leaning to one side and shuffling their weight with difficulty. In this effort, one leg was bent inwardly at the knee and, because of the frequency of the chore, in some, it had become a permanent malformation. Presumably, they did not want to place the containers on their heads, as it was not considered dignified for a male to carry loads in the way a female did. Nonetheless, this work was entirely unsuitable for either boys or girls of this age and size.

I had not left these jerrycans, so we stopped to ask what they were lugging, and they replied with "water". We talked a little while and discovered that those we pitied were older than they looked. One of them, giving the impression of being around 10, was 14. But, regardless of their real age, their task was just not good treatment. Around hour, these children belonged in a classroom, preparing for the future and not fetching water. According to local knowledge, the girls shrank—their height stunted from what they carried. They lacked confidence and self-esteem because of being forced to do the work that left them feeling like slaves.

Congolese girls like to look beautiful all the time. It is a whole culture, almost a religion, out there. But water on their heads every day, their hair was often neglected or, worse, baldness developed from the friction of the basins, a big shame in this society for female teenagers. Many had their ears pierced since infancy but no longer wore studs for practical reasons—the inconvenience of the jewellery while on duty had turned into a habit of not wearing any, no matter where and when. This labour left them no time to beautify themselves, consequently rendering them to feel unattractive, besides causing emotional, mental, and physical harm. Everywhere we looked, we saw children at risk because of the necessity of water. We yearned for a change.

Priority

There was no end to our discoveries. Some of these children contributed to the family income, while others had long been the sole breadwinners for their households. Their parents could not find employment, and because most thought of work only in the formal sense, supplying water to those who had it easy in life was out of the question. Theirs were negative pride and culture that advocated that a child's responsibility was to obey and serve when asked to.

Despite their young age, some found themselves compelled to take the reins to avoid catastrophe for the whole family unit. A few of those we spoke to were just about managing to combine feeding their households with school because they believed that a better future would come from classroom learning. Some of their earnings covered the cost of education. Among them were many eight-year-olds. We admired and felt for them, doing our best to hide the tears their situation provoked in us. Their awareness that there was more to life than carrying water could not be highlighted enough. Others, unable to mix the two, had completely dropped out of school.

With sadness and empathy, we asked ourselves about the likelihood of a better tomorrow when growing up under these circumstances was all that was there for these kids. Nine-year-old Julie told us how her mother, Esther, had had a very difficult pregnancy and additional complications upon giving birth. Her father, Bernard, was a civil servant who worked in the city, some 40 kilometres away. Monday to Friday, he left home at four in the morning to arrive at work by eight, while his return journey began at five to get home at nine or so. It was clear that he could not help, so she dropped out of school to cater to her mother, the newly born, and three other younger siblings, no one asking her to. We could not believe that she could be so wise and conscious of the situation around her in this manner. And who was looking after her?

"God does!" came her answer, which left us speechless.

Julie told us how to get to her school. But we still got lost several times as the streets were not sign-posted. We asked the locals for help. She was classed as lucky because her establishment was under three kilometres away.

Once there, a man guarding the unfenced compound greeted us warmly. He was there to prevent pupils from leaving during school hours without written authorisation from their teacher. He also intercepted those arriving late so they could get their punishment. That one brought back some memories of what corporal sanctions were like in my days. It consisted of kneeling on hard pavement for hours or having knuckles hit with a wooden ruler. Laura and the others looked on strangely as I laughed through my tears.

He directed us to the headmaster, where we asked for Julie as though we knew not that she was elsewhere. We did not want to expose our investigation. Child protection applied not there. So, despite not being family or known to the school, we were given all the details about her, including confirmation that she had not been in over a month. Customarily, nobody contacted parents when children showed not up. The secretary opened the eight class registers and pointed out that less than five percent had their addresses recorded and none a phone number. If pupils fell ill at school, they would be sent home alone. Obviously unaware of the poor impression he was making on us, he told us about one unfortunate six-year-old.

Laurent got terrible cramps in his tummy within an hour of sitting at his desk and stayed on as long as he could. The pain became unbearable, and he started to cry loudly. There being no toilets on-site, the inevitable happened. He was asked to leave. After that, all the school knew were assumptions based on the accounts of those who claimed to be eyewitnesses. But knowing my people, this could be several degrees of hearsay by the time we heard it.

"In the middle of his journey, he was incontinent again," the secretary said. "To hide the mess, he took off his shirt and tied it around his waist so it would hang down over his shorts. He was busy taking care of this operation while walking and paying attention to nothing else.

"Usually, that would not have been a problem, as there was hardly any traffic on this broad road. But a car came from nowhere and hit him as he was pressing his tummy in the hope of easing the increasing pain. He died on the spot! The driver sped off, leaving no trace.

"His body lay there for about three hours, crowds stopping by but unable to identify him as he was not from the neighbourhood. In the end, some decided to see if his shirt had a badge on, as it was with most schools; and, yes, there was."

"What did the parents do with the school?" Laura asked.

"Nothing," the secretary answered. "They should not have let him out unwell."

It took us a few minutes to pick ourselves up from the remorseless attitude thereby manifested. A child had disappeared off the face of the earth like an object. The police, passing by, took the body to a nearby clinic with no morgue before contacting the school.

His mother became worried when he was not home at his usual time of two, so by four o'clock, she was frantic and rushed to the school where the bad news awaited. She went to find her husband at his workplace. Sadly, by the time they reached the clinic, the person who held the key to the room where the corpse was kept had already left for the day. They returned in the morning to be handed a bill before they could even be sure it was their son. The invoice included first paying what was due to the police for their hand.

We went to meet them. They were both 51 at his death. Their relationship started on the first day of their sophomore year in high school when her family came to live in Kinshasa from the *Equateur* province. It was love at first sight, which somehow stuck despite threats of dismissal if ever found holding hands on the school premises, and their parents trying hard to break them up out of fear of something happening between them early. They tied the knot at 22, neither of them in employment. Still childless after 20 years, the doctors treating her confirmed she was barren. Determined to seal their union with offspring, they turned to traditional medicine they had all along been uninterested in. Surprisingly, she fell pregnant within two years of taking up this practice, at the stroke of her 44th birthday. It took them time to believe it was real.

When they had to claim Laurent's body, they did not immediately have the money. Earning a combined $200 a month meant no savings, and it took them three days to fundraise from friends and family. It was only after paying both the police and the clinic that the corpse got released.

"This was four days later," the father said. "So, you can imagine what our son was like when he was brought out of that room."

Who was truly to blame?

DIY Spirit

Jacques owned the school. He saw a gap in his community and capitalised on it. The number of children reaching their teenage years without formal learning was shocking and ever-increasing. His own were not spared. Establishments received more applications than they had places and rejected nearly half each year. Out of compassion, he made four rooms available in his unfinished house, making his family share with pupils and teachers. DIY spirit applies to everything in the Congo! Everyone does the best they can with whatever they lay their hands on.

His priority was those whose parents paid tuition in advance of the school year. He did obtain registration with this proof, giving some of the money to those who handled his application at various levels to avoid being held back or turned down. His good intentions to see children educated should have warranted approval, but the reality on the ground was different. He nonetheless hired teachers with ease as every year, more of them qualified to fight over the vacancies that were hardly there.

He himself was an unemployed teacher looking for work for four years. He was tempted to talk himself out of setting up but the bulb having gone off in his head illuminated the more. Having 13 people on his payroll resulted from seeing the positive in his own situation. He would not have brought himself the success we found him enjoying had he asked others for their opinion before taking the plunge.

He ran four classes in the morning and four more in the afternoon. They were grades one to four. He was a blessing to his community and an inspiration to us. His connections and networking ability helped him secure places elsewhere for those leaving for the fifth grade. He wished to grow, but for that, he needed funding as well as a piece of land to purchase. The lack of proper town planning by the authorities meant that there was no suitable space for this kind of development within 10 kilometres of his home. He kept speaking to anyone who appeared to have the finances, hoping to have them buy into rescuing the children's future.

If both land and funds became available, Jacques would have the potential to quadruple the size of the school because of the number of children whose parents had come knocking since opening. His desire to expand was due to those who honoured their commitments timely. They also permitted him excellent employee retention and performance as he paid on time, regularly, and better than the local rate. But, despite all this astounding work in the community, banks told him that they lent not to educational institutions.

From there, we came across an overwhelming number of disheartening accounts that left us devastated. It was scary how much these children were mistaken for adults, and being expected to look after themselves in circumstances beyond their capabilities. No one seemed concerned that they made their way to and from school unaccompanied. It was normal for their parents to come with them on their first day and pick them up at the end of the day. But thereafter, they were on their own and expected to remember the route at the tender age of five, when they started pre-school. Those lucky walked with siblings, neighbours, or friends they had just made, thanks to striking friendships there happening naturally.

At Jacques' school, each class was overflowing with 60 children. Due to the lack of proper seating, they wrote with notepads on their laps, the upper part of the body bent over—a position prohibited in Pedagogy for evident reasons. It explained why all the fourth graders we visited wrote like someone starting out.

At the ministry of education, the answer was that schools were supposed to conform to the pioneering pedagogues' ideology of having no more than 30 pupils per class and that such was not the case was beyond everyone's control. One inspector would tell us that they had not received their *motivation* (the money paid to them to go around) in a long time to make sure guidelines were adhered to. A bit later, he blamed the lack of buildings. The government had not kept up with the demographic surge of the last 47 years. It is believed that there were about 200,000 students in the capital back in 1960—an estimated four children to every couple. We left him when he said that the immediate solution should be rather to get as many boys as possible into schools even if it needed disembarking girls already attending. We suspected to know what that implied.

Discrimination

Our observation, and on hearing the locals, concluded that the carrying of water was a females' responsibility, and males came in only in support. It showed clearly how the former were discriminated against, which made Amy and Laura discuss what it could have led to if such had come up in the West. They emailed a few *NGOs* (Non-Governmental Organisations) back in Europe and North America that funded gender-based advocacy projects in the Congo. But these, obviously having not seen any importance in their inquiry, bothered not to reply.

Apparently, their job was limited to discrimination related to where women suffered physical abuse at the hands of their husbands. Females on water drawing duty at the cost of their well-being and future was not part of their mission statements and, therefore, not something they were willing to address. There was also the fear of interfering with long-standing traditions such as household roles distribution.

Furthermore, the fact that many of these institutions were managed from overseas aided not the situation, for they relied on scanty information from local collaborators who themselves offered no better treatment to the women in their own households. They were raised with their mothers and sisters providing water, so they were not prepared to make it different for their wives and daughters. In fact, they remained unconcerned even with us stating that water carrying was one of the major stumbling blocks to the advancement of women in the Congo.

Discussing gender-based discrimination concerning work in the house is seen as inciting women to rebel. It is taboo bringing up the subject, and the situation will remain unchanged in this part of the world unless everyone highlights and seeks to eradicate it. However, it was not our place to initiate this, especially as we would soon pursue some economic interests. We were warned that human rights advocacy did not mix business.

The question divided even us, in part, due to our varying backgrounds. My experience growing up in the Congo differed greatly from that of the children we sympathised with. Hence, I understood the culture and the need to have it changed, even if it could not be brought up to the same level as in the West. But for my partners, solutions needed to be found and implemented right away, even where we had no say.

I passed our recommendations to some members of the Parliament and those in management at numerous NGOs, asking them not to be simple observers. To succeed, local situation needed to count greatly when elaborating on these projects. Generic tactics had long proved ineffective when evaluating work of this nature. It was true that sometimes the law of the land restricted these foreign institutions so that they could not operate freely like in the West. However, they could still negotiate and bring about life-saving changes if they truly tried.

I was relieved when my partners observed the warning to be careful about what they said so they did not cause problems. I, however, was allowed some leeway to challenge the authorities to some extent. Therefore, I would often see my friends whisper their discontentment, questions, and suggestions in my ear, so I could relay to whoever we were speaking to in a tone of voice and manner acceptable there.

All this was to make a difference in the lives of girls and women but also boys and men. No one in the family was unaffected by the encumbrance of living without water. But, seeking to take the responsibility to bring this commodity home from women and children proved not to be the only challenge we were to face. The closer we got to solving one problem, the more others emerged. Nevertheless, we did not fail to demonstrate why we believed to be fit for the Congo.

By-challenges

Alvin and Amy were impressed everywhere they had been before, but the welcome they received from the Congolese exceeded their expectations. Likewise, their difficulties in other countries could not be compared with what they would face on this side. This made them believe they had gone elsewhere to prepare for the Congo. Hence, they were not alarmed when both of our drivers did let us down on our third day in Kinshasa.

Our rentals were kept overnight at the hire company's site. Taking them home was an open invitation to thieves to help themselves to mirrors, lights, and tyres if they could not steal the whole automobile. They had to pick up the cars before collecting us. They had fallen short before but were not getting away with it this time. One claimed to be stuck in traffic between the parking lot and the hotel, which were only five kilometres apart.

Alvin took control of the situation. He asked him to honk, but he did not. So, he told him that he was not behind the wheel. Embarrassed, he hung up and would not answer again. Alvin and I caught a taxi to the office. The receptionist confirmed neither had picked up the keys. Alvin asked for and obtained the waiving of the charges for two days on both cars to compensate for the inconvenience caused both times.

We were still filling out forms when one of the men arrived. He was shocked to find us there. Ten minutes later, as we waited for the computer and the printer to communicate with each other, his colleague entered. We asked that they be replaced, else we were cancelling our contract, asking to be refunded in full, and going to a competitor. But the manager came out to advise of no standby driver. Instead, he offered to put both guys in a budget accommodation near their parking lot for the remainder of our booking to prevent this from happening again. Alvin was weakened.

"One must be heartless to not appreciate this goodwill," he said.

He had seen enough of people not being time-conscious on this continent when they ought to be, so he joked that Africa had eight days a week when the rest of the world struggled to manage with seven. Hence why so much negligence and inconsideration of others, to the point of being four hours late picking up the keys. We had to be strict with the use of our time as we only had two weeks to see all that we needed to and reach a conclusion about the trade to engage in. As much as we wanted to support local businesses, like the small pool of car owners that offered price cuts, we were lucky to have booked with a global brand. This branch did not want a bad review.

After the altercation with the drivers, we found ourselves demotivated to go out because of the time now being past two. Things were closing at four o'clock, and the traffic towards the suburbs, where we meant heading, becoming dense again. Therefore, Laura requested we sit around the table to discuss in detail what to invest in. She spoke less, allowing us to express our feelings and thoughts abundantly. We took on brainstorming, steering towards tangible profits in farming and the food industry, imagining ourselves thriving in the nutrition sector as well as providing employment and an income to families. Amy was almost halfway through reading what she had typed out, the rest of us impatient to go to dinner, when Laura interrupted.

"Guys! I am supportive of everything you have said. However, I am aching that we would leave the evident and biggest societal pain point untreated."

We lent an ear.

"I am not at peace since coming out of the airport to children selling water, most of them into the night. It has broken me.

"If you see and admire other things as we drive around, all I spot are kids with yellow jerrycans. I am sleepless at night. I cannot stand it anymore, nor must we go away without making a real difference, though little that might be. One can survive without food but not water.

"Furthermore, I want these containers off my fellow females' heads. And that is not all. I want water in the proximity of their homes so their children can attend school. I know this to be too ambitious. But we do not need to go after the entire city, let alone the whole country. Just one girl or boy free from this ordeal and in education would mean the world to me."

We looked at each other, the seven of us, and then into her eyes. Her speech had won us over. We were unanimous. Not just because it was her investment and idea to come to the Congo but mainly due to the immense humanity aspect of her recommendation.

"Let us drill water," Laura concluded, thanking me for a team capable of this.

But where do we start?

Location

We reverted to those we had met before to help us determine where to drill. All seemed laid back, and none came forth with suggestions of where to start. But Alvin, converted to African traditions, insisted on looking for and listening to the elders. He wanted their blessing, convinced that water would be found in abundance and of good quality where they would point at. Günter, Jan, Laura, and Tino broke to pieces when they realised that he was referring to ancestral power. His wife knew it, while Themba and I were impressed by his transformation. What mattered, however, was that all jokes shared and over, we should not lose our focus.

The children trapped in the cycle of fetching water were aware that missing out on schooling would leave them with a bleak future, but they had no idea how to break away from this tradition and had no one to speak for them. Witnessing this danger was painful but worse for the victims, who always opened up easily to any foreigner who asked what they wanted from life. We felt a deep sense of revulsion but were grateful for the heart-transforming this experience was bringing us that could not have come otherwise. Consoling was the knowledge that if these could survive this hardship, they would have the strength to withstand anything else when adults.

But until such time, we encouraged the parents we sat down with to seek ways to increase their revenues, so their children could be freed up. The obvious option was to set up a side business. But, with no funds, the great ideas they had at moments were no more than vague ambitions and distant dreams. Jan suggested saving up no matter how long it would take. But he understood not what it was like living hand-to-mouth. This was a country where most people had never heard of disposable income. Nevertheless, despite this money problem, many never lost hope. They believed that good health and peace would contribute to bringing about the change needed.

"My prayer going to bed is not to have a job or money," said 32-year-old Louis we chatted with at our hotel. "It is, rather, to see another day."

We were buying souvenirs from him at the time of this conversation. He had a master's in Economics but was yet to secure formal employment—a song we had become all too familiar with. He said to be in possession of the report of a few foreign researchers who had revealed appealing corollaries for achieving easier access to clean water, persuading us to let him lend a hand where he could. Water shortage was of personal relevance to him. His two sisters had succumbed to HIV contracted from the rebels who fell on them on their way to drawing water.

The men had been travelling for months and may not have known they were carrying the disease. They might have passed it on to other women as well during their journey. He was convinced that water accessibility would save lives beyond the scarcity itself. That made Alvin view him as a leader because of putting the general interest before his own, asking not to be paid to share that data with us. What was written led us to the most deprived areas and indicated what to expect in terms of quantity and quality of the water we might find and at what depths. It also detailed possible difficulties to be encountered while drilling. The knowledge we received brightened us up.

Rising

We hoped to keep up the momentum gained interacting with Louis. He certainly changed our mood so that we started seeing the brighter side of life in the Congo rather than just the negative many filled us with. Hence, we came across a few that had turned their lives around. The simple belief that they could do great in the days ahead had led them to go after their own luck.

Roger, 34, owned the restaurant Louis recommended. We waited just past the entrance while arrangements were being made to seat our rather large group of 10—Alvin, Amy, Günter, Jan, Laura, Tino, Themba, two drivers, and me. Chauffeurs joined not those regarded as their bosses at meals, but Laura invited ours to wherever we went. She could not stand some being considered lesser than others. She believed that if you could not give someone something, at least leave them feeling unhurt by your attitude.

We noticed that we were being given special treatment. Our glasses got replenished more than we asked for. We were served larger portions of food than stated on the menu. Whereas we chose no dessert, ice cream and fruits were brought to us, more than we had room for. Also, a dozen bottles of water were ours to take away, free of charge.

"Never run out of drinking water in this country," was Roger's reply to my insistence that we had enough complimentary supplies at the hotel every morning.

The total to be paid was null. A handwritten note from him read: "Thank you for the visit!"

He resolutely rejected payment, leaving us wondering why such generosity. But we did not depart until he had agreed to join us the following day, with us footing the bill. He committed painfully, giving the impression of thinking that we appreciated not his kindness. It was when dining with us that he would let out his jaw-dropping account. Meeting him was an eye-opener. Through him, we realised, once more, that Kinshasa was full of smart individuals who only needed encouragement, or to some extent coaching, to shine. Graduates or not, they could draw a lot of ideas, strategies, tactics, and wisdom from their own or others' experiences and go on to thrive.

Our benefactor owned seven more outlets of this type, spread around different communes of the capital. He had endured a great deal on his way to the life he now had, beginning with his dad losing his job at the Finance Inspectorate, where he managed a district of the city. He (the father) took what he had in savings and went on buying foods in the province of Equateur to resell in Kinshasa. On one of those trips, he ran out of bottled water and turned to the Congo River. Sadly, he was buried on the riverbank alongside other victims who also travelled on that boat.

Within two months of the news of her husband's passing, Roger's mother lost her battle against cerebral malaria, a condition which had worsened after his leaving for Equateur. Although only 11, Roger crumbled not. He had six younger siblings, aged nine, seven (triplets), five, and three, to look after. When things were going well, his parents had not invested in a house of their own in a less urban area where the cost was more affordable. They loved it near the city centre.

With them gone, no extended family returned to check on the children, despite Roger reaching out repeatedly. They used up the rental deposit, and the landlady allowed them to stay a month free, giving them the chance to vacate with dignity, as though someone this young knew what dignity was. He approached a local orphanage, but it was full. Many other children were also turned away, so he did not take it personally. He pressed on to churches, but no change in fortune.

Two days before becoming homeless, he headed to the market. Kids made a living out there transporting goods. He was turned down all afternoon until an hour before closing. Clearly seeing his desperation, a kind merchant asked what he charged. He knew that was a foot in the door.

"I will take anything, Mum!"

There it is not *madam* or *sir* if someone is old enough to be your parent.

He emotionally referred to that moment as the basis for everything he continued to accomplish. She paid him significantly less, but he took it politely and with gratitude. In the short time left that day, he got three more clients, each more generous than he could have imagined, making up for the shortfall left by the first client. He was too busy rushing around and getting more business to count his earnings, but the bag was filling up nicely.

In the end, having put in four hours of work, thanks to those not observing opening hours, he found a relatively quiet place on the side of the market and counted a little over $20 in local currency. Now, $50 was their monthly rent for their three-bed flat, while $2 fed them all for a day. He went down on his knees and loudly uttered a fervent prayer. It was his first-ever personal conversation with his Creator. He opened his eyes to a crowd surrounding him. Many began singing to the Most High. He knew not what to say. In the meantime, someone went around with a carrier bag and collected the equivalent of $33, as per the local practice, to support a pastor or spiritual intercessor.

He explained the reason for his imploring the Heavens, and more money, to the amount of $15, was donated. *Lebeka* (Rebekah in the *Lingala* language), a woman in her forties, was as tearful as most females there present.

"I would have taken you all in if I could," she said.

She and her husband already had four children under their roof—two of their own and two nephews. However, her heart was too heavy to allow her to move even an inch from that spot without acting. She took his address and, with her spouse, went to meet with the landlady and covered their rent for an entire year. She kept a close eye on them, making them her extended family. Their parents' meetings, graduations, and birthdays became part of her diary.

Moseka, from that same crowd, owned a busy downtown supermarket. She asked the manager to squeeze in the lad, reminding him that he was but a child, so he should not be given heavy lifting duties. He gave him afternoon shifts five days a week and all-day Saturday, bagging groceries for customers at the till. This was how he had plenty for himself and his siblings.

When Lebeka's commitment elapsed, he stayed on to be in walking distance of work and school, missing no payment. Besides, this was the only address they had ever lived at. They felt safe being next to *Koko* (Grandma). Roger, the oldest of his siblings, and the triplets only found out she was not blood-related when their mum passed because of how she had always treated them. Even when both parents were alive, Koko fed them in her flat or brought a plate to them in the yard every Sunday evening. She had bathed them, changed their nappies, and carried on doing so for the youngest two when they became orphans.

Overcoming

At the age of 28, Roger purchased Koko's property at the asking price of $90,000. She was 85. Her children wanted the inheritance shared to avoid family feuds after her death. Her husband had gone before her. We came to a four-floor 30-room hotel that had replaced the old clay brick-rusted roof buildings that once stood there. He also bought the three neighbouring properties to accommodate a five-bed house for himself and a three-bed one at the back to keep Grandma on-site, free of charge, thus returning the favour.

Koko was permitted two members of her family permanently and for as long as she lived. Sadly, more invited themselves over, attracted by the roomy and much cleaner dwelling, and because the new owner was but the kid they had always known and had, sometimes in the past, washed and fed with a spoon. It annoyed him, but he said no word to not worry Koko. He knew it would end, although not wishing it to be sooner, as Koko's presence still gave him and his siblings the strength to stay on their feet.

She died at 93, holding his hand, him being one of the last few to be with her in the hospital when she closed her eyes for the last time. He buried her jointly with her family, proving that whoever said that "no act of kindness is ever wasted" was right.

Roger made money from short and long-term foreign workers who lodged at his hotel. Several nationalities filled his downtown restaurant at midday and in the evening because of strategically choosing to be close to embassies and international institutions. He had come up with a wonderful marketing idea. Every Tuesday and Thursday at lunchtime, customers could book to join the kitchen and cook a specialty from their country, which would be sold at a premium. A watchful qualified chef ensured food was safe and industry standards observed.

The money raised was used to support the children of the soldiers who had fallen in war, providing them with school fees and uniforms. As one can imagine, with the proceeds from this activity being used for such a good cause, there was a long waiting list of improvised cooks, and the event attracted more customers than would normally have during this time of the day.

To show his appreciation for the participants, only music from their countries played during those hours, most of it their own selection. Each member of my crew took the opportunity to showcase their culinary talents. I, too, had a go, but my adopted fish-and-chips failed due to not being blessed in this department. But I blamed not having the right kind of fish in the local market. So, what I cooked never made it out of the kitchen. Roger's staff ate it for me. The chef bailed me out with a similar impromptu dish. He announced that I had messed up, hence the last-minute change to the menu. I still got applauded and tipped greater than anyone else at any time.

Roger had attended Uni in the evening and graduated. He had read pretty much every business and related book available locally. He had likewise educated all his siblings, all of which was unstinting on his part. Daily sales at this downtown location were over $17,000; his other restaurants brought in at least $11,000 each. More importantly, he employed over 200 individuals, many with families to look after.

Among his employees were Lebeka's son, an accountant, and Moseka's niece, who managed the nine bakeries he owned across the city. Hiring them was a token of his gratitude to these ladies. He made it a habit to always return a favour in this manner. Taking us around his businesses, there was always a moment he stopped by someone and told us what it was that he was paying back for by employing this individual.

Alvin was the first to commend Roger, letting him know that he, too, had not had an easy ride growing up, starting with alcoholic and drug-addicted parents to their unemployment that was aggravated by the poor job market where they lived and more.

"See!" Roger said. "Over here, we believe that God helps those who help themselves. Where you start out is none of your business; where you end is."

He was referring to his courage to go out seeking work in the market so young and where we found him when it was easy to just sit there complaining about the miserable situation their parents had left them in.

Refusing our payment that day was how he gave back to the many expats who had helped him along the way but had not had the chance to pay them back. He did this once a week whenever he spotted a new foreigner in one of his restaurants. He remembered how, in the past, many of them tipped him hugely because of taking their purchases to their vehicles. He was doing so without any thought of getting something in return, going beyond his call of duty without being asked to. He was very familiar with most currencies from a young age and used to convert them all into US dollars, saving up for a rainy day that never came again since that afternoon in the market.

Giving away free bottles of water to customers was to raise awareness of the necessity to "always have a stock," in memory of his dad. Sure, as a businessman, the expense was indirectly passed onto the beneficiaries, but he could have pocketed all of it without question. He reminisced how his parents used to make them drink plenty when water out of the tap was potable and always available, telling them that "water is life".

With that in mind, they bathed them thrice a day, believing that "water heals", and they, the children, knowing how injections hurt, preferred bathing to going to the doctor. They had formed this opinion that the latter hated them, so they administered jabs when tablets, even bitter ones, could have done a better job. All this cracked up my partners, but not me, for I, too, grew up fearing the doctors, for the same reason. He recalled coming back from school to first be given a bath, before eating, to get rid of the sweat accumulated throughout the day. He reassured us that it invigorated both the body and the mind and even influenced performance at school. Hence, he was confident his customers were safer with every bottle of water he sent them away with.

Having ridden against the storm and overcome, he hoped his compatriots could do more with what the country offered, for he believed there to be more than enough and only needed to be processed into end-products. He made sure we did not just take his word for it.

Doing More

Roger arranged for someone to take us around a few nearby villages. Words failed us when we found ourselves walking on rotten mangoes, papayas, oranges, and other fruits. These had ripened on trees and fallen, having attracted no partaker. No wonder flies there were big and green—enjoying good health. Yet Kinshasa queued in supermarkets with juices containing less than one percent fruit. I had returned such onto the shelf upon discovering that it cost four dollars a litre when I paid £0.39 for a slightly better quality in the UK.

Further evidence of waste was witnessed at the Kinkole fishing village. We stood next to the busy fishermen barbecuing their catches for customers on the bank of the Congo River on burning wood with local pepper, basil, onions, garlic, turmeric, and other spices. The scent thereof filled the air, and the food was so tasty. We were shocked to see some dead fish floating, and others cast onto the shore by the mild midmorning waves.

"They die of old age all the time," one of the fishermen told us.

In the meantime, people longed for, proudly bought, and ate tinned sardines and mackerels and dried, salted, or frozen fish, all imported. The same applied to animals in the bush. We found them, while hiking, dead next to dry lakes that formed whenever there was abundant rain, just 15 kilometres from the Maluku suburb. All around us was a profusion of food not exploited.

A man told us about his village, in the Bandundu, where crude oil came out of almost the same spot as their water. The locals could barely afford imported paraffin. Therefore, they made use of what was free to them, even though it damaged the founts of their lamps. He worked for the ministry of oil and was aware of what this resource was worth, but he never dared discuss it with his hierarchy, who never appreciated being educated by a subordinate. Instead, he had the pleasure of lecturing us that though the refining thereof was expensive and lengthy, investing in it would create employment, not to mention wealth and reduce dependency on importation.

Roger was a total contrast to many in that he tried to have an answer to every question life had for him. Fruits and juices served in his restaurants were not from shops but his own. Upon deciding to go into the gastronomy business at 20, he carefully chose a location favourable to planting fruit trees based on what was already growing there on their own. Hence, he now owned hundreds of acres where he harvested tonnes yearly.

He also bought other lands for his livestock, poultry, and pisciculture, all reproducing themselves at an unimaginable rate. His main cost was getting people to deliver water from a stream two kilometres away after failing to buy out landowners between him and the stream.

It was gruelling for humans to fill up his ponds—27 when we visited. He could not have done it without them. They also helped maintain his trees, seeing they needed to be watered twice daily until they were old enough to sustain themselves. He kept planting at least 5,000 new ones a year, lining them up in a disciplined manner, leaving sufficient gaps between them in anticipation of when they would have branches. A plate was attached to each one of them saying when they were planted and when they first produced fruits to plan their revitalisation or replacement. Doing all this were industry experts he employed.

More impressively, Roger supplied his produce excess to his competitors for the benefit of the public. And it was out of the desire to deliver to more restaurants, supermarkets, and others that he was keen to bring in partners rather than investors, as did many in the Congo. He was different: he sought not just financial participation. Expertise in automation, production, logistics, and even export—he was getting ahead of himself—was part of his pitch. He wanted us to dip our toe in the water, saying we would not regret it. However, it was too early for us to promise anything, let alone commit.

"I am certain to produce more with greater access to water," he said.

We commented not about water and just kept admiring the guy for his achievements. It made us wonder why everyone else in Kinshasa was taking pleasure in moaning. Accounts like Roger's were not heard of abroad. Even the Congolese diaspora themselves would only tell what was not working, consequently discouraging even a visit.

Sure, it was necessary to let the world know of wars, degradation, slugging development, and all that was detrimental to the mind and body. However, they were overdoing it, only wishing to play down this land, so they could take advantage of the country's mineral resources.

Their bad campaign also created room for the Congolese overseas to collect funds for fake projects. One of our drivers confirmed that all this negativity had long cost the nation more than its people's own failure to stretch themselves.

"Bad press has kept investors away for decades," said he.

His words came out just as we hit a pothole on the road and bounced up with our heads striking the ceiling, sidewise against the doors, and then each other.

"Often, we need not money from *rich* countries or *reigning* financial institutions that are good at plunging us into debts, to the point of lending irresponsibly, but experts prepared to work side-by-side with us, so we can avoid making the same mistakes repeatedly," he added.

His statement aligned with Roger's wish to set up a proper industrial production line for each of his farm products. It made sense to have a foreign input. Local experts were unable to pick up his ideas and deliver. His past made him long to include water purification and bottling in what he would like to run. Laura taking time to make up her mind unknowingly handed Günter and Jan the opportunity to get on the case, find investment, and team up with Roger without the rest of us, them having been craving for a chance of their own.

Listening

As a group, we remained determined to leave a landmark now that we were unanimous in providing water, so our visit would not be reduced to tourism. Nothing foreign media had said could now hold us back. Any chance to laugh was taken with gratitude, for there was little around to cheer us up with. Almost everything we came across left us angry and teeth gnashing, struggling to believe the atrocities people endured could lead to achieving a lot and improving life with small but persistent efforts and good intentions. But many supposed to make a difference were yet far from being honest with themselves.

We saw this when we came across a so-called *World Water Day* caravan one day, and it further upset us. We engaged in an intellectual discussion with those running it. The event was promoted by an international NGO no reader would not recognise, if mentioned, and executed by its local representatives. They were situated in the city centre, away from the areas most affected by water shortage.

We could not help but advise our interlocutors that their show had no bearing on the country's calamitous situation unless the population benefited from the funds raised on their behalf. Additionally, it was best to invite private investors to help provide a hand-up rather than continually issuing grants and loans, politically dictated, that the

Congolese had grown to dislike. They could see that their land was getting nowhere with these schemes.

The message of the day was that there were 20 million Congolese without drinking water, as to say that 85 million were served. But the information in our possession, from the government's agencies as well as our own findings, during the short time in the country led to the conclusion that this was a lack of respect for a people in great need of a commodity so basic. No correlation between what was advanced and the reality. The harsh truth was that less than five percent had access to piped water, and, dishearteningly, none of it was drinkable quality.

Sure, conditions had worsened with wars during the 13 years preceding our visit. However, it still was immoral to attempt to change the brutal fact that this nation had never had a water system capable of supplying to even a mere 20% of its people at any time in history. This is why the Congolese turned to unhealthy water when unable to keep suppressing their needs if this was all they could find.

This shortage also came with some related major necessities, such as sanitation, that will sadly remain unresolved for a more extended period, despite offering a huge business potential for those able to answer the call of a country in distress. However, humanity must be at the forefront of coming to the rescue of a developing land with dire problems like those faced in the Congo, else any desire to invest will disappear with the first unsuccessful attempt.

Not helping the cause were those still nostalgically referring to Kinshasa as *la belle* (the beautiful) in relation to how it once was radiant in the days it was Leopoldville. But that beauty had died by the end of the 1960s with a dictatorial regime replacing the colonial influence that, despite having left scars in the memories of many, had some level of welfare of the people at heart.

The post-colonial Kinshasa keeps up with the largest cities in Africa: Lagos and Cairo. Its current second or third position, population-wise on the continent, depending on which international reference book consulted, was on everyone's lips and surely a national pride. Many had a script ready to be unleashed flawlessly and to the point when we met. They came forward, unsolicited, wherever we stopped, to introduce the capital to us. Some audaciously followed up with a remuneration request for their time and the history lesson. Whatever they related registered, though, leaving us yearning to contribute to their development.

Lying along the Congo River, the city once was only a small fishing site where residents of the nearby villages met to fish and sold what they caught. But this had since become a metropolitan agglomeration. On the opposite bank sits Brazzaville, in the Republic of the Congo. These two are the closest capitals in the world. However, it is a fact that neither of them takes advantage of in terms of tourism. A few fast boats providing day trips in both directions could boost their economies manifold.

We were on the south bank digesting their shared history as the hotel manager recounted. He had joined us in the meeting room he had let us use. Being on the 19th floor, we had our nose right into Brazzaville. Together with the river, the sight was breathtaking. We could have spent the whole day looking through the glass had we nothing else for the day.

"Your stay here would have cost a bit less had this river been drinkable," he said. "Water in this building counts for a big chunk of our tariffs."

His showcasing of the country continued, inciting in us the desire to make a hasty entry into the local business sphere after realising there was no end to prospects. We could not agree more with every reason he gave us to set up, despite sensing an exaggerated ego in him for his nation. We nonetheless focused on the good in his sayings.

"This city is a province on its own," he said.

There were 11 provinces when we first arrived in 2007, but 12 years later were shredded into 26. Kinshasa occupies a mere 10% of its vast territory but has long outpaced Paris in terms of the world's largest French-speaking metropolis. The Congo being four times larger than France, has earned itself an imposing presence on the *francophone* map, and rightfully so in Africa.

French remains the language of communication in administration, white-collar work, schools, the media, and even everyday life. People who speak local languages still enormously borrow French words to express their thoughts better or just out of habit, if not to show that they are educated. This influence is noted even in how children born to Congolese parents, but living in non-French-speaking countries, are fluent in or at least understand French.

"Sometimes, they mix French words, unconsciously, with their English, German, Portuguese, or Spanish, when talking to their parents or peers of their descent," the hotel manager told us. "It proves the extent to which we contribute to the survival of the French language."

He had graduated from three universities in the Congo and on the continent. He knew how to bring his knowledge into context and in a manner that benefited us. We wished he could have the chance to address those at the state level as he did to us. Such a shame we are unable to fit his hour-long lecture into these pages for the readers' sake.

"Ours is a country ruled by NGOs, all promoting human rights and the like," he argued when I dared to ask his opinion about children carrying water the city over. "Yet none understands that our kids' future will be best secured through education. They are at peril unless we eradicate this water scarcity. Our supply is obtained with too much legwork inflicted on our youngsters and their mothers, which is painful to watch."

He pointed out an NGO that had put a single water point for populations in a six-kilometre radius to flock to, leaving children still missing school because of this distance. The intended beneficiaries ignored the gift. They continued with their old habits of using their nearby unhealthy water, despite knowing the danger staring at them.

At that point, it seemed like he had been briefed about what we intended to do. We, therefore, could not help but ask for his advice on how to have the population on our side.

"A 10-minute walk to the well and no queuing would be appreciated. And, for the solution to be effective, parents need to find work to support their families. Otherwise, many children will keep playing the role of breadwinner."

He indeed gave us a lot to think about. We suddenly found ourselves questioning the efficiency of our contribution, becoming aware that water provision alone sufficed not to fully rescue these children. In all cases, he had softened the edges around our hearts.

Time-wasting

Heading into deprived areas to establish wells proved to be a wise decision. Interminable contracts awaited us there due to the immense population in such places. No wonder we received varying numbers whenever we inquired about how many lived there. Officials themselves insisted that even their own figures were to be taken cautiously and that if it pleased us, we could add 20% thereto. How disappointing that the government did not have exact statistics. But what do you expect when census had not taken place in 30 years. Therefore, going 10 kilometres off a tarred road to find out the number of people without water in their vicinity was the last thing that could have crossed these well-dressed office lovers' minds.

Surely not worth our time, despite their hospitality. Their polished French and job titles failed to impress us because of the many people off the main roads seeking water where they could. They went up the mountains and down in the valleys in and around the city just to bring some litres home. Their numbers led to conclude that millions said to be already having access to healthy water was tangible bad faith on the part of those who stated so.

We loved Laura for hurriedly leaving these executives on many occasions. She would sit in the car while the rest of us were still trying to say goodbye properly, thinking there was no point in burning bridges. She was rather eager to provide water and give people the chance to better their lives. She was totally right: time-wasting is a great enemy to the Congolese, but they seem unaware of what it costs them. Hence, the following day she picked up on the long-lines walking towards the city centre and suggested we drive where they were coming from.

From that moment on, we spent the first half of the morning in the SUVs battling through throngs of people to reach the off-the-beaten-path Commune of Kisenso. The tiny roads up there made our drivers alert and committed to making room for the oncoming vehicles, as a single scratch sufficed to get sacked. Water, not to mention clean, was the real luxury there, it being high on a mountain.

Contacts

We stepped out of the vehicles to admire the view over Kinshasa from the mountain. A curious driver went on to park just past us and walked back to introduce himself, joining a few improvised guides already surrounding us. Makengo was a surgeon who had moved on to work for a global NGO and was up there attending to the beneficiaries of the service he administered.

Masina—a different commune—was where he lived until 17 months prior. His house there was just a short five-metre from the now-unused railway that linked the *Gare Centrale* (Central Station) to the Ndjili airport via the proximity of the Ndolo military airport. He used to perform operations on patients with the help of candlelight in a room not approved by the Authority. But that was all he had. He could not deny people treatment or starve his family. The position of a regional director with this employer enabled him a move to Gombe, a huge social shift as well as a massive change in luck and status; an *upgrade*, as they call it over there.

He managed the Congo, advising government officials and medical professionals on industry standards and monitoring the application thereof, reporting back to his headquarters in the West. He received and distributed financial aid to the institutions that needed it—none ever said no, though. Hence, $15,000 in salary every month, a four-bed modern townhouse in a gated community costing his organisation $7,000 a month, two cars, private schools for his three children, and other benefits were his.

Very commendable of this NGO to put him in the same conditions as his counterparts in other countries. This was contrary to the organisations that justified their discrimination of the locals with the excuse that they could not go against the government-imposed miserable payscale. Had they not put him in this comfortable position, we would have seen an unenthusiastic representative, like many we kept coming across.

His reports appeared in global industry periodicals that influenced policies and funding decisions. But he was humble, counting himself lucky for what he now had, despite all the efforts put into finding his way out of the poverty that, for a long time, had seemed to be all he was destined for, even 15 years after being awarded the title of Doctor of Medicine. The country produced many medical professionals yearly, but almost 90% went straight into unemployment if they could not find jobs in unrelated fields. Another physician told us he was teaching secondary school to avoid turning into a beggar.

All this had resulted in so many small clinics run by individual doctors and nurses in conditions that rendered the profession untrustworthy. However, rather than criticising, now that we understood many things, we thought of how to reach out and help where possible.

Makengo gave us over 100 contacts that lodged in his handset unexploited, whereas they were a source of additional income. He was the opposite of a government clerk who asked for a beer to give us a piece of information. Handing him 500 Congolese Francs, the cost of a 75-centilitre bottle of the brand he had mentioned, he rejected. He charged back that he only drank liquor. Laura fell for it and parted with her $20. She badly wanted to obtain the list of the biggest employers this man had. These were presumably the top taxpayers in Kinshasa. Luckily for Laura and the rest of us, approaching these companies, they responded to the quest to give water to less-resourced communities.

As for Makengo, he took not the compensation we offered him but instead asked that we further our work with it. His unselfishness motivated us more to turn to the needy.

4

THE VICTIMS

Basil

In *Kingasani* (not to be confounded with *Kisangani*), east of the Ndjili river, we stopped at a street corner and exchanged with Crispin, who sat at his stall selling pay-as-you-go phone credits. At our request, he left the business with his friend to take us to seven wells in the area, where children under the age of 12 formed crowds. It hurt seeing them wrestling with a rusted hand pump or a palm-cutting rope to bring water to the surface. Pushing and shoving each other to be next in the queue was taking up even more time and energy and leading to fights.

What an awful thing to see some of them as young as six resolving matters with fists, inflicting bruises and cuts to each other, all this to have a few litres of water. Some were lucky to have parents with work to go to. But most carried water to bring an income home because the responsibility to care for the family had long shifted hands.

He mentioned an additional well he was not comfortable with us visiting. But that only intrigued us, and pressing, he told us of Basil, who had set out to do what he had always done devotedly and daily. He was forced out of sleep at his usual time of six by the demands of the several roles known as his despite being only eight. He brushed his teeth with the water he had to use sparingly, it being the last drops out of the white 25-litre jerrycan that sat in the corner of the kitchen. This one was used to store drinking water. Two similar but yellow ones used for water for other needs were wrung out. Therefore, he wiped his face with the dampness of his hand.

He went for the broomstick that stood against the wall and proceeded to tidy up the large unpaved yard. Then, he went back indoors to dust off the furniture and sweep and mop the floor on his knees. They were repeatedly bruised, cut, and healed because of the rough and broken cement floor he was exposed to.

A heap of dirty dishes and pots was usually next on his to-do list, but not that day, as the family had had no meal the night before. He had mastered his routine and completed it in a timely manner, giving himself an hour to kick a ball against the wall by himself. The only time friends joined in was when school was in the morning, and they had the afternoon free.

Basil was too young to carry a full 25-litre jerrycan. So, he made five daily trips to the well with a five-litre one to bring home drinking water. His brothers, Kabeya, 12, and Mulumba, 14, made six rounds with 25 litres each after school to provide the family with 300 litres for general usage. This was how the water task was divided between them, and it was their foremost job, even ahead of school, else there could be no water in the house.

They were lucky in that their water source was just a kilometre away. The only difficulty was queuing due to the number of people relying on this well and, of course, the arduous pulling out of the bucket. Also, the constant bending and weight involved caused terrible pain in the back and arms. Hence, their mother, Brigitte, had taken it upon herself to deeply massage them every night with a towel dampened with hot water. She also gave them some painkillers when they could afford a stock. Otherwise, they could not sleep well.

Basil had often confided in his friends that he did not carry out these tasks by choice. But because he too had to help, as it was taught in the family from not sure when. He had been contributing since the age of five when he could not lift his five-litre jerrycan more than half-full. Life was difficult for them all, and he knew it. The father, Mukendi, and Brigitte worked hard. They left home at four, thinking he was asleep, whereas he always heard them. His siblings attended school in the morning, so they were out of the door at six, just as he was lifting himself out of the very same bed the three of them shared.

Like his brothers, he had washed his own school white shirt by hand the night before and hung it on the line in the yard with the help of a stool before moving it indoors. It was dry by the morning and almost wrinkle-free, thanks to it being predominantly polyester. Because ironing a damp white shirt turned it yellowish, he always gave it more time to catch some sun rays if it was not ready by the morning. His other difficulty was blowing into a charcoal-filled iron to keep the fire going, running the risk of sparks burning his face.

He put his full uniform set, including socks, on the bed and trainers on the floor. His books were on the chair that was in the room. Then he headed out to the well. He bumped into a couple of adult neighbours and greeted them while two peers with water assured him of no queue. He had learnt to start with the other chores to avoid a long line.

Brigitte did not return home for lunch that day as she had not sold a thing all morning. She did not want to ruin any chance of feeding the family that evening. She arrived home after seven and a furious husband asked her where on earth Basil was. His siblings had returned at their usual time of three to only the preparation he had made for school. It was unusual and worrying, and with no one to ask, they held their breath, hoping it was not what they were thinking.

Since late afternoon when people usually resumed drawing water after school and work, no one had fetched water because the news had already gone around. Then someone appeared with a jerrycan that the family identified. He had found it half-filled on the side of the well at about nine, which those who had seen the boy confirmed to be about when they had spoken to him. This person was on his way to the street leader's house, as was customary with lost-and-found items. The container used to bring out water was inside the borehole, and the other end of the rope was tied to the nearby tree, as it had always been.

The casing of the borehole was a series of 200-litre steel drums cut at both ends and welded together, filling the 60-metre depth of this well. The mouth of the well was wide open, with no covering. Its 900 millimetres diameter posed a threat to swallow up anything. It was established that Basil had most likely become dizzy, lost his footing, fallen inside, and died. The house on the site had nobody in at the time believed to be when the incident took place. However, the next two properties on either side had people at home. They claimed to have heard a single sharp scream and that it was a child's voice.

Basil had not eaten a thing for 36 hours, and it was not the first time the family had gone without food for that duration. Mukendi's income had never made ends meet all the boys' lives; hence his wife was required to take control.

Because it was already dark, the police ordered that the investigation be resumed in the morning. The father sent the family home while he held a vigil at the well, crying and hoping his son was somewhere else and alive. He called him all night in vain. A year earlier, they had lost their nine-year-old daughter to dysentery, and the last thing they wanted was another death.

Having exhausted himself and fallen asleep, Brigitte woke him up at four, with a crowd joining them from six. He had no voice left to talk to anyone, nor could he hear anything that was said to him. His own crying and screaming had turned him deaf. His eyes were terribly swollen and could barely open. Standing up was possible only with two individuals with their arms under his in support. Eventually, a body was brought to the surface, and seeing it was his son, he collapsed and remained unconscious for a week.

Basil was buried to the disbelief of the entire neighbourhood. This could have been prevented as the lack of safety measures around the well was clearly visible.

The lad was known and loved because he sang beautifully wherever he went and danced whenever appropriate. He and his siblings had formed a band open to other kids in the community. A lead singer and showman, he knew how to captivate crowds with his moves, even in the absence of music. They were solicited every time there was an event in the area, including funerals. But, at his, no one dared to sing, saying they could not do it as nicely as he would have sung for someone else. He also played football and won trophies in his community and at school.

When the family was finally allowed to visit Mukendi, he had just opened his eyes. Although struggling to finish a sentence due to a speech impediment suffered, he smiled at their approach. He held the boys at either side of the bed and down onto his chest. Then Brigitte, and there was the other hand in vain navigating the empty space on the other side before calling out loudly with the strength he did not have a minute ago:

"Basil! Basil!" and "Basil…"

The tears in his wife's and children's eyes were the only answer to his yearning for his baby son. Mukendi instantly went back into the coma to never wake up again.

At his funeral, his widow was branded a witch, beaten, stoned, and burnt to death with a tyre of a car around her neck. These horrific acts were carried out by her own community, many of whom were close friends of the family. Hearing them sending for a couple more tyres, the boys escaped through the back of the compound, knowing with a surety that they were next. They were not found when the tyres arrived. It had slipped the *law enforcers'* minds to keep hold of them.

"How many years did they get?" Günter asked.

The killers were heroes in the eyes of all for sending out a strong message that would prevent someone from bewitching their own or anyone else. With that, no one admitted that the cause of this catastrophe was that a child was left to draw water while the parents fought to put food on the table. The unsafe well was since abandoned. It was referred to as a ghost place and a source of every bad thing happening in the neighbourhood.

It was like we were watching a horror movie. We were defeated and incapable of thinking straight. We questioned nature and ourselves, furious with everyone, but not permitted to show it. This tragedy had happened over a decade prior but felt fresh as the story was recounted to us, mostly by those Basil's age and best mates of his back then. They were 18-year-olds now, and imagining what he would have looked like and achieved by now made us the more upset.

"Why?" Amy was heard asking continually.

An unsafe well had claimed the life of an innocent child and wiped out an entire family!

Mentality Shift

Having clean water in proximity and available all the time was taking centre stage in our minds and becoming the heartbeat of our design—so adults could find the time to devote to other household needs before setting out for what paid their bills. It would, likewise, liberate children from drawing water so they could focus on school. Walking for great distances to and from remote springs and rivers would be forgotten if water is metres away.

Crispin taking us around the wells was not because of having time on his hands. Hence, Laura asked what to pay him. He said he would balance his books with $10, sharing some of it with the person he left manning his stall. Although they would be overpaid with what he asked, she happily quadrupled it in appreciation of the discovery.

At that point, and with a wallet weighing more than usual, he opened up more and told us about the good having a well brought to his uncle's household. Frequent clinic visits with aches ceased. Kids found themselves with extra hours to revise their lessons, and their father started to buy a book a month to help them improve their reading and broaden their general knowledge. His wife had eight hours a day to invest in learning to bake. And, once confident, she made bread and sold it to sustain her family. This saw her husband's income go straight into a savings account.

She did not have to worry about her children's safety to and from their old water source, a river where they had been verbally abused by some unruly males and females old enough to be their parents. Their sin was asking to not jump the queue. She and her husband could now have evening chats and were able to bond with their children daily. They got to know them better than when water was a long walk away from home. There was peace at home for not having to force some of the members of the family to fulfill their water-fetching task, especially when playing with their mates was all they wanted. Nearby and readily available water also provided the opportunity to build safe latrines and curtail the diseases related to the lack thereof.

All these stories were but untapped opportunities for my partners. Therefore, I continued to create occasions to learn from the locals, who, the more they interacted with us, the more they bought into the idea that access to water would transform many things. These changes would also allow them to return to their previous way of life, which was socially oriented and promoted sharing whatever little they could.

"In the past, people could stop anywhere on their way to somewhere and ask for water to drink, " Crispin said. "But not in 2007!"

This attitude had nothing to do with no longer being kind to strangers, but taps had ceased yielding water all day long, or when they did, it was rusty and dirty and not worth gambling on.

Another problem is that the Equator cutting through the Congo causes high temperatures all year, leaving people sweating a lot. Many have limited access to water to allow them to wash their clothes regularly and keep up the tradition of bathing at least once a day. Even worse, over three-quarters of the Congolese have no choice over what they drink. Hence, out of sheer necessity, they consent to consume disease-laden water, resulting in sickness and, if untreated, death, as bacteria of pathogenic natures are frequent in corrupted freshwater.

Waterborne Diseases

We visited hospitals in Kinshasa to learn more about water-related problems, which was key in drawing conclusions because if the most cosmopolitan city failed the test, no other town could do better. Kinshasa was where to get the feel of the country's welfare level. For example, poor medical facilities there gave no hope for any other city faring in this department. No clean water there meant a disaster everywhere. Yet Kinshasa is home to the wealthy, politicians, celebrities, and international institutions, even if they had second homes and offices in other cities.

We heard of rampant waterborne diseases contracted through drinking or bathing in contaminated water. A report from nurses, doctors, and other medical officials categorised distinct types of waterborne infectious agents, such as bacterial, parasite, protozoan, and viral. Our informers concurred that drilling wells could directly result in controlling, reducing, and mitigating these severe diseases. Furthermore, easing access to clean water would have a tremendous socioeconomic impact on the inhabitants and be a blessing to many future generations.

Moving through the wards led us to Lisa, 32, lying on a bed in this downtown hospital. She was a victim of consuming unhealthy water and could now barely open her eyes while speaking was already behind her. Caring for her was her sister, who exchanged with us on her behalf. The patient walked three hours to and from the school where she taught. At home, she stayed up late, preparing lessons for the following day. Facing acute necessity, she resorted to a river relatively near her home despite still requiring an hour round-trip. But, even if time was not an issue, there was just no source of safe water to which to turn.

She knew too well that river water, although not stagnant, was filthy and infected, as she had disgustedly witnessed human discharges floating on it on numerous occasions. That alone should have been enough to dissuade her from carrying it home. Instead, she convinced herself that boiling water turned it potable. She drank it once, and she had no negative effects. So, she made it a habit for her children to partake of it. Because of the cost of heating water, she stopped going past 100°C when most bacteria died, ignoring that others resisted beyond 130°C. Unfortunately, being budget-conscious had its consequences.

Her meagre income contributed towards the never-ending bills that included consultation, tests, hospitalisation, prescriptions, and more. The cost of the bed was separate; else, she would have ended up on the veranda, in the cold and rain, because of the high demand. Being outside also meant facing the cumbrous mosquitoes that worked around the clock and fed on human blood, the option that only those who had completely run out of resources took.

With Lisa incapacitated and waking up rarely, her sister did not leave her bedside. Therefore, she paid to stay past visiting hours and sleep under the bed when the chair became difficult to manage. By the time we came to her, two months into her internment, Lisa had already been released from her employment. Same with the sister who was a tax collector. This made us realise how waterborne diseases affected more than just the ones infected.

Medical practitioners seeing our concern told us more about the consequences of using unhealthy water. The situation was not limited only to those in those beds. It extended to the public at large as even the doctors, nurses, and their families were without clean water. They lived with the fear of being next to fall if solutions were not found and implemented in the foreseeable future, if not immediately.

Lisa had contracted amoeba—a protozoan infection—possibly by placing her hand on her mouth after touching contaminated water. It could also have come through drinking untreated tap water or the one she had heated but left uncovered to cool down, and a fly had landed on or dropped its liquid in it. Whatever the cause, she was experiencing acute abdominal discomfort, bloating, diarrhoea, fatigue, fever, and weight loss.

Cryptosporidiosis and Cyclosporiasis were also found in her laboratory results. This often occurs with oral intake of water spoiled by animal manure. Another cause could be consuming seasonal run-off water, such as from a pond or infrequent tap delivery, or where there was sewage interference. Hence her cramps, flu-like symptoms, increased gas, no appetite, muscle aches, nausea, vomiting, watery diarrhoea, and so on.

Cases like hers were legion in Kinshasa. Faced with no choice, residents settled for what was within reach. For those reading this, let it be known that it would be no different the world over if anyone consumed the above types of water. We might be too conscious about saving money, relegating questions that matter most backstage. But consequences strike up eventually, and very complicatedly, as was also with the patient next to Lisa. She was diagnosed with Fasciolopsiasis, Guinea Worm Disease, Schistosomiasis, tapeworms, and possibly more, as tests were taking time to come through due to insufficient tools and having less *motivated* staff on the task.

Her diseases were spread by certain types of snails that carried Schistosomes, stagnant water that contained larvae generally found in parasitised Copepoda, drinking water polluted with eggs or encysted Metacercaria, and the list was endless. Hence, she had aching muscles, allergic effects, asthmatic bouts, blood-filled urine, cholangitis, cold, cough, cysticercosis, diarrhoea, fever, intestinal disturbances, itchy skin, jaundice, nausea, neurological signs, swollen liver, urticarial rash, vomiting, and weight loss, among many other things. All these in a single person!

The doctors only tried to show us a portion of the danger of drinking unclean water. Sadly, these were what many in this ward were left to process. Their health had deteriorated because they could not afford the bills. But the doctor on duty forbade Laura from pulling out her purse when trying to do so. He was happy to take her money only if she was agreeable to helping those who had not yet gotten this far. There was no hope for recovery for anyone in this unit. Our eyes filled up with tears hearing this.

Put it in a monetary context, there would have been a need for not less than $2,000 for each one of the 64 in this ward had they come in early. It was customary in this city to raise funds by selling the patient's property because of the belief that assets could be replaced but not life. In the case of these, the doctors had advised against this practice. But where heartless professionals were involved, families were made homeless because of being given false assurances that their parent or child would be healed. Such staff were being accused of earning a commission out of prescriptions due to imposing on people where to purchase the medicines, and each chemist charging what seemed to them good. This was yet to be proved, but that the regulator never investigating either led us to doubt these accusations less.

Also sickening us was that most efficacious medications were imported from Europe. This caused a delay in reaching the hospital. Besides, it was not guaranteed to have prescriptions from the Congo accepted at pharmacies in the West. Furthermore, with express couriers costing a fortune, doctors took time so they could gather a few prescriptions and reduce delivery fees for themselves but not for the patients. The latter could not individually afford the full cost of a courier.

Three days later, we returned to that hospital but to another person in Lisa's bed.

Neglect

The water that took Lisa's life was only one of the many types turned into weapons. We were shaken to learn that even someone touching a door handle without washing hands with soap properly following a visit to the loo posed a threat to the next person to lay their hand on it. Others also got infected when they bathed, washed clothes or dishes, and cooked with water not trusted. Many overlooked that eating the food they had grabbed with hands washed with unsanitary water was lethal. We were far from done hearing of the infections that occurred as a result of drinking or coming into direct contact with unhealthy water. But we knew by then that they were referred to as waterborne diseases.

Where there was no water at all, the locals used what they found, bringing home waterborne diseases and consequently jeopardising their households. They had little choice to make between being without water and taking some uncalculated risks, but not all were fully aware of the significance of their actions. Even after witnessing a fatality at close range, few still considered how the outcome would have been different had the victims fully understood the aftermath of using germ-ridden water. The fallen might have thought there was little or no harm in using the water they knew was infected to wash their bodies or laundry with, forgetting that their skins could equally react badly to infected water as did their internal organs.

That was how some indescribable negligence gob-smacked us when curiosity led us to stop by a large pond that appeared on our way to visits. That pool, and many others throughout the city, were the result of torrential rains that Kinshasa received all year round but during the dry season.

Kids as young as six were packed in that artificial lake, ecstatically throwing their arms in all directions. Most of them were walking around in there with their feet on the bottom of the tarn, pretending to be swimming but nonetheless enjoying the moment. No sign flagging the damage they were self-inflicting. Some unconcernedly acknowledged randomly swallowing the inactive mud-filled liquid when burying themselves in and coming out of the water. The reason for being there was the lack of a single drop out of the tap for weeks, or they could not afford to buy water from those who delivered it or travel far to bring home the relatively clean water.

A close look at the colour of the pond confirmed the filth that had come to mind with stepping out of the cars, while the horrible smell justified the fear that had enveloped us at first sight of that lake. Those coming onshore had their feet covered with mud, and their bodies and hair tainted with small particles of leaves and other objects blown in by winds. Not a pleasant scene, but to the swimmers, by the look of it, just normal life. But, in all fairness, it all came down to just what happens when people are limited in their choices.

Others there busied themselves washing their clothes or dishes on the bank, barely half-a-metre ashore. Obviously, the ordeal this lasting lack of clean water caused was multi-faceted and deep-rooted. Huge efforts would be needed to reverse the situation. A subtle enquiry led to the adults assuring us they would pay for clean water if wells became available in their communities. It did not bother them that we were not an NGO, which we had initially appeared to be to them, but businesspeople who would infuse cash into a project to make a profit.

They were in favour of an investment rather than the old-fashioned donation approach that had never brought lasting joy but depleted their self-esteem for generations. Charity had turned them into a people that could not do anything for themselves without foreign aid.

We took their word for it, seeing they valued mutual advancement and offered to contribute. They insisted that if we could not give them water for whatever reason, we should at least accept the challenge to campaign on their behalf for a group that would fancy to succor them for a fee.

Being Warned

We paid attention to everything people told us. But, we could not understand why the organisations that had preceded us with the intention to give these populations water had failed to overcome administrative caprices. They warned that our situation would be no different, and they were right. Those granting permits continually devised new ways to make life difficult for anyone not bending to them.

We did not want to make our predecessors' experience ours, especially with some findings leading to the deduction that they had possibly not secured funding. Their stories were like those of several groups that had contacted me in the past but showed no financial capabilities when required. Instead, they told people of the difficulty of working with the Congolese government to come out clean, when they had yet to travel to the Congo even once.

Some of the parties coming over to undertake this kind of project had gotten away with misrepresentation, as they were determined to justify why they did not go all the way until the propagation of the Internet commenced to expose them. Many dissatisfied recipients started to take it online to help stop the damage done in their name, for there were ever-increasing numbers of non-profits collecting funds that never reached the intended beneficiaries.

The humanitarian aspect of a social development project, like providing water, was in decline. Funding was becoming more obtainable only where there was a speculative promise of helping people to uplift themselves out of poverty. However, many NGO executives were still getting their pockets filled. They constantly sought and received donations that never served to alleviate the pain of those they were meant to be helping. The outcome could have been different had the donors adopted the investment approach my partners and I saw as the solution.

This was why whether someone had the funding or was still seeking to secure it, they could not win me over if they spoke of *helping* the Congo. I wanted to make life better for my people, but only while constructing a sustainable business that would yield a profit and live long beyond my coming back this way. That is how to best help someone, in my opinion. The people at the rainwater *lake* sustained this belief. Those who had the courage to speak admitted having fallen into the trap of those coming in the name of charity several times. Nothing worked with just donations. Often, upon realising they were being taken advantage of, the recipients sank such NGOs by pointing them in the wrong direction at every level of their undertaking.

At this point, a man standing a couple of metres from us, having all along given the impression of one not interested in our presence at the pond, finally broke his silence. He upheld that charging for water would make the investment go further, so the same privilege can be extended to more people without needing new funding each time. Otherwise, their dependency would continue, and the nation would be permanently impoverished. Most adults gathered there reasoned the same, proving to understand what would work best for them in the long run rather than being content with precarious solutions to a problem that had gone on too long.

Some adults there mentioned their good level of education, leading the youth to also brag about their parents' professions. It was shocking still that they had lowered themselves to this lake rather than getting together to fight their water scarcity. But we carried on learning from whoever was willing to impart with us, especially when they came off the street unexpectedly.

Lydie

Street-contacting left us with some sour taste in the mouth, nevertheless lessons upon which to build. Being naive, we spelt out our intentions to whoever had a minute, allowing them to make up what we wanted to hear. They could tell we were new in town and made it count, milking a dollar or two out of us. Certainly, the Congo had moved on without me! The proof was that I could not detect the games played on us.

Growing up in Kinshasa, we had water. I must, nonetheless, admit that living in the part of the city that came out of the ground a decade after the country had gained independence, we struggled until the early 1980s, when the government won our hearts bringing water to every street in my commune of Masina. But we knew nothing as chaotic as when returning with my partners. However, that water system had since deteriorated due to not being serviced.

Unpaved streets were victims of erosion, which led to pipes becoming uncovered and bursting with the weight of the passing vehicles, helped by drivers' inattention or inability to do otherwise. Hence, streams appeared, and any water that remained in the pipes entered the taps already contaminated. Misusing the consumers' monthly payments left municipal water plants with no treatment products nor what was needed to acquire replacement parts. Civil wars across the country had also forced the government to divert its priorities elsewhere.

I understood—peace is everything, especially after seeing for myself the level of insecurity people now lived with as opposed to back in my day. But the biggest cause for this water shortage was that I had left my city with three million inhabitants to return to one that had grown five times, and no one was keeping tabs on this expansion.

Back then, people came to the capital for a visit, or uni, and went back. They only stayed on if they had a job. Life was better, more peaceful, and safer away from Kinshasa, but not since the culture of wars became commonplace and a passport to a ministerial appointment or another position of power in the government. They now felt protected in the capital that could not be taken easily by insurgents and where killing was not so rampant. Hence, all the people carrying water on their heads everywhere to provide for families.

My time away left me to rely on others to find and visit at least two water drilling companies, for there was no phone book or anywhere else to which to turn. The latter pricked Laura's mind as a business opportunity, especially with the Internet becoming trendy. It would cost less to list companies online than going to print. But I convinced her to park that prompting, for the time being, so we could just carry on with fact-finding.

We approached Lydie as she walked towards the *Rond-Point Victoire*, a buoyant crossroads harbouring shops and roadside markets, where all Kinshasa congregated. Conservatively but smartly dressed, she radiated an executive aura and was comfortable sharing much about herself with a simple question as though we had not just met. She had a bachelor's in pharmacy but worked in an unrelated field and was on leave. At 29, she had become under pressure from her family to get married to her unemployed chemistry graduate boyfriend. Asking her conjecture about the number of drilling firms in town, she advised us of a huge deficit and encouraged us to use this to our advantage.

We trusted her with taking us to the companies she brought to our attention, as well as functioning wells that she knew. She assured us she had access to all the information we could ever need in this department. Her daily rate of $50 for up to 10 hours of her time was reasonable. We offered lunch with us so she could go home with her remuneration untouched.

Our city centre hotel offered the tranquility needed to plan out the week. But Lydie objected to meeting there, advancing transportation difficulties, and we bounced back with a lift commitment on our part. Once there, she spent prolonged periods on the phone, away from us, saying that she was gathering details. By the end of the day, she left us with two A4 sheets chock-full of scribbles, auguring a busy week ahead.

But to our disappointment, she did not show up in the morning! Her phone was out of reach, despite several attempts. We worried about her and made a detour in the afternoon for a chance to bump into her again where we had met but did so in vain efforts. That she had been paid for one day's work now defunct to us was not as upsetting as the thought of having to start all over again to find a replacement.

The next day, we were in the queue for breakfast but struggling to regain the level of excitement we had been enjoying the past few days. The chef was about to place a couple of crispy-edged runny-yolk fried eggs on my plate when the man ahead of me turned around:

"What a great morning this is proving to be!"

I forced out a smile to not seem unfriendly. It was only 6.15 a.m. but so sunny as though it already was 11.00 a.m.

"Paul," he added, stretching his right hand to me.

He was an architect. His clients had won a weighty contract to build 6,500 quality houses in prime locations of the city. Having returned from a Belgian university, he was making himself a fortune ahead of his fellow diaspora who had not found something valuable to come home to or with which to contribute to the development of the country. He was serving foreign land developers who had seen the *high risk* the Congo was labelled with, investment-wise, as an opportunity to multiply their wealth several times whilst competition remained low. I had no choice but to help his curiosity.

"You have been away too long, Brother," he said, making me feel guilty.

He made a phone call and requested that I stay in the lobby or in my room, then asked to be excused once through his plate. An hour later, the receptionist had someone for me downstairs. Lee would make us forget about Lydie, as he took no time to prove he was very connected.

There was an outcry for water everywhere he took us to. Potential customers asked where to sign and demanded our banking details when we declined their cash. All this without seeing our offices, equipment, or employees. They could care less that we were yet to register. That we were on an exploratory trip could not dissuade them either. We finally convinced them that it was not a good idea for us to take their money as anything could happen, despite boasting with confidence to return and accomplish whatever little we could.

We came to know that there were trustworthy people there. Lydie had walked away with a tiny slice of a very small cake, earned slyly, while Paul and Lee knew how to build brick by brick to accumulate more income with time. We just had to be selective in choosing who to hand ourselves to and refrain from writing off everyone because one individual had let us down. Both lads made a living being honest despite hardship sparing no one. Dignity meant everything to them, as evidenced by how people opened their doors to us because we were in Lee's company, thanks to his strong relationships in the suburb where he lived up to graduating from uni.

Consensus

We entered a community leader's yard and were treated to an hour-long chat. Lee was aware of this area's zero percent tap connection, making it a great candidate for drilling and the distribution system we had in mind. Therefore, we came seeking the leader's involvement. In the West, calling unexpectedly on someone, you would be met by one standing in the doorway and, before even greeting you, asking: "*What can I do for you?*"

"Please, come in the shade," was instead how Lambert reacted.

He wanted us to go on and on talking, in conjunction with the culture that asked not to rush guests, so they could feel at home. He sat us in the best conditions he had, under his large mango tree that was in the shape of an umbrella. A soft drink, although as warm as a late afternoon tea, was in our hands by the time we finished introducing ourselves, and it said everything about his hospitality. Not long after, trays full of bananas and roasted peanuts landed on a coffee table. My non-Africans raised curiosity to the point that even those busy cooking stopped momentarily to find out what brought us there.

Lambert's jurisdiction was 10 streets of about 200 properties each. These were made up of 20 occupants each on average, divided into some three to four households. His area and four others formed a locality. There were four localities in this part of the Commune of Kimbanseke and about half a million people, a sixth or so of this commune. Kimbanseke is one of the five communes of the Tshangu District, which in turn is one of Kinshasa's four districts. Tshangu is nicknamed *Chine Populaire*—implying that it is *over-populated like China.*

With Lambert's consent, we briefed him succinctly about our errand before allowing in a few people. These were young and adults, men and women, educated and uneducated, those in employment, job seekers, and retirees. A group of 10 people made a good representation of Lambert's street, and it gave everyone an equal chance to express themselves on the good that establishing wells would bring about for them. A fourth-grade schoolboy recommended restoring a dysfunctional nearby borehole instead of drilling a new one. He reasoned like an adult, explaining how it would cost less and take no time to refurbish, and that its closeness to his home would eliminate his daily journeys to the stream and permit him to be at school on time.

The Ntshuenge river, substituting the *SWC* (State Water Company), was 50 minutes away. School started at 7.15 a.m. But children chose to visit, waking up early because of the body hygiene their parents had instilled in them, that their schools also insisted on it.

The tone of the discussion echoed the participants' desire to be part of the solution, despite rendering it difficult to follow all of them at once, as they did not speak in an orderly fashion. We appreciated, however, that women had a say, contrary to the tradition that quietened them or relegated them to the kitchen when important matters were being discussed. Such was the case with Leah, a mother of seven with twins on the way, who could not wait to thank us for her chance to participate. She begged us not to change our minds.

She had resigned from her job at a shoe manufacturing plant to monitor her children's water drawing, so they were not late for school and was aware that much time was wasted hand-pumping water and of the physical demands with which this exercise came. Therefore, affixing a solar pump to the well was, for her, "life-prolonging" and would be more than they expected.

Lambert thought it was not best for this group to decide for the entire community just because he was their leader. Therefore, for the next two days, he took us to meet with each street's leader and some of their residents. Every household supported our proposal. We achieved a more consensual and compelling decision faster, working with a mixture of delegates than we would have with a homogenous selection of, let's say, leaders only. Together, they pushed for a fulfilment date which we dared not give out, for we were still weighing our options.

Another difficulty during this decision-making process was determining whose opinion to take and leave. Everyone wanted their wording included in the short write-up we dictated to one of them, who improvised as our scribe. They were all ambitious and determined to win—a grit that would serve us later when we asked them to take responsibility for improving their conditions and quit waiting for someone to come from overseas to do it for them.

They repeatedly told us that we were the saviours they had longed to have around, to cause their voice to be heard, which had been our plan coming to them anyway. Giving them access to water should not deprive them of the right to choose how it should be provided, and by no means undermine them in establishing this solution just because of their weak position.

Furthermore, their males' keenness to lighten their women's burden and give their children the time to focus on education made it worth investing our money and time. They led us to doubt the general assumption that made them look like they cared less and only exploited their wives and children. The men we found there understood that overall improvement of this water situation would be a big step towards bringing healing in their midst. They believed that we would be better than non-profits because of giving them the chance to be accountable. But we paid little attention to the praises they showered us with and just went on navigating through all the avenues at our disposal.

Relationships

Laura made friends wherever life took her; be it in her neighbourhood, at school, on holiday, or at work, she just connected naturally with people and kept those relationships much longer than most of us. Her friendship with Judy went back to their first day of nursery in Montreal. They had remained in contact, thanks to their mums also becoming friends when destiny would make them live across the road from each other. Their mothers took turns driving them to and from school, sporting activities, and more, so they could attend college or work, despite not needing the latter to sustain their families.

Their husbands fully provided for them, but they got it that it was always best to prepare for the future no matter how rosy life was. They took pride in adding to their households' revenues and being role models to their children and the African community they frequented. Their down-to-earth personalities facilitated their integration into a culture new to them. They served those who needed it, and taking up paid employment would be handy in meeting the unforeseen, which eventually struck.

Judy's dad was a wealthy diamond dealer who sent his family to Montreal so the children could study there and have a competitive advantage when they returned home. He came to them every six months for two weeks. He was all over the world but spent much of his time in the Congo, carefully buying stones deep in the bush. One day, he came home to Kinshasa robbed. His established buyers had shown an interest in the manifest he had sent to them and invited him with the stones worth $12 million to Moscow, whereas all other times, he had sold to them in Antwerp. He woke up to him alone in the room he recognised not and without any knowledge of how he had parted with his consignment.

The family found themselves living with no light nor gas in temperatures that plummeted to minus 30°C. The leased car went. Public transport came with snow up to the knees; without counting how often they found themselves on their backsides due to the black ice that formed easily on the streets of Montreal, they not being used to walking them. No more private schools for the children. Being evicted from the rented house was the last nail in the coffin and terrible humiliation for the mother.

Her husband had not sent a penny in nearly a year because of keeping trying to bounce back again with top-notch 10-carat plus stones that used to set him apart from other suppliers. It was for that purpose that he sold every possession. He was, therefore, left with no accommodation of his own, let alone a vehicle to get around, when the family finally joined him with the help of a few friends who came together with just what was needed for airfares.

Fortunately, his brother had lent him a modest two-bed flat in the Commune of Bumbu. Such a big favour, although with no running water nor electricity. It was tough for them! The youngest, just four, passed away within two months of their return. They all contracted malaria because of the abundance of mosquitoes in this enclave of the city. Life took its toll on the rest of them, but the worst off was the father, who sank into depression and succumbed within three months of his son's death. The doctors had warned him that he would die if he did not stop worrying about his situation. Easier said than done! Judy was the eldest and only 12 when she saw her dad buried in a very modest way that she could have never imagined for the man whose pride she knew too well despite her young age.

Fearing for the remainder, a friend of his put them up in his six-bed villa in the rich suburb of Macampagne, giving them two years to get themselves sorted. He had served as a minister in various governments and managed state-owned companies for a combined 28 years. Another friend offered the mother work in his department at the bank. Thus her Montreal-acquired degree in finance and a couple of diplomas in accounting and management came in handy. This was proof to all of us that "luck is what happens when preparation meets opportunity", despite the fact that all the professional experience she had brought back was hotel room cleaning, a curse or blessing that is African's in the West.

Their new dwelling being on a steep hill, was not exempt from the calamity of water. Without the mother asking, the children took it upon themselves to go down in the valley to fetch water from those who had it out of the tap unless it rained due to not being in the position to pay someone to bring it to them.

After a year in a public school where pupils sat on the floor unless they brought their own chairs, the mother's employer placed all three in a private one, later giving Judy a bursary to attend uni in France the moment she completed high school with distinction. They all had been very good at and loved education, such that even their mates mocking their Quebecois did not put them off their studies. It took some time to pick up the local accent, but until then, teachers made them repeat themselves a few times for their own understanding and that of the other students.

Aware of her luck, Judy took learning seriously and obtained a bachelor's in business management, followed by a master's with a focus on global supply chain. She added a year-long placement within a bottled water company as a trainee planning manager.

The international brand supermarket where we found her as general manager was recruiting talents throughout France via universities for overseas vacancies. Her uni recommended they check her out because she could return home easily if good benefits were offered. The recruiter arranged for an undercover agent to observe her on the job for a month, for the role they had in mind for her required someone with much experience. In the end, they brought her over to be their procurement administrator with a package only a valued expatriate could be entitled to. Before long, she made her way up to head that department.

She also proved to be the best customer service manager they had ever had when she was handed this role. We witnessed this while in conversation with her the first day we visited, and queuing was building up at check-out. She asked to be excused, opened a till, and got customers through so they were not kept long. Another day, we found her sucking up spilt water with a mop. Our last trip to her outlet led us to her serving at the cooked food counter, wrapped in the department's attire, a hat covering her hair, to be compliant and like everyone there.

Each time the public announcement called for staff, they found her already helping. She handed them back their tasks with a smile, whereas she could have barked at them for being slow to respond. To Amy's comment that she was a different breed of manager, she asked not to embarrass her, before insisting on having learnt from gentle leaders and not ruthless bosses. She explained that it took time to absorb lessons and, even more so, to adopt imported work mannerisms, such as greeting, thanking, and saying goodbye to every customer.

Her compassion for others led her to beg us to do something for the water problem in Kinshasa, when we disclosed our intentions to her, because she had been there herself. For her, even relieving a single locality from this ordeal would have an impact on the city and inspire other investors to come to dip in for the benefit of a population almost forsaken.

She advised us that bottled water was among the most sold items in her supermarket, which we had already noticed, as shelves were emptying or being restacked each time we were there. They resourced from France that produced about 200 different brands. Equally, hundreds of millions of dollars went through the tills yearly in transactions relating to the sale of this product.

"But not all can afford bottled water," she said.

Dignity

The Congolese do face their challenges with courage. They do not let go of their dignity easily. More than most do live within their means. All they possess is earned through extreme labour. Wherever we went, my people accepted nothing free from us, despite obviously needing pretty much everything. When we insisted that we wanted to help, they did all they could to return the favour, whether on the spot or at a later time. Such was the case with Benj, an 11-year-old we spotted selling water along a commercial street in the over-crowded city centre. He was better dressed than any other kid we had seen on this job or a similar one since our arrival.

We followed him for five minutes. The crowd made it easy to move at such a slow pace. He skillfully interacted with his targets to create a desire in them while they, despite the excruciatingly hot and overwhelmingly humid weather, were manifestly reluctant to part with their money. No doubt they had their children at home in mind. Sadly, for them, he too would need food in the evening, so he was determined to entice them. It was noon, and most children his age were either about to come out of school or getting ready to enter one. There, some attended from 7.45 a.m. till 12.15 p.m, making room for those starting at 12.45 p.m. to finish at 5.45 p.m. There were not enough buildings for all to attend at the same time.

Amy told him in a parental tone of voice to go to school, to which he politely retorted that he first had to deplete his inventory. There were 16 units of 50-centilitre each on his head. The bucket filled up with 50 that sold at $0.10 a-piece. Günter pulled out his wallet, beating the rest of us to it, and handed him a couple of $10 bills and three of 500 Congolese Francs. The rate was 450 francs to $1. Therefore, the local currency alone made up for more than the $1.60 stock.

"Now, go!" Günter ordered.

Tears running down his face, Benj tried to give all the money back to him. But he declined, saying he had grandchildren coming up to his age and could not imagine them not being in school, let alone on the street selling goods. My friends were having trouble accepting the reality these children faced, so I left them to process their pain, after telling them many times that what they saw was not fiction. They were, nonetheless, optimistic that the Congolese could surmount their challenges if these kids, conscious of their calamities, adapted and aptly fought on courageously as they did. They all knew this boy was not selling water but managing poverty, if not little by little kicking it out of his life. Nevertheless, they refused to accept that this should be a child's fight, especially not at the cost of education.

Benj walked away, repeatedly putting his hands together and not fearing the container falling off his head.

"Thank you! Thank you very much! Thank you, *Papa*!"

The benefactor sobbed at being referred to as dad by one not his own and for the gratitude manifested. The boy looked back several times while disappearing in the thick crowd like a shadow at the going down of the sun. The strong-willed German, being of average height, got on the tips of his toes for one last glimpse of the kid, barking orders in broken French that made people laugh.

"I will call the police on you if I ever see you here again!"

But he was now too far away to hear any of it. I reminded Günter that he had yet much to learn as, over there, the officers would do nothing but charge him for calling them out. That fee will go into their pockets, and there will be no receipt. Then, they will release him around the corner. I wanted to tell him this was not the West, but I left it there as they had heard enough of that from me since coming over. I had something more close to me to say instead.

"This could have been me," I said to them, now emotional as I cast my mind many years back to when aged 13 I almost lost my mother to illness. It was also the darkest time in my father's career because of splitting hairs with those who used their leadership position to influence the justice system. Nonetheless, my partners were grateful to me for the privilege to experience all this, as they would not have come down on their own after all they had heard and read about this country.

We had parked at the zoo, so they could see what was left of the place that drew tens of thousands of us each day during the school holidays when I was growing up. Now it was a shell of its former self, much like the city I struggled to recognise each time we came to a location I once admired.

Back in the day, the zoo was the best touristic place in the capital, maybe second only to the *Garden of Eden,* which was taught to us in our childhood to have been somewhere in the Congo. They, too, would buy into such a belief by witnessing the biggest crocodiles they had ever seen. They lay in mud, most of it dry when these ponds should have been full of water. Because of that, they remained static all the time we were there, as though dead.

Jan asked why there was no water and got his answer from our guide:

"It has not rained for three weeks now."

That was also almost how long these creatures had been without drinking. They gave them a little now and then but not enough to satisfy their thirst. None of us could believe what we had just heard. Even the zoo was a victim of the shortage. Amy spotted a tap within five metres of the crocodiles' enclosure and rushed to it, but nothing came out of the tap. The guide laughed, saying it had also stopped working a few years back. He picked up the hose out of the wildly growing grass and showed us that it was split in bits—proof that it had not been used for ages.

"When lucky, we get visitors who buy us water from the kids outside the gate, so we can give it to the animals of their liking."

Laura asked for another worker to come with her. I prayed Jan to go with them—just in case. They returned 15 minutes later with a convoy of 10 children, all under 12, with their buckets full of water bags. The crocodiles that had had their mouths wide open all along like dry tree trunks, no doubt telling everyone who came by they were thirsty, suddenly rolled their eyes over at the appearance of the suppliers, seemingly aware of what was about to take place.

Then, they could not close their mouths once their tongues refreshed with the first load we threw at them. Their eyes came to life and began following us everywhere. However, they were still glued in the dry mire as we moved next door to the monkeys' area. The message we were getting was that they were not done drinking yet. But, as much as we were full of compassion for them, we could not discriminate against their neighbours that had spotted what was happening this end, proving that all these animals knew when there was water around.

"See! There is a reason for all those acrobatics," said the guide, pointing at the chimpanzees.

They knew very well that we would not come too close to them. So, with our approach, they stepped back to the farthest possible to allow us to put the bags through to them. In appreciation, they clapped their hands, then picked up the sachets and drank. They hit themselves on the tummies to say we had not given them enough. Then they moved to the rear again. We furnished them with more. Again, they gave thanks before picking up and drinking.

Next was them somersaulting concertedly and competing with one another from the few individual cages. They changed their dance steps with each song the guide came up with. We were very impressed to see them moving rhythmically. Each time we turned round to head to another section, they came banging on the cages to get us to tarry with them. They certainly loved our company. And when we returned, they entertained us more until the zoo guys told us why.

"They are expecting bananas."

Thinking it would be cruel not to oblige, we sent for some. They chewed them down like they had not eaten a thing for days. Since water was unaffordable to the Zoo, it was understandable that fruits could not have been easily made available. Whether realising that we had no more to give or that they were full, they sat down like they were not the same agile and super-hyped chimps we had witnessed a moment ago. We were, at that point, free to move on our way.

I could not wait all that time to get to *Vieux Marcel.* He used to be my favourite out of the entire zoo. Luckily, he was still around. This was the charismatic gorilla that entertained us into my late teenage years. But he was tired and unable to put up the best show he used to do. He still tried hard for us, pushing himself to the limit, but nothing compared to the good old days when he went on for hours, audiences replacing each other throughout the day without him sitting down.

In our excitement to make the best of our time there, we would be warned to keep away from the little creature with a white line on the back. The reason being if it sprayed us, a horrible odour would stay on us for days unless we washed with tomato juice. Wow! We learnt something there. Hence, we kept our distance, not wanting to bathe in that manner. Furthermore, we thought someone could do with the budget, despite fresh tomatoes costing not much in the local market and most of the supply going in the bin due to the public's limited buying power, no matter how further the price dropped towards the end of the day.

While still trying to handle our disappointment seeing the animals without food and water, the guide would further upset us, pointing out that the $50 that went towards that water was enough for a month's supply as it needed not to be potable. We were, however, grateful to learn that 20,000 litres of the type of water most families used for general usage was obtainable at $45. But, still he was being inconsiderate of the others' welfare. Therefore, Laura reprimanded him because those children also needed her money. She knew well what it meant to them when they all, one by one, thanked her en-route to delivery, saying how she had just fed their families for a day, which was why she tipped them each $5.

The Reason

Three hours had passed quickly, and we returned to sparkling SUVs, whereas we had left them covered with dust. The ground around them was wet without the rain falling. The car park guard described who had washed them, and we needed no second guess to establish who it was. But to be sure, Jan instinctively stood on the side-step and popped his head over the roof.

"Benj's height has prohibited him from reaching up here."

We looked at each other in awe.

Two months later, we spotted Benj again, but in the administrative part of the city, wearing the same clothes he had on the other day. He confessed to having turned back and followed us as we crossed the street and into the parking lot, where he saw us leaving our backpacks in the vehicles. The state they were in offered him the chance to give back. He rented washing stuff from another kid at the car washing bay 180 metres up the road and completed the job himself, avoiding further sharing what he had received from us with that boy. Tears filled our eyes hearing how he had achieved this, as well as his refusal to remain indebted.

"But why are you here again?" Amy asked. "It is half past two!"

"I have mouths to feed," he replied, emotionally stammering.

"What do you mean?" she followed up.

Not too long before, Benj lived comfortably and attended a prestigious private school in town. His father was a major in the army and an accountant trusted with payroll responsibility for over 16,000 personnel in the Kasai *Occidental* province. Therefore, he was well taken care of where remuneration was concerned. He spent two weeks in the capital and two away dishing out salaries. Committed to him were three officers to prevent hold-ups or robberies since they carried cash due to banking facilities being available to less than one percent of the Congo.

He avoided bathing at the hotels because the water there, served in a bucket, was always unclean and messed up his clothes no matter how hard he used a clean towel afterwards. Instead, them four visited rivers in the region on their way to and from their assignments, as well as every morning and evening while working away. Because of the respect owed to bosses, he was always at the head, out of the subordinates' view, and them at the bottom. It was too hot on their way home on this occasion, and their vehicle's air-con had given up, so he decided to stop where they had never ventured. The calm and clean Kasai River was not far from the road they traveled on. But seven minutes in, swimming, the guards heard a cry of one in trouble.

They picked up their guns, and off they sprinted, in their swimwear, calling out to their leader. A glimpse of the upper part of a massive crocodile sailing away with a human arm sticking out of its mouth was all they managed. Two of them fired, and the animal submerged. The other attempted to jump in, but his colleagues restrained him. No word was uttered between them for close to an hour, frustration mounted as they kicked stones, pulled at herbs in anger, and wept bitterly. His clothes sat there, looking at them. They waited two hours, hoping the animal would reappear, but it was not to be.

The army gave the family a month to hand back the villa they lived in and leave the barracks altogether. Their only indemnity, eight months later, was the equivalent of $300 in a large envelope that misled many who saw it being given to them to believe it was all banknotes. Instead, it was filled with eulogies from his hierarchy and colleagues for his loyal service to the nation. Still, Benj found something positive in those long-winded letters.

"They wished us well, and that suffices," he said. "I take it that they meant it. It does renew my strength every morning to challenge myself to move the barriers out of my way."

When his mother offered to take them shopping to cheer them up, Benj, nine, declined the opportunity to have new clothes. He kept his share—worth $12. The deceased's younger brother, André, 29, rightfully became the father but refused to take the widow to wife, opposing his tribal practice. He was of the rising generation not in favour of polygamy, let alone inheriting a sibling's widow. Their excuse was that life was now more expensive to have more than one wife, which presented the risk of making 10 children or more.

Strangely, the older generations believed having more than one wife was synonymous with wealth and glory. Some husbands ceased working to have their multiple wives feed them and hoped their children to take over in the future. Others laboured harder and looked after their households very well, but in the process bullied and mistreated their spouses who would not leave their children behind no matter how bad it got.

As for our friend's mum, aged 30, the in-laws returned her to her people for the chance to remarry. André's wife of only three months, Muika, 21, consequently became a mother of five overnight: Benj and his siblings aged seven, five, three, and one. Fortunately, it was instilled in her that they were her own.

The kids ate only once a day since coming to their uncle's. The oldest two understood their new situation from day one, but not the younger ones. They would eventually give up crying over it a week later, no one asking them to do so. The poor man could not operate miracles despite loving them to bits. He luckily earned $100 a month, which was better than many who had no source of income. His six-day a-week-trek to and from work was a couple of hours each way. Hence, Muika had to let go of her employment to devote herself to child-rearing.

Benj asked his now-father if he could sell water. André reluctantly granted permission after instructing him about when to go out and be back. His funds purchased a $5 bucket-turned-cooler, water purification products, and bags. He used the biggest pot in the house, gathered wood and all that was needed, and produced his first stock. His eyes were beaming with joy, imagining success even before heading out. The night before, he had seen in a dream that his circumstances had changed for the better, just to be woken up by the youngest of his siblings crying because he had gone to bed with tummy pains. But they had no painkillers. He knew, therefore, that he had there a good reason to abandon everything else and fight for them.

Our knees wobbled with hearing his tale, and not knowing how to now tell him whatever we thought was our right to say, Benj moved on to what he had done since we first met. He had tripled his inventory, which was impossible during the previous year because of living hand to mouth. He now employed his sister—the nine-year-old hassling customers on the other side of the road. She was thriving despite competition. Another child his age was selling the same, for him, up the road.

Benj was a true businessman material and already proving it. He had used the money from Günter to acquire two new coolers at $5 a piece, spending a dollar to fill up each of them with merchandise. He gave the rest to his auntie, who was his bank. Each bucket load made him a $4-profit, and he managed six rounds a day with ease if he worked 9.00 a.m. to 6.00 p.m. with no break, six days a week. His employees worked half-days because of staying in school, managing only a bucket a day each. Netting in a combined $800 out of 25 days of work a month was colossal for anyone of any age, which explained his cheerfulness.

His production consisted of boiling water and letting it cool off before adding chlorine. He bought a supply of plastic bags in town and used a cup to measure the quantity to bag up. The lack of a freezer and electricity led him every morning to a butcher's cold room downtown, where he left off what he made the night before and picked up what he had brought there the previous morning. He and his team worked close to each other and the butcher's place, so they could replenish quickly if they were having a good day.

He gave money to Muika every evening so the family could have three meals the next day, despite himself being able to eat only in the evening. With his mum at heart, though now 2,450 kilometres away, he sent her $100 at the end of each month. André met him downtown every other Saturday at noon to bank $200 in the account he had opened for him. His siblings' school uniforms and fees were at his charge, except for the one who worked for him, as she got $50 monthly for her contribution to the business.

The two fed the household, but they never missed an opportunity to express their gratitude to their new parents for taking them in. Benj was doing his best so his siblings, those of them who remembered their birth father and mother, could put the past behind them and just enjoy their new family setting. He was, in a way, an additional dad to them because of the amount of advice he seemed to always have ready for them. Because he valued education, he did not allow his sister and friend to work full-time, except during the school holidays. The latter had lost his parents when he was four and lived with his grandma, so Benj treated him like a brother.

When those desiring to buy from him called him *the water boy*, he always refuted selling water. He said to be learning about business hands-on rather than in a classroom. He joked that he would one day graduate from this trade with a doctorate, which was why his pals addressed him as *Docta*, in anticipation. It was also in this environment that his name went on to be known as *Benj*, as he wanted to be done with the past where he went by *Benjamin*. He believed the water industry would make him rich because people would always be drinking water.

While conversing with us, he gave water to a couple of guards he was friends with at the SWC tower and reminded them that he was their future CEO. His humour had earned him permission to sell in front of this building. He also delivered to managers who tipped him, always, because they fancied not taking the stairs up and down. They likewise avoided the lift because of frequent power cuts that had seen them stuck inside it several times, dripping in their suits.

These gatekeepers looked forward to Benj's visit every day and paid for his delivery despite his insisting that it was free to them. They revealed that even the national provider's premises did not have a reliable supply out of the tap. The executives upstairs knew well of their poor service to the nation but blamed it on the politicians.

"But forget what you see," Benj said. "Life is hard!"

His dazzling smile had all along held up well. But he became emotional, tearful, and shaky when I switched to Lingala. My partners insisted I tell them what was going on. There was nothing more than that sometimes, while on his job, he felt the pain of losing his dad and ending up with the responsibility to provide for his brothers and sisters at the cost of his education. But, because of the sharpness of his words and their significance, I interpreted some of his statements and left out the most poignant bits. Sensing my struggle, he reverted to French, which he spoke fluently, so Laura, and to some extent, Günter and Jan, could follow his elocution, equally tactically eased—the wisdom no one his age could have had.

"See! No need going about telling people all your sufferings," he said. "In Kinshasa, everyone has got their own load. Bearable or not depends on how each reacts to it."

"Are you sure he is 11?" I could hear Amy whispering to her husband before hurriedly answering her own question. "The face is of a baby, though!"

We offered to sit down at a sandwich bar up the street, but he politely declined, saying that he only rested at home, implying that we would be causing him a loss of income. Even for a soft drink at the kiosk opposite us, he replied that he only drank what he produced. We had heard it all from this kid. His conviction that things will certainly work out made us ponder more on ways to instill his positivity into those who did nothing but moan about their circumstances.

"Life is getting better with every challenge," he concluded, perplexing us.

Alvin and Amy asked to meet André and Muika, who came to our hotel two days later, on Sunday, with the youngest child, now a buoyant three-year-old.

Living Water

Muika offered to take us to some schools, including the one she taught at before being required to become a stay-at-home mum. But a nursery in the Commune of Matete would appear on our trajectory. We liked that it was called *L'eau de Vie* (Living Water), and both Amy and Laura desired to have a feel of how the little ones were cared for there. Fortunately, Muika's cousin taught there. So, we booked for the following day.

Midway through the visit, Laura became thirsty and asked for a drink. The metal roofing not covered up on the inside made us sweat terribly. The kind teacher disappeared to come back with a bottle of soft drink that had cost her money at the kiosk outside. Guilty Laura, now aware of what the profession paid, insisted she only wanted water. But there was no tap on the premises. Parents dropped their kids with the bottles visible on the shelves at the other end of the room. When a three-year-old finished their water, they waited to get home to drink again. Nationwide, less than a 10th of a percent of schools had taps. The not-air-conditioned rooms demanded sipping frequently, but it was a luxury those perspiring toddlers had learnt to live without.

How they stayed alert and participated in lessons for four hours daily was a miracle to my partners. No wonder they all seemed deflated within an hour of taking their seats. The headmaster asked that we spend 30 minutes in every classroom, purposely setting us up to experience what those kids were going through so we could possibly offer to invest. She had heard of what we were planning to establish in the Congo.

At the end of the shift, we witnessed with sadness parents demanding their children to walk steadily in the overwhelming heat, directly exposed to the sun. After being suffocated indoors that long, it was not easy for them to be pulled by hand at an adult's pace, especially for those with some distance to cover. The only thing that pleased us was hearing those same parents offering to support any initiative to bring water to that school. That reinforced our desire to get on with what we had already set our minds on.

5

BUREAUCRACY

Carefulness

Unable to find indications online as to how and where to start the process of registering a company, we turned to the front desk at our hotel. They could not help either and later told us they were not allowed to give out any information unless it was related to their work for fear of getting sacked. Even something as courteous as calling a taxi for a guest was prohibited because of past experiences whereby people had ended up in the wrong hands when an employee had trusted a third-party service provider. We understood.

So, we drove to the commercial part of downtown and parked to walk a kilometre, inspecting the different businesses there. Our targets were those with names that stipulated that the owners could be foreigners, approaching the receptionists if we could not have access to the bosses. They came across as being unhelpful, or that was what we assumed, maybe because of seeing only our interest and being now so desperate to get somewhere.

Persistence paid off with stopping by Hassan. He had come from the Middle East three decades prior when things were different, and people gave out assistance more easily. His advice was that we use a solicitor to spare ourselves from all sorts of trouble, including delays and bribery probes. He warned this was not a country to be at fault, for we would be alone and against all. The presence of non-nationals in our group was all the government needed to call for even tougher punishment; those imposing sanctions aimed to give the impression that the law was in force.

He cited his countryman, Moammar, who had ignored his counsel six years earlier and, unfortunately, paid a heavy price. He had arrived with a good sum to invest in the transport sector but thought to have little to gain from those, like Hassan, who had learnt how the country operated step by step and over time, forgetting that shortcuts did not always land a pleasant outcome. His attitude was that he had no room for others' experiences. He believed both times and governments to be different than they were when those trying to warn him first arrived in the Congo.

The poor man got all the way to the office that signed off registrations. Trying to make a good impression, he took the person with the last signature out before the certificate of incorporation was in his hands. Sitting across the table at a restaurant, the officer pulled four banknotes of $100 out of his pocket and asked Moammar if they were real. They parted to finalise his case in the morning. Instead, the police approached him. He was accused of attempting to bribe the man to push his application through without ticking all the boxes, whereas his accuser had asked for a bribe, and Moammar had resisted.

Recognising himself and the person with him in the picture he was presented with, him holding the cash with his hand and giving it to the officer was the last nail in the coffin. Arguing that he was unaware of the photograph being taken did not help. He was lectured about the role of an undercover detective. For the inspectors, it was sufficient evidence of his guilt that he vividly remembered the place and described the related circumstances. Any further argument on his part was noted as angling the situation in his favour to cover up his evil.

Moammar was sentenced to a year in prison and fined $2,000, and to be deported when out. Therefore, Hassan never wished anyone to fall into any trap like this, especially with the knowledge that ill-intentioned administrators were around and continually damaging the reputation of a very welcoming nation. This was only one of the many stories he had time to tell us. He insisted that we be careful who we dealt with, for there were those who, when their demands were not met, were prepared to ruin anyone who resisted them at any cost.

Recommendations

We stopped for a soft drink, a block up from Hassan's, and because the owner was too inquisitive, Laura told him what we were trying to achieve. He took us through the process but explained that it was in relation to a sole trader, which was the type of business he ran. He put us in touch with a friend at the ministry of public administration, where we would spend the afternoon within the walls of a massive building, sweating and getting acquainted with its occupants rather than being advised on how to go about registering.

We appreciated that people loved to socialise, but that was something we just did not have time for at that moment.

Our next port of call was the ministry of energy and water, seeking to secure an appointment with the commissioner to inquire about well drilling regulations. The guys at the previous ministry had told us that this was where to begin, to avoid being trapped once the registration was completed. The person manning the lobby asked us to come back another day but refused to say which day and made it clear we were bothering him by insisting he be specific. We challenged him as we saw that his job was signing people in and out and pointing them to the relevant locales. Our proof was that he had no diary to book appointments. His being irate and ordering us to clear out made us conclude that he was having a bad day or must have just taken a dislike to us. It was not that he had to help other people, for only he and us were there.

Unimpressed and now outside, we turned back to someone calling and running after us, asking for a word with me. He had overheard us from his room just past the lobby. According to him, I was too linear with the guard, which was not the way to get something out of anyone there. Whatever that was to him!

"I am Michel," he said. "Can I help?"

He begged us to come back with him, past the now-powerless guard. I would have preferred listening to him outdoors had I known how crammed it would get in his office, and for fear of suffocation as his large window opened not, and there was no air-con in there. But I would have denied him the joy he felt for hosting us. Thankfully, the main entrance was nearby. But, still, the hallways not having lights would have made evacuating difficult in the case of an emergency.

Regrettably, we had contributed to the breaching of health and safety rules by not signing in to go past the reception area. Our host added to our guilt when he told us there was not a warden in place and everyone just looked after their own. It sounded terrible for a 12-floor edifice despite him saying it was less than 20% occupied. He was implying that there would not be much traffic in case of something as bad as a fire breaking out, which had never happened in his 33 years of service there.

His concern was, rather, the appallingly modest environment he was compelled to have us in. Having only two chairs, one of which was three-legged, dampened his hospitable spirit. An old, rusted typewriter confirmed the rough working conditions we had sensed when we neared the main door. Spider-filled cobwebs in every corner of the room and missing bulbs and sockets disheartened us. There was no way to justify such neglect. The ministry overseeing water was so under-furnished while the northern desert nations on the continent were begging to resource themselves from the Congo River for a large fee.

This being home, I was ashamed beyond measure about the situation, while my friends were convinced that someone was surely playing with the country's wealth because they had always heard that the land was extremely rich. My attempt to correct their view with *"potentially rich"* succeeded not, especially with Laura, who had learnt from jewelers in Hong Kong that the diamonds in their shops came from this Congo. But she was witnessing the advanced deterioration of everything, second only to hell according to her, as though she had been there. Günter was aware of the use of semi-precious metals in manufacturing hailing from the country he was falling in love with. Therefore, he, too, was disgusted to see a government building in this state.

Laura, so versatile when it came to business ideas, figured out that because of its prime location, this tower could be turned into a 5-star 100-room hotel under a private-public-partnership arrangement. She wanted me to find out who to negotiate with, offering to build modern offices adapted to their needs elsewhere. She talked provocative numbers, spelling out marketing strategies on her feet, and how to engage in a price war with where we put up. But I asked her to leave it alone until we had made a name in this city.

It was best to focus on the interest Michel took in us. He facilitated a meeting with the minister's advisor assigned to the water-drilling sector a couple of days later. His help came at the cost of an hour of our time as all he said required not more than five minutes. He was keen to acquaint with us and exchange contacts. Then, he referred us to the OSS (One-Stop-Shop) that was set up to make registering companies less stressful and from a single port of call, sparing people the trouble of dealing with a multiplicity of services scattered in various locations of the town.

The OSS sounded innovative, but we chose to go by the list from the ministry of public administration, hoping to familiarise ourselves with as many authorities as possible in the process. However, we soon found out that it was not a wise decision as even just going from one office to another, though only in an eight-kilometre radius, was challenging. The traffic was horrendously detrimental because all the key offices were located in one corner of the capital—not a good idea for a metropolis with scanty but too-busy paved roads. Hence, everyone going one way in the morning and heading back in the opposite direction at the end of the day was a real nightmare.

All this caused people to be late for work and close early, so they did not get stuck in traffic or were not without transport home. These reduced opening hours affected us, and we reverted to the OSS after we had wasted resources visiting ghost offices or disinterested administrators with no intention of being there. They asked us to return in the afternoon, then the next day. We gave up after four visits, two days later, not having obtained even a piece of valuable information, let alone starting the registration process.

Anyway, with the existence of the OSS, we questioned the need to have the other offices open, as running more than one, providing the same service, only created confusion and weighed on the taxpayer. Going through this agency also had its share of frustrations, it being an extension of the government and subject to the same *laissez-faire* prevalent everywhere. Staff there still took far longer than needed to serve people, claiming to be very busy. Therefore, we decided to split into two groups to not waste the remainder of this expedition caught up in administration dysfunction. We hired an extra car—an unplanned expense—so Laura and I could pursue registration while the rest continued visiting sites.

Abusing Power

We pulled into a petrol station, knowing we had a quarter of the tank. It was not self-service—presumably a manner of creating jobs for others, the customer unknowingly paying for the resulting wages. So, we waited close to 15 minutes for an attendant juggling eight pumps and serving lines of cars, as well as motorcycles and jerrycans, whereas we could have helped ourselves and gone. When it was finally our turn, I became under obligation to stop him as the counter hit 75 litres but was still going. A small vehicle as this could not take so much. I pointed out that something was wrong with the pump, to which he objected with why I was the only one to have ever questioned their equipment.

The driver, Mashimba, did not know his tank size despite having had this car every day, from new, for eight months. I checked the manual, and it stated that our maximum intake was 60 litres. Hence, we should have filled up with 45 or, in the worse scenario, 60, had the fuel gauge been faulty and we had come in completely dry. Combining the quarter on the dashboard with this 75 meant we had a 100-litre tank had it been full at that point.

Despite all this logic, the man declined responsibility, arguing that all he was there for was to pour in fuel, read what was on the counter, collect money from customers, and write up receipts. Anything beyond that was none of his business.

I called the car hire company. They asked for a minute and then gave me the figure that was in my manual, possibly reading from a similar one. Mashimba turned on the engine, and the gauge went not past the three-quarter mark, which further worried us. It was evident that only 30 litres had been added to our 15. Still, the attendant would not explain by what magic his pump could have delivered 75 litres in a tank designed for 60.

We had looked at the pump from when the nozzle was lifted, the counter showing zero, until that debatable 75. 'Where had the 45 gone to?' was the question no one answered. So, I got out and stooped down. No leakage under the car! I went into the shop and told the manager to take the details of the car hire company, seeing our only address was the hotel, so we could be allowed to leave and pay when the pump would be investigated, and the amount of fuel provided confirmed. Instead, fearing having to bear the cost and possibly lose his job, the manager called the owner.

Ten minutes later, an unmarked SUV entered the forecourt. A well-suited man and three *bérets rouges* (parachutists) stepped out, each holding a possibly loaded Kalashnikov and wearing a bulletproof vest. None smiled nor said a word. However, their stern look and coming as close as standing on my toes failed to intimidate me. I uttered nothing but looked at only one of them straight in the eyes, not blinking until the civilian broke the silence. Heaven knew what he was told on the phone. He introduced himself as a colonel in a tone of voice that was like giving me orders, which was met with me forcing him to pause and listen to me too. But he was having none of it. As far as he was concerned, we owed what was showing, and the manual was our problem, not his. Nonsense, I thought!

Laura, struck with fear of the guns, went into her purse, and I watched all four men's eyes shift over to the brand-new dollar bills she had in there. I was glad it was daytime, in the city centre, and that many other motorists were watching. She counted the money against my will, unaware of the envy she caused in those armed guys. Then, we sped off.

Mashimba discouraged us from entertaining any thought to report the incident to the police or take legal action, deeming it a waste of time and a further loss of funds. He believed everyone in the justice system hoped for an opportunity like this one to feed off the petitioner. What happened there was more proof that nothing worked properly after decades of dictatorship, unpaid civil servants, and the rebellion that gave whoever was in a position of power the right to make and impose their own laws.

The change my countrymen hoped for was yet a long way coming, especially where protecting the vulnerable was concerned. Having not shown us his credentials—as though he would have, anyway—the so-called colonel could have been an imposter. Or, if he was real, the possibility that he was paid to play the owner could not be dismissed. It mattered not what he really was. But I wondered where on earth Mashimba drew the strength to speak again when, just a moment ago, he had gone dead cold at the appearance of these men, leaving me fighting alone.

He asked that we focus on what we had come to the Congo for, which would save lives. Ripping others off in this manner was popular, and those with no one to stand up for them suffered all the time. Despite his encouragement, it was frustrating to be forced to part with $81 for the 45 litres of petrol we never had. It left me furious and ashamed all afternoon.

When I had come to myself, Mashimba handed me the hand-written receipt that Laura had previously refused us to take. He had snatched it off the attendant's hand when we had already turned our backs. He feared that with no proof of payment, the garage could sue us, saying that we had not paid, and we would be defenseless, especially with no camera on-site.

Arriving at the City Hall to have our identities checked so we could move on to register our company, we would meet yet another challenge, which defeated the efforts made to be on time, besides the trauma of the previous couple of days to secure this appointment.

The administrator supposed to see us was not in yet—at 11.00. His secretary phoned up, with us paying for the credits. Telecommunication companies rendered the use of a phone a luxury and beyond the average civil servant's reach. The guy was not coming in because it had rained the night before till four in the morning. It would take much persuasion and me taking over the conversation to change his mind, but only if we would reimburse his taxi fares. Mashimba reacted with the suggestion to pick him up, as his claim could be any amount.

All the way to his, some five kilometres of clean and clear paved road, we saw no city under water as he had put it. He peeped out the window to see if we were serious when we announced ourselves as being outside. We waited in the car while he jumped in the shower, ironed a shirt, and shined his shoes. No apology, nothing, when he finally took his seat onboard more than an hour later. All he did during this short journey was complain to Mashimba for dragging him out when he was on a miserable salary, ignoring that I spoke Lingala. Working for the government had its perks, and the ability to stay at home because it had drizzled was one of them. With this kind of attitude, it was difficult to see the nation starting to move in the right direction.

At his office, we were asked to cover the cost of a few sheets of A4 paper, the photocopying of our documents, and someone to type out other documents at a *cybercafé*. The owner had strategically placed his business right opposite the City Hall. Saying goodbye, the administrator asked for $50 for his taxi home. Although Laura was unwilling to lose more time, giving him a lift back was cheaper. That was when he finally spoke to me in Lingala, insisting we owed him for coming in only for our job. Facing my rejection, he got his revenge asking to be dropped off some 18 kilometres in the opposite direction, where he suddenly had other things to do. That was the entire day gone.

The optimist Mashimba apologised for all this and warned us that the worst could still be coming but that we should not tone down, for many will cheer us on when our persistence has paid off. His words meant the world to us, especially as he had nothing to do with our project directly nor shared the money we were compelled to part with in this manner. It only worried us that our plans were still far from jellying.

Deception

A fellow applicant we had met at the notary's, like Hassan, recommended using a solicitor going forward, and even one who had experience representing foreigners and their interests, to avoid becoming victims of unprofessionalism that could result in heavy costs. He gave us 10 names to look into. We narrowed down our selection criteria to the proximity of the lawyer's office to the government's edifices we needed to visit. Next was how presentable the building they operated from was. Zacharie's practice topped the list as it was located in an externally bright-colour high-rise that charismatically towered over the city.

I called the number on the board outside, and the receptionist asked to meet at a nearby restaurant in the afternoon. The solicitor himself attended, diffidently advising that the business was only him and that secretary. We did not see any reason for his apology, as most businesses in developed countries nowadays were small, until he confessed that he was operating from a room inside his rented 15th floor three-bed family dwelling.

A humble man, he had no intention of sugarcoating anything. Hence, he revealed the reason why he had turned up sweating and did not want us to go up: there was no electricity to run the lift. By this time, we were no longer interested in hearing about what was not working in town but those trying their best with what they made available to themselves and their community.

Despite the warning, we decided to take the staircase the following day to see where our money was going. But it proved not to be a good thing, not only because of the steepness of the stairs that left us and even Laura with her gym body aching. I had not played football, the only fitness regime I maintained, for a while. So, I will not dare describe what I was like by the time I reached the 10th floor.

To climb the unilluminated flight of stairs, we relied on touching the wall and making sounds to send out warnings so not to collide with many coming down. How deceived we had been, as this tower was a beauty to behold from a distance and the area where it sat was reassuring. This was an area full of embassies, quality hotels, expats' residences, high-end boutiques that sold trendy clothes, as well as supermarkets frequented by the wealthy and politicians. Evenings were adorned with restaurants' regulars and posh cars fighting over parking slots. These offered Uni students and teenagers the opportunity to earn money by keeping an eye on their automobiles and sometimes washing them while they dined and drank past two, any day of the week.

Dense traffic on the stairs was people delivering water in those famous yellow jerrycans omnipresent the city over. This was a 20-plus floors building, and it was a battle already getting past the third floor where sunlight ended. From that point on, it was all dark due to the windows in the stairway being tiny. Frequently stopping to catch our breath and rest our legs, we caused queues but blamed it on the narrow stairwell that did not allow overtaking without coming head-on with those moving in the opposite direction. All this slowed down those determined to maximise their income through their hard labour.

We heard about collisions that led to teeth coming off, head bumps, cuts, and bruises. Worse were indecent contact incidents, most unintentional and from venerable men while groping for the wall. Many of the victims were of the vulnerable age group of the under-12 to as young as seven. They had to carry water. But for them, coming from less-privileged suburbs, it was a blessing that this commodity was not pumped into these high-rises for close to half a year. They earned a quarter of a dollar for every 25-litre delivery, pushing themselves past their limits to make a tenner a day while caring less about how sore they would be at the end of the shift. School was no longer part of their vocabulary.

Mashimba did reinforce our desire to go up the building because of some past experiences known to him. A client of his had regretted staying in the comfort of his air-conditioned 5-star hotel penthouse flat that cost him $4,000 a night. Understandably, splashing out that kind of money entitled him to service providers bringing him whatever he needed right where he sat. Then, one supposed to be a customs agent filled in forms for him as he could not even make an effort to complete them himself. He ended up close to $200,000 poorer.

We, too, had almost fallen for something of the type when we were approached at the airport with lawyers' business cards. We accepted the first five and rejected the rest. Come to finding them, the addresses were all residential, and no lawyer lived there, nor did the names ring a bell to anyone dwelling there. Mashimba told us of people copying each other's tricks blindly. Even what does not work! You open a shop, and everyone follows suit, selling the same products. You tell a lie or use a certain method to cheat, and all do likewise. Hence, the same outcome all day long when we dialed:

"This phone is either switched off or out of the coverage area. Try again later."

Yet they would text back immediately asking for our location and the time to have them meet us if we could only confirm to reimburse taxi fares. But we had made up our minds to go to service providers and not the other way around. We were careful.

Bribery

Strolling through many impoverished neighbourhoods, we always heard of a well that was supposed to be drilled for the community, on a church site, in a school yard corner, or on someone's property. In some places, there were boreholes that had since been filled up with dirt and stones, the efforts and money invested come to nothing. The locals lectured us why good intentions were not all that was required to undertake these projects to completion. The authorities played a big role and would not process an application for a permit unless they had received money under the table. *Motivation,* the culprits called it and never admitted it to be bribery.

My partners entertained the idea that it could have been a false accusation, for they struggled to believe that someone would fail to put the public's interest before their own.

Because of the similarities of the realities of our less-developed countries, Tino knew of this erroneous practice. Having come across the same through her interests in the continent, Laura was not shocked, but she was nonetheless unimpressed. We, however, all agreed that corruption was immoral and needed not to be entertained as we went about our business, no matter what.

Being warned that the administrators would expect money from us had put me on the front foot. I consequently devised a strategy that denied them any grounds to cause retardation in processing our application, offering a more valuable alternative. I had to share the bigger picture repeatedly before they grasped the merits. This was not attained until after several trips to and from the Congo. Emails and calls went unanswered because of their limited connectivity and to avoid leaving any traces. The cost of flying was exorbitant; however, a better option than condoning their malpractice.

I offered to hire their relatives once in business so it could go down as helping, and elaborated the greatness of the resultant earnings over five years. I intended to show how their beneficiaries would lift themselves out of poverty with a job going forward. Still, the officials we dealt with had no faith in promises. The reward had to be prompt and palpable: cash or nothing. "A bird in hands is better than two in the bush," one of them put it to us in the Congolese adage that replaces *bird* with *fish*, *hand* with *mouth*, and *bush* with *sea*.

Realising I was uncompromising, they expanded their bureaucracy, turning their initial four checkpoints into 12 to charge back with a claim for an equal number of positions. But I was giving out four and not more. Therefore, I left it to them to decide which of them 12—the real four and the fictitious eight—were to benefit.

A long list of academically qualified siblings, cousins, children, in-laws, and so on, 24 of them, poured in, making me wonder if my French was not up to speed. Where they hoped I would be considerate to chop off the list in half, to revert to 12, I threatened to withdraw the favour altogether. It was all about taking advantage of dealing with a compatriot, away from the rest, to try and force their demands, even to the point of resurrecting the request for motivation, but I remained hard-nosed.

But they were not retracting either. Because those days, telephone companies charged even to receive, the administrators tried to pass their bills to me when I had no record of them picking up whenever I dialed. Even saying to have made contacts with their hierarchy, whom we too knew to be hardly in the office, to advance my application was met with rejection due to not having agreed ahead for such an expense to be incurred on my behalf.

Despite giving me the names of their candidates, not giving them a penny was sanctioned with delay, making a point that I was not out of the woods yet. I appreciated that they had had what they saw as bad experiences in the past— gaining nothing from someone they had put forward for employment. However, as far as I was concerned, there should be no obligation on the person hired to remit a portion of their income to the facilitator, who should just be pleased to have helped their own. But that was not how it was seen there. Gratitude is expressed through salary-sharing for months or, at least, parting with the first pay-cheque in full. Hence, they play it safe, seeking to get their *motivation* beforehand and on top of what they would still impose on the recruit.

I was going to hold on for as long as their caprices went on before turning my back on them, but they came down with a reduced sum that still failed to move me over the curb. Instead, I started to make less contact, and it played on them, fearing I could be onto other paths that could see me land what I was after and the chance to get something from us go to someone else. They attributed their reluctance to several facts: (1) vacancies not being instantly available; (2) people recommended competing with anyone else through an equal recruitment process; (3) no *job-for-life* guarantee as under-performance or the breaking of the rules sufficed to get fired any time; etc.

Decades of non-governance ruined the economy and morals in a country where a person's integrity once was a national identity. Many now had their own definition of a salary and, as a result, created ways of remunerating themselves through bribery and other malpractices because what they formally received from their employers was nothing short of mockery. Still, it made no sense to try to obtain compensation from someone seeking to register a company. It was incorrect for them to claim to be rendering applicants a favour when, honestly, both the nation and the investors needed each other.

An insider aware of our ordeal called it a battle lost in advance and not worth pursuing because the habit had been long-running. But we believed that people could change if the efforts to help them improve their conditions were evident. Irrespective, my team expected me to use all avenues at my disposal to land all needed licences, so we could serve the people we had now seen with our own eyes crushed by the lack of water. That those administrators were short-sighted was a choice they had made, but that could not stop me from preaching that a job, though for a third-party, was better than the one-off meagre hand-out they wanted slipped into their pockets.

In the meantime, the many curriculum vitae I received were great, and each candidate was a gem when I got to meet them. That alone did, for a moment, overshadow all the misery we had witnessed. Certainly, the poor rating the country was subject to was not fair for a people trying hard to pull themselves out of the rubble. Come the recruitment, it pained us that those over-qualified settled for labour work. Our biggest challenge, though, was the inability to hire everyone. Not faring at deterring the spirit of corruption and being way outside the timeframe we had assigned ourselves, my partners were compelled to be away from the Congo, despite the guilt of leaving me fighting on alone.

It was best for them to come back only when they would have an active role to play. Gladly, it took not too long for them to be needed, as we resorted to other options to end this time wasting from the hands of those determined to hold us back, if not totally discourage us.

Connections

Laura returned with a list of people in governmental positions and notable public figures. She had told her contacts in the Congo that she was coming. They had attended school and church together in Montreal, where there was a remarkable Congolese presence, but she had until now decided not to let them know she was over, let alone that she intended to invest. Their parents had sent them there with their mothers to get a better education. Therefore, once back on home soil, most of them had it a bit easier positioning themselves so that, when we came knocking, they had the connections I did not have.

Emissaries paraded at our hotel most evenings to meet with Laura briefly before escorting us to the various residences she was invited to for what turned out to be a buffet ritual at every reception. At times, we visited into the early hours of the morning. Where it was not her friends but their parents or relatives, many recognised her for having met her several times back then, while others apologised for not remembering her. She was no longer the young person she used to be and had changed over time, as most had. Hence these apologies were reciprocal. What mattered was that our meeting them got us hoping again.

First coming to our rescue was Billy. He was a senior executive at a world-renowned airline. We had just spent three days visiting the bank, where we faced one problem after another trying to get Laura's accountant, Rex, to transfer money to us. There was a local ruling we had not heard of before: no one could have $10,000 internationally wired to them in a single transaction without prior governmental authorisation.

Rex had sent over 10 times that amount to help us take care of foreseeable bills now that we knew the trend of our expenditure and our pockets were running low. Surprisingly, Zacharie had overlooked this restriction when we told him of the need to bring in funds in a week. His bank had asked for a written explanation of who we were, our relationship with the recipient, the reason for bringing in the money, and any supporting documents of our activities where we resided. We were told to check back the day after, but still, nothing had been posted to his account.

We got more uneasy with the bank demanding to see our business plan, despite telling them in advance of having initially come to explore opportunities. And, because we did not have one, the money was returned to the sender. Rex subsequently acknowledged receipt of the funds returned to him, minus some bits as movement charges applied. To be compliant, Zacharie, bouncing back, asked that this sum be transferred in 10 batches.

Three days later, Zacharie called to meet at the bank in two hours because they had received the new wires. But we were told of our new breach trying to get around the system. So, where we could have been allowed the first of these 10 batches, they all returned to their origin. The best thing was to leave each transfer clear before sending another one. We understood where they were coming from but were at breaking point. We did not want to be owing anyone.

Should not Zacharie have known of this law in advance? Well, maybe he saw himself as being contracted only for company registration, whereas taking care of all our legal needs in the Congo was available to him. But he would confess to having never handled an international payment in his career or any other capacity. He was learning with us. However, that did not erase doubts building inside us about how safe we would be, in the future, in his hands. I was further less impressed when he questioned why we had travelled without sufficient funds.

We informed him of the restriction to fly internationally with over $10,000 in cash, which was why we boarded the plane with only $9,000 each. We had hoped to sort out hotel bills with credit cards, but they never worked, let alone debit ones, despite advising our banks of our travel plans before setting off. The Kinshasa we had come to, with all its 15 million population, operated with less than 20 cashpoints, all accessible only during working hours. So, we tried to withdraw cash wherever we spotted one, to no avail. Foreign cheques passed not either. International money transfer companies were on a stringent limit of $800 per wire, not to be repeated within three days of the first remittance. Banks gave us the impression of being less customer-oriented.

"Money laundering regulations," a manager said. "Not us!"

Billy suggested that we first complete the registration, for it would influence the lifting of the transfer cap and stand as proof of planning to have activities that would need big sums. He entertained the thought that Zacharie was either prolonging registration completion to keep claiming payment from us or had simply proved his limitations. He understood not why a solicitor used a personal bank account when it was business between him and us. Either way, he had a lifeline for us.

His sister, Alice, who worked at the OSS, found out that our application was not yet submitted to them. Zacharie confessed to having passed it to a specialised law firm. We ordered him to bring us the file by the end of the day. But it was incomplete: no *casier judiciaire* (Criminal Record Bureau Report) included. At that point, I was totally fed up with the man.

However, dropping him would have incurred office charges. This amounted to $18,000 in deposit for a modest downtown two-room locale, sharing the toilet, kitchen, and waiting room with other businesses. A $3,000 monthly rent, paid three months in advance, regardless of whether we were trading or not, was also required. This, while a suburban address four times bigger, was 80% cheaper. The problem with the latter was the lack of electricity and water, unpaved access road, and what it would say about our firm.

Before bed that night, I found an email in my inbox from a compatriot, Bob, from Gatineau, Quebec. I opened up to him, and he told me about Richard, a friend of his from Quebec City, who had returned to the Congo and had been appointed as an advisor to a minister in the newly formed government. He promised to get me his details by my morning.

Reputation

It was half past seven, and I had just said hello when Richard stopped me.

"Diamany! Could you be *Maître* Diamany's son, by chance?"

Maître is a *prefix* reserved for a solicitor or a barrister over there.

"Indeed, I am! If we are thinking of the same person."

"Let me see! Are your sisters Yvonne, Monique, and Henriette?"

"Correct!"

"What a big surprise this is! Where are they all these days?"

"Monique passed away at 19, and Henriette at 23."

"What! I am so sorry! What of?"

"Medical casualty for the former, and road accident for the latter," I said, wounds never healed properly reopening.

He knew me until I was three. He grew up with the above. So, he promised to invest himself because of what my dad was to them, the youth in the neighbourhood, back then. We agreed to meet at 10 at his office. I rang Laura's room and told her we had under three hours. He took us to the minister, a relative of his and a decade his senior, who also knew Dad very well. Hence he greeted me with a hug instead of a handshake.

One of his staff took us to the ministry of justice, where an inspector awaited. He, too, knew me in my infancy. There, lawyers mobbed me, saying many good things about my late father. The ministry of justice's official passed us to an administrator at the Casier Judiciaire office, so we could have our police record established. He made sure no one blocked us unnecessarily but insisted on the need to do things right, for governments changed frequently, and he did not want any law-bending catching up with us with time.

The clerks who had turned us away there before were stunned to receive our files from the hands of their boss, paying the required fees out of his own pocket while we stood by silently. These had previously said that they knew not how to process our application due to not having all the details they wanted about us. That abruptly changed with orders coming from the top, as we had added nothing to the file.

Pictures and other particulars were taken, and clearance certificates were issued in no time, thanks to the initiative we had taken to come to the Congo with passports obtained within three months of our departure, as well as those held the previous 10 years. Both turned evidence that we did not have any problems back in our respective countries of residence.

From there, the agent taking us places drove us to the OSS, where Alice would not be too pleased to see us being led past her desk to the managing director. He called her in, instructing her to serve us within an hour. I spontaneously advised that she was a cousin. Surprised, he wondered why she had left us struggling all this time. He would later reveal he knew I meant a cousin the Congolese way, where friends and acquaintances were all extended family. It led to him inviting her and us to his for food. Her face shone to that, and off she went to execute the orders.

Next was the *Journal Officiel* for the publishing of our registration in the relevant periodical, which was accessible *nationwide* to whoever was interested. Copies, in the form of a booklet, were unavailable until three months after we got confirmation that it went to print. It did not bother us as we could present the payment receipt and other documents where required.

Returning to Richard's minister to express our gratitude for moving a huge mountain, if not several, for us, he had left early because of a flight he had to catch that evening. But he had left instructions for the same person who had been with us everywhere to take us to the bank to open a business account. Five days later, we received a letter from the ministry of finance permitting us in-and-out money movements to seven figures each time, owing no one a justification. This was my major contribution to the project since coming over. I suddenly regained the confidence I had lost to Laura coming up with all useful contacts.

"I remember you telling me that your father was one of the first judges *Zaire* (the Congo's name when she and I met in 1994) had ever produced. But I was unaware he was this respected. You must be proud of him, dude!"

Dad was two years from completing his medical school when the country's independence became imminent. The Belgians started training the locals so they could take care of their own justice system. He jumped ships because of the knowledge that men and women of integrity would be needed. Soon, he moved across to defence as many people were imprisoned arbitrarily. He took many from his Kasai province under his wings and sold them the profession.

Hence the reputation he cared about all his working life earned me all the hailing that day. But, he was just a low-key person who did no more than what all other men did for the youth: tirelessly advising them of the importance of formal education. He passed not a beggar by without saying "hello" if that was all he had for them. He opposed injustice in all its forms and hated seeing someone in distress. In his own eyes, he was an ordinary creature deserving no special mention, for he did no good to be repaid. The praises I heard that day would have embarrassed him. This was the best I described Dad to my partners when they became interested to know more about him.

Inner Circles

Two other people joined us at the OSS boss' house: a Chamber of Commerce director and a Customs and Excises senior executive with their wives. They had been friends since high school. Our conversation was mostly about how to help the country, so it could become like those they had visited on other continents. They each held a Ph.D., hence they were committed to bringing changes in their jobs and society, remaining positive that this land would get going one day.

One of the areas they wanted to see progress in was everyone adopting a tax culture to help the nation rely less on foreign aid. They welcomed the idea of providing a commodity as valuable as water. Their contribution to this effort was seen in how they instantly invited us to affiliate with the Chamber of Commerce. This would qualify us for a heap of tax reductions that existed for those in this sector of development, so we could reinvest and expand faster. It meant paying 10%, whereas a non-member producing the same commodity paid 40.

"But do not abuse the system as many do," said one of them.

Our host had had these two over to introduce us to better practices that could propel our getting ahead in business in the Congo, privileges we would not have discovered this early. Agents kept such details to themselves as they fed out of the claims they made on behalf of their clients. But these three, seeking the welfare of all, further facilitated assistance from the institutions that supported projects of this nature. They warned of the possibility of long delays before we could see the results. They insisted we use the wait to set up and get going with the means we already had so that come these entitlements, we should be ready to scale up.

Another meeting followed, this time with a trusted Health and Safety executive. He was related to the Chamber of Commerce guy. He could not let the opportunity to have us over slip him by. The Congolese are more hospitable than one has ever known. The people cited here, so far, had everything to offer. But there were yet many with very little who still gave us it all. They all wanted us to up sticks there. Hence, hearts, homes, and circles of friends opened to us. This additional contact took us through industry standards so that we would not go on endangering the public. He told us stories where children remained so exposed.

"I hope you guys can prove to be different," he said.

Therefore, we made it our goal to do nothing less than what could pass the test in developed countries for the sake of the people but also to not dent our reputation, as it is such a fragile commodity. We learnt of funding available to organisations that operated to the expected level and received promises from the industry's commissioner to accompany us to be compliant and qualify. Life was treated lightly, and despite these incentives, many companies still preferred to take shortcuts to make huge returns without considering the society they were part of.

He could not have stressed enough the need to stand out and earn recognition. We beamed with excitement because of what was unfolding, realising we were receiving where we had come to give before even putting a shovel in the ground. However, we kept our eyes on the ball—we were there to deliver water—committing ourselves more to take care of everything needful along the way to keep moving forward.

How we wished all other administrators we had met up to this point could welcome and support newcomers in this manner and be part of any success that would come. Unfortunately, this inner circle of the OSS man seemed to be the only people with the desire to see the country evolve. Until meeting them, we had struggled to find someone to direct us. However, these four's briefing, being all verbal, was not conclusive. Their offices still had a say when submitting applications.

Files piled up on every desk, and most had not moved for more than a year, either because they were incomplete due to the applicants not being advised properly beforehand or they had stopped following up. Jan wanted to know why chasing was necessary, but I declined to find out for him. Ours had obviously jumped the queue or moved to schedule because of who we knew. Minty offices for the bosses versus the almost unfurnished ones for the rest made it two contrasting worlds under the same roof, hence no jellying. At one end were leaders with great ideas, and at the other, unhappy subordinates who saw no reason to give their all.

The conscientious few did what they could in their job, regardless of their conditions, and were grateful for the opportunity to serve. They cared little that their contribution, for the most part, went unnoticed. Even in the absence of manuals and other work gear, they relied on their memory, hardly recounting to external parties how badly remunerated they were. Their only apologetic moment was that the delay in completing cases handed to them was aggravated by the entrepreneurial culture hugely embraced by the rising generation. These, unlike their parents, asked themselves what they could do for their country and answered with an ingenious spirit. Like them, the time had come for us to pass to action.

6

GROUND-BREAKING

Proximity

Throughout this journey, we unequivocally realised that people not only needed water but also longed for it to be in proximity to their homes and they were ready to contribute in whatever way possible for it to be so. This was not difficult to achieve given the tradition whereby everyone aimed to be useful. Ingrained in their minds was the belief that receiving without reciprocity turned one mentally a slave, for it led to always feeling indebted to and diminished in front of the giver. Therefore, it was imperative to show that we understood where they were coming from, establishing a rapport of equality from the outset in our endeavour to serve them.

The communities we approached shared that they preferred not to be simple recipients because they did not have much, and that it would not be appreciated if we turned up and just started drilling for them. They wanted to be part of the process—a privilege granted—even in determining where to place our first well. Only, we would be torn between going first to those who could afford the service and those in a desperate situation.

"Suppose you are the only coastguard on duty, and five people are drowning, all calling out for help," Alvin pricked our brains. "How long do you need to decide who to rescue first?"

We all agreed we would have instinctively jumped into the sea and reached out to the one closest to us. Where water scarcity was concerned, no one was closer to us than Basil. It did not matter that this closeness was emotional and that we had to go past millions of people, teeth-gritting, to get to his death's spot. The pain his story had left in our hearts since we heard it forced a proximity that surpassed physical boundaries. He was in our conversations every day. Even in his neighbourhood, the impact of this sad tale was still evidenced in the deserted family house turned into a police station, so it was not further vandalised.

Seeking permission from the Council to reinstate this well or build a new one in that parcel, in his memory, raised eyebrows. They wanted to know who we were, our relationship with the family, or who was behind us. Our good intentions were not sufficient to convince them. We heard that we could not be allowed because the search for Kabeya and Mulumba had not yet ended, despite knowing that the authorities had given up the morning after their escape. Their fear was somewhere else: we could be after what had become the Commune's inheritance.

We found ourselves filling out forms of all types and going through lengthy procedures. At one point, I asked myself what on earth we had gotten ourselves into when a few other places were available. However, Amy and Laura were convinced that if we could be granted permission, this would be an accomplishment not to be forgotten. They viewed this as a tourist attraction by linking it to a few other nearby landmarks the population had advised us of, which showed what this commune had been through.

We needed not to dig deep into history: we were within two kilometres of what was once a market but had had the misfortune of an overloaded cargo aircraft dropping down on it within three minutes of leaving the Ndjili airport. It had not risen properly, and all the way people stood still, watching it struggle. They held their breath. More than 250 innocent merchants, shoppers, residents in the nearby homes, and passers-by were decimated. The date was October 4th, 2007, and the time was 1.24 p.m., the busiest time of the day.

That site was now a large sandy patch where kids played football, despite the trauma from witnessing the tragedy. To some, it was where their family members had perished while they, themselves, had escaped only because they were at school. This was the month before our coming over. We had read about it online as we turned to the news daily from the moment we decided to embark on this adventure. But little did we know we would be standing on that spot one day, and even worse, my sister and her family were a near miss because of being only two properties to the right of the last house to catch fire in that incident. They had kept this from me. I felt as though I was myself a survivor. Erecting something in memory of the victims would maybe remind the government of what had happened there and the need to reinforce regulations in all industries.

We believed to see the light at the end of the tunnel when we finally got authorised to drill close to Basil's well. We were allowed to tweak an income-generation scheme. But some officials asked if we did not have anything better to do with the investment, seeing that the community had been coping without. Furthermore, Basil's family being *Luba*—a tribe labelled as sorcerers—everyone argued that their dark works had gone wrong, so they deserved not to be honoured. Ten years on, their animosity towards this family was tangible still and stronger, as seen in their words. They certainly had not moved on with their lives or forgiven themselves. Their burden was too heavy to carry. Hence, to some, this project was a chance to reconcile with the dead.

Delivery Partner

We had the opportunity to enter the market with a project that responded to a societal need. Commercial gains became second at this point in our minds. Likewise, fancy planning, heavy-duty machinery, meticulous operations, and even ego were laid aside. A roadmap to how to get started was needed, especially with no equipment of our own yet. Relieved we were to have not binned Lydie's notes. The companies she had listed turned out to be real and where she had indicated.

We took a non-trumpet-sounding approach, with me going to them as one of theirs first, seeking to find one that could drill for us, to avoid being over-quoted. There was a lot to learn, and they kept nothing they knew from us. These visits shaped our attitude and strategies, overcoming Lydie hanging us up and out to dry. We recognised the difference in dealing with those in the business, on one side, and listening to those we met in the street and at the various government offices, on the other side.

But the best way to learn, as we already knew, was by being part of the work. We wanted to get as much as we could out of this contract, even though with only one well to offer. Each of these operators made our selection difficult as, hoping to tie us in for ongoing collaboration, they emptied their knowledge on us in their effort to sell themselves better than the competition.

We were grateful to Benj who had helped us secure solid contacts at the SWC. It was hard to believe how big a role a child had played in introducing us. The executives there had advised us of the areas with great needs, and that, as a company, they had no plans to serve those communities in the foreseeable future. When the timescale is expressed in this manner in the Congo, one must not expect anything to happen in 30 years or so. The authorities welcomed anyone capable of reducing the deficit, although nothing was done to find qualified players. The population's discontentment and desperation touched everyone but those in charge of finding solutions. They were, however, embarrassed if water containers on people's heads appeared when in the company of their international visiting counterparts, for instance.

Putting Lydie's notes and the public's recommendations together, we narrowed our choice down to three drilling firms, thus rendering Themba and Tino's selection of the contractor to have on our first job easier. Their industry experience called for rigorous scrutiny of a delivery partner.

LaSource operated only in Kinshasa and had invested in a warehouse much bigger than they required, thus straightaway casting doubts over teaming up with them as we had long-term in mind. Many of its workers sat around all day because there was not enough work for everyone. The boss said more sets of equipment, tools, and materials had been ordered, just for the unoccupied employees to reveal that they had heard the same the last 18 months. Some had given up, as they were not paid, while the majority still turned up due to having no alternative and out of the fear of the consignment arriving the day they chose not to bother.

The rig this company functioned with was old and took 24 days to complete a single well. Its vehicle explained best this under-performance as it hardly did 20 kilometres per hour. This image alone cost them business, for potential customers could not trust a firm unable to put up a decent automobile on the road. It was a fatal marketing mistake in a country where making more than a good impression was crucial. The Congolese buy into appearances, a culture the owner had not grasped, despite having come there in the early 1970s.

The business was popular among some customers only because of his sensitivity to domestic issues. He always donated to hospitals and schools and contributed to the clearing of canals to help prevent flooding, mosquitoes, and more. Hence, when the drilling of a well was needed, some people chose to live with his slow delivery and get on a six-to-nine-month waiting list, even after paying 50% of the $20,000 this owner charged.

Dev-Plus was another Kinshasa-based operator. Its activities were not noteworthy. A church-owned organisation, it took advantage of its widespread presence to have an office in every province. Sadly, this was as far as it went. It had not drilled enough to match the number of its congregations as its mission statement stipulated. For instance, in the Bandundu province, it had only ever completed 21 communal wells, seven of which were still operational when we made contact. These were on its church premises, and access to water was solely given to those who worshipped there.

"Is that not discrimination?" asked one not of their faith briefing us.

Having no knowledge of why this non-inclusive policy was in place, we did not comment. We feared the same to be said about us when we, too, would have to turn away those not qualified to benefit from the water we would bring to communities.

This company acquired many private contracts but took more than six months to complete them, although receiving 80% advance payment. Its work included no over-ground finishing. Customers were comfortable with it hiring independent individuals to perform the job on its behalf as it reassured them that work would get done, else their money would be returned. Ninety percent of the equipment and tools used under this arrangement belonged to sub-contractors, and these were no more than shovels, picks, buckets, and the like.

Past, current, and potential customers advised us that Dev-Plus was never present where third parties undertook work. We were overall not surprised to hear that those assignments fulfilled in these manual conditions had, in a great part, an unsatisfactory outcome. Clients, if of the faith, had no right to a complaint against the church they were part of. The management yearned for investors so they could afford suitable equipment to match their intentions to better the lives of their congregations and safeguard their own employment.

Omega's proprietor was a local entrepreneur who, out of a burning desire to serve others, was breaking himself into pieces trying to be everywhere at the same time. However, this was impossible to accomplish with only two sets of equipment. He made losses year after year because of travelling wherever work called. Most of his customers were not willing or able to pay for the extra mileage or time away from family.

A good portion of his contracts came through a contact who worked for a big international NGO. His inability to say no to these assignments was due to being offered up to 200% of what he charged in the capital, and not wanting to let his facilitators down out of fear of being dropped for good. This client paid for mileage, however, did not consider the unpaved road conditions that slowed down travelling. Its executives flew to these locations, up to 1,000 kilometres away, so they were unfamiliar with what Omega faced.

Frequently breaking down and jamming in mud during the rainy season or in sand in the summer months prolonged an assignment and ate into profits. Repairs, per diems, and not getting to the next contract timely were heavy unforeseen expenses hindering growth. Had there been other companies in those distant locations, he would have sub-contracted, settling for a small share of the income. But, out of the necessity to help as many people as possible with drinking water, he risked his assets and was, several times, on the brink of packing it in.

He insisted it had nothing to do with unmeasured ambitions, or greed, which some observers attributed him. He blamed the difficult terrain. It demanded sacrifice—a key characteristic of an entrepreneur, and even more so if operating in the Congo. Under-capitalisation was also a problem as it was, in his situation, a lone person getting up one day and saying, "enough with this shortage", to start drilling water with only what was in hand. He was trying hard to save to afford more equipment, but he was never left with much for himself.

Hence, he resorted to running with no permanent crew, except a driver, a geologist, and a technician, on each of his two lorries. He hired temporary staff for any job beyond 30 kilometres of his hub so they did not spend nights away from their homes. Then he saw savings in the range of 70%, which he shared a bit of with the temps, on top of their wages, to encourage them to work well. However, always training new employees to operate the equipment, teaching them industry standards, and testing their knowledge killed the business, for at least a month was needed to bring them up to speed.

He told us of one of his drillers chopping off his own fingers as he activated the blade he had his hand on. With no insurance covering the company beyond the capital and these temps not licensed, he spent two years in prison. The initial sentence was five years, but his lawyers brought his goodwill to the attention of the judges. He still paid a beefy fee in lieu of the remaining jail time, leading the victim and his family to accuse him of bribing. They wanted him out of business, despite the weighty sum which the court had forced him to pay to the injured.

The authorities saw in his weakened position an opportunity to assign two officials to go with his crew, wherever work called, to provide health and safety training to new recruits and test and certify them. In other words, he now employed these full-time, paying their salaries and for their absence from home, which turned out to be heftier than having permanent travelling staff of his own. He worsened the company's financial situation by trying to save money.

The time spent behind bars had seen activities halted as all the equipment was seized, yet he was compelled to keep paying his employees. The machinery was imported with a loan from a local bank that had accepted his three houses, valued at a combined amount of $800,000, as collateral. The lender took possession of two of them due to no payment during his incarceration. "When it rains, it pours" is not an adage to some people but the reality of their life. We wondered why he was still in this business, and he replied:

"People cannot live without water!"

They all three deserved a chance because of their equal desire to give water to the people. But we were divided between LaSource, with its imported quality materials that demanded a long wait and struggling equipment, on the one hand, and Omega, which had two sets of equipment but local materials that passed not the test, on the other. However, we wished not to compromise on quality and were not ready to give out our business on compassionate grounds. Basil was sure gone, but we were determined to honour him only with the best quality we could find.

Also influencing our decision was that although Omega's owner was present in the capital, both his sets of crew and equipment were over 900 kilometres away and on an eight-month-long commitment. Therefore, we went with LaSource, paying him the total due rather than an advance and a surplus to have his consignment delivered within weeks by a much-trusted air courier.

However, expediting delivery was not all that was needed. Customs being based on the transporter's premises turned out to be more of a challenge than going through the maritime port. Everyone added a figure to the clearance fee, building up barricades, especially when we made the mistake of getting involved. They no longer saw it as LaSource's cargo but ours. So, they asked for our import licence and more. Gladly, we had already finalised our registration. But, not wanting to back up, the agents hid behind the not-yet-published Journal Officiel despite the law not saying that we had to wait for publication to start trading.

Sight of Water

Come the drilling, the community still fought over where to place their well. Most people had rejected the leader's support of Basil's property and asked that we revive the old one, which was not on the boy's compound. Nothing else was acceptable. We approached the environmental department at the Commune, given that the reason behind the abandonment of this well was that the corpse had contaminated it. Money and an entire month would be spent to get the ever-slow bureaucracy telling us what they thought.

The officials denied us using the old well, despite LaSource guaranteeing it would be disinfected to industry standards. The person whose land it sat on claimed the right to have the communal well for this close-knit neighbourhood only at his. He wanted control of what the population would pay to draw water.

Worse in all these negotiations were those opposed, accusing us publicly of coming to divide their community, creating anarchy, and silencing them when we had let the authorities take the reins. The clock was ticking. We were another month behind schedule, whereas we had intended to have Basil's well pumping out water by now. The officials' alternative consisted of drilling within the same property. So, they had to send someone to examine the place, which meant us incurring administrative, transportation, and lunch fees.

The go-ahead granted, we kept our fingers crossed so that LaSource's vehicle would reach the site without any problem, but it had a mind of its own. A flat tyre 13 kilometres to the destination, and an incompatible jack, left the driver and another crew member spending the night in the middle of the road. This disturbed other motorists throughout the day as they had to pass on either side and presented even greater danger at night due to the road being unlit, despite it being the main boulevard and the only road leading to the country's number one airport.

The tyre sorted, it only covered another four kilometres when the radiator gave up. We dismounted and took it away for welding. That was another week gone, and nothing we could do in the absence of another company to call immediately. By then, our visits to the site to advise that we were confident of surmounting these challenges were met with traditional beliefs. For the neighbourhood, the boy, in his grave, was still showing what he was capable of. They were adamant it was best to just abandon the project altogether.

This explained why while talking with the community, we were the only ones who pronounced Basil's name, besides the leader, who was said to be untouchable by evil spirits. The same applied to the rest of the family members' names that were disclosed to us only at the Commune. Hence, the community decided to come up with what to call their new well.

Meanwhile, we got the struggling lorry on-site, thanks to Günter chipping in his know-how to accelerate repairs. Almost the entire neighbourhood gathered to watch and direct work. Everyone was an expert in their own mind. The crew held us liable for the disturbance because we had refused to fence up their space so they could work in peace. Our defence was that we did not fancy splashing out more than $2,000 on wood and corrugated sheets that would be needed for only up to a month, and then have the public fight over them if the workers did not sell them.

A crowd very determined to maintain a leading role relegated Themba and Tino to the second or third row, whereas they were to be watching work closely and learning a thing or two about how to handle the soil they were discovering. I was glad to be the only one of us able to understand every word said aloud. However, the improvised work directors had an even better way to let my partners know they were adding value, using gestures as best as they could and changing the tone of voice when needed, barking orders if feeling ignored.

While overseeing this drilling was worthwhile in their eyes, we thought they could have used their time better. There were at least 300 hours invested badly daily over the first 18 days on the job. Jan and I discussed how else those spectators could have occupied themselves had water already been in their midst. But because of what we were doing there, kids missed or were late for school, and parents went not out looking for work or deserted homes and other responsibilities. Water scarcity steals time in many ways in this nation.

A few more unproductive days followed because of the rig's inability to get past the carcass of a car buried in the ground, possibly long before the area was inhabited. Also, the earth's formation had not given us a hint of the big stones therein found. Luckily, we could not be held back eternally. Singing and dancing eventually broke out with a huge splash coming out, higher than the lorry, when the rig hit the bedrock. The crew was mobbed and lost ownership of the site as children swarmed in, showering like in the rain. Adults who had the foresight of having buckets ready violently pushed them aside to fill up before they could be restricted or asked to pay. Throughout drilling, people sat on containers, unbeknown to us what they were up to. I assumed they were going to their usual sources, but I should have inquired.

Seeing the population's devotion to coming out every day to watch the progress made, we felt they were entitled to this madness and privilege. It was a customary celebration at the arrival of water in a community with none. Hence, we left them to it for the rest of the day. The workers were used to this, so they just safeguarded the borehole as best as they could to avoid accidents. We worried about flooding but, regaining control, they diverted the forming-lake into the street before stopping the springing water with dusk approaching, sadly putting an end to the jamboree.

It left us feeling guilty seeing some go home without when they could have walked their usual long distance to fetch water, but it was getting late and dark for us, too. Because the crew stayed on-site overnight since setting up, they asked for permission to leave access to water on till 10.00 p.m., but, being aware that any mishap would be on our back, we declined. The agreement with LaSource and the regulators clearly stated that we were not to operate before 8.00 a.m., or go past 5.00 p.m., so we had to be careful. We had already taken the risk of letting the crowd have water till 7.00 p.m., which we were not proud of, although glad for the euphoria.

Quality

Before drilling further, in the quest for top quality, Tino, I, and a member of LaSource planned to visit the government's laboratory first thing in the morning to determine whether we already had potable water. This meant 11.00 to him, despite Mashimba being at his at the agreed time of eight.

His excuse was that no one was going to be in at nine. We did not take him seriously. But lab staff showed up at noon, causing us to return the following day.

The gatekeeper advised that no one attended without an appointment and having paid a fee, which was separate from what was due for the analysis. But we did not see the reason for advance booking as the place was empty. As painful as it felt, we took it on the chin and asked for the proper procedure to follow, wondering why on earth this LaSource worker was unaware. But he said to have been under the impression that his office had it covered. He suggested making life easier for ourselves by getting the lab scientist to collect samples from us and bring back the results. All that was needed was his *motivation*. But thinking it disrespectful to make an official come to us, we went by their schedule, to be seen after five attempts.

The results were much below what Tino, with his expertise, expected. We surreptitiously submitted the same water for another test and got a new certificate that said it was now potable. What a joke! The colour attributed to *this* sample was nowhere near even what my naked eye could have given it. The *excellent* grading received caused us to doubt the overall quality of the lab. Their guess or incompetence was a blessing in disguise; otherwise, we would not have sought to do better. We wished we did have testing instruments of our own.

Drilling resumed, going 10 metres deeper to 70. Surprisingly, the lab gave us worse grades, despite the yellow colouring having diminished to the point that it was hard to tell of any without being an expert. Hence, we reverted to our ministerial contacts who placed calls around, and not only were samples picked up, but Tino, Themba, and I also joined the workroom. Tino participated and pointed out where processes and standards were not observed. Three different bottles had the same outcome: very potable! This was a quality neither Tino nor Themba had ever witnessed at the same depth in their career.

With the public's interest at heart, we deployed efforts to 100 metres to avoid any quality variation after covering the well. The solar pump went in, and the exterior got embellished. We equipped the station with 10 outlets, so queuing would be minimal. Eighty cubic metres was available every hour, making it 960,000 litres of healthy water daily, based on a 12-hour daylight period that often extended to 14 in this region. Every household of five was entitled to a daily supply of 300 litres. Therefore, this station alone catered to 3,200 families.

Our problem became, however, what was a *neighbourhood* now that water was accessible at a push of a button, thanks to the solar system and word of mouth travelling like the wind. The nearby communities flocked in, either their eligible extended families or friends beckoning them or uninvited. The boundaries comprising 2,000 households we had in mind, all within a five-minute walk of the borehole, were dismissed. Therefore, we left it with the management over the well to sort out who of the outsiders to let in. Thus, the surplus representing an extra $65,700 in revenue yearly did not go to waste.

Envy

It was difficult to prioritise the primary beneficiaries of this well because every family had more or less the same timetable, going out before dawn and returning at dusk. Relieving kids from drawing water also seemed on the way to being defeated, for it was they who left home after their parents and came back from school when it was still daytime. Hence, the adults excused themselves from fetching water still, especially with the solar pump not working at either end of the day justifying them more.

In this situation, only children with stay-at-home mothers enjoyed being released from the arduous chore they had faithfully carried out, and could now focus on their education and find time to play with their friends. Not content to deliver a partially fulfilling solution, going the extra mile became imperative. The community's monetary contribution empowered us to create work for a few of the many who sat around unoccupied. Those willing to let go of their pride were useful in taking water to homes so busy parents and school-age children could reinvest their time and energy as we had hoped.

A litre of clean water was available at $0.0005, equalling $0.15 per 300 litres. This was $54.75 a year to a family of five and far better than the $1 per 1.5-litre bottle from the store or walking long distances to meet the demand to the detriment of education, work, health, and family time. This offering became the envy of even those corners of the capital with taps because the SWC charged a flat fee of $20 monthly in less-privileged suburbs, regardless of how many days in a calendar month water came out of the tap—those lucky were served 10 days out of 30.

This neighbourhood had not thought of water coming to them again after Basil's death. Hence, they considered the proposal established with our coordination as charitable, despite them paying back for it. Chariots had greatly served the city for decades. They came in handy again to bring water to families. Nothing inventive from us, except that Alvin and Amy tweaked them into our programme to give business to existing *chariot-men* who earned a living transporting goods, pushing or pulling a two-wheel cart. But money had long become a problem for everyone; hence they were many hours a day without customers. So, we could not have come up at a better time.

People had been loving their new way of life for a month when their leader was summoned to the police station. He was kept there for two days until we heard, visited, and assigned Zacharie to investigate. His evil was to have given water to the community before it was analysed and declared potable. Our defence outweighed the accusation as the crowd storming out at the appearance of water had not started with us. Ironically, the defendant confounded one of his prosecutors, who was from the neighbourhood, as his wife was among those who waited and went home with water when it sprung out of the ground that day. But that was deemed irrelevant and by no means sufficient to influence his release.

So, as the hearing dragged on, three kids and their parents came out to witness. They apparently had had terrible stomach aches over two days after consuming our water. We were charged, despite them drinking it of their own free will and choice. The fine included their treatment. However, we were denied access to their medical records. Zacharie advised not to insist.

Meanwhile, the leader was still not free. Another case had developed: they accused him of depriving the authorities of the ribbon-cutting honour to declare the station officially operational. There, even a private achievement was turned into a state affair should the officials choose to, erasing the person behind the accomplishment. However, we recalled not the clerks briefing us about this protocol despite multiple visits to them seeking various permits. We had not taken them seriously when four of them had asked, jokingly we had assumed, for us to have plenty of refreshments at the inauguration.

We sent out the invite as the now-law-abiding neighbourhood leader counselled with regaining his freedom. We went weekly, in person, to obtain a date suitable for those to attend from the Commune. "Wait to be contacted," we repeatedly got told, and to expect it to take up to three months because diaries were full. In the meantime, the ban on giving people water remained on. All that time, lab analyses continued to be carried out and confirmed water to be drinkable, for a certificate produced within a week was required at the inaugural ceremony. We heard that it was all about envy and that nothing would change unless we sent over *motivation*.

"Iron sharpens iron," said an elderly man, implying the need to respond to force with force.

He stood with a five-litre jerrycan in one hand, bent to one side, and holding his waist with the other. These caprices punished him.

"I took out early retirement as a bank clerk, aged 55, to look after my wife until her passing 17 years later. Two decades on, I still miss her terribly. We were not blessed with children but had each other. At my age, having water nearby will mean the world. For 30 years, my wife walked far and wide to bring water home without a moan."

In a country with no pension scheme, he relied on the investment they had made early enough on a piece of land. It was the annex buildings they had erected and rented out. His tenants now took turns—the ladies it was—providing him with 50 litres of water daily. But, not wanting to give up completely, he contributed with that container half-full.

"This hour-long journey, every other day, presents me with the chance to get out of the house and give myself drinking water."

Hand-pumping was too hard for him. Hence not filling up his container. There were times when people pumped for him. But, in the eyes of mothers with feeding babies waiting at home or students running against time, old age mattered not. They took the pump out of his hands and brushed him aside. This compelled him to drink sparingly, despite the heat.

A 92-year-old thus pleading got us off to the City Hall, where we no longer needed an appointment. The Commune was summoned to the inauguration to take place in a week.

Ndôto

It was beyond celebratory finally having water back. Community notables had never tired of giving us tips to overcome red tape. I regretted at times questioning the efficacity of their counsel. Nonetheless, even as much as I now valued them, I still held it against them for not allowing us to name this asset what we desired. But not wanting to spoil the party, they had our blessing to go ahead with whatever they thought right to call it.

For them, two children dying of malaria whilst this inauguration was pending was Basil haunting back. They feared him coming back for more, hiding behind several illnesses known to be prevalent in the country, going back to Heaven knows when, if this station was left to have any association with him. We hated listening to how inconsiderate they were of him besides denying any wrongdoing on their part. We did our best to hide our anger. What mattered most was to alleviate the penury that was destroying generations.

We rejected the offer to call it Amy's, then Alvin's, Günter's, Jan's, and Tino's, in that order. The culture to honour a foreigner who had done something of much importance for them did not trick us. Laura had joined us two days prior, upon hearing we now had a date. But, she and Themba were not foreigners enough in the eyes of the community.

In the end, a lady sitting in the front row raised her hand. She was the oldest person there. Noticing, the entire crowd progressively went quiet. This is how they revere old age there—those who still do. She was two days short of her 110th birthday. The person tasked with finding out the people's will took the microphone to her. Suddenly, her vocal cords got working again, and she spoke with confidence, which most of the younger generation in the audience had never known of her. She had had this same dream six times over the past year, wherein some foreigners had come to install a well next to the one Basil had perished in. However, she dared not tell anyone because, in it, she had seen herself dying three days following her revealing her dream.

"What is it to me if I now go?"

"What shall we then call this well?" the City man asked.

"*Ndôto*," came the reply. A *dream*, in Lingala.

No one said otherwise. They just enjoyed the food and the music provided.

We got a call three days later from the neighbourhood leader, saying she had not woken up that morning despite going to bed with no sign of being under the weather. Amy pointed out that her age was being unwell anyway. But, how interesting that her *ndôto* came to pass!

There was only one concern with her passing: a coffin and other funeral costs were not met. Therefore, all the streets in the area got blocked off; no one was permitted to come in or go out unless they donated a minimum of 50 francs to help bury her. This was the equivalent of $0.10, but few had it. Assistance was sought from us, timidly. But, it made us feel more like part of them.

Laura paid what was required, although most of it was just for the crowd to have a good time. But we were surprised when the leader reimbursed us in full, out of the first month's income from the well, despite Laura's rejection. He argued that we had not come to leave everything out there. We had given them water, a responsibility, a source of income, and dignity, which was a lot, in his opinion. He intended to send us away with more than we had put in if he could.

Certainly, they were returning more than the monetary value they had in mind for us. We had gained knowledge, wisdom, and experience that money could not buy us. Ndôto, in local philosophy, means more than a dream. It is a *solution* to a problem long holding someone or a society back. It is a wish, a yearning, a goal. Water scarcity was a crisis that had become a way of life. This lady had dreamt of a solution that would help turn the page. In the Congo, people do not reveal their dreams until they become a reality, else they would not come true. That is just how it is. Although when it comes to pass, most would question one's claim. We, too, had a ndôto: we wanted to assist more than just this community, and we chose to keep quiet about it yet.

Expansion

All the difficulties encountered to this point had left us with an incommensurable level of confidence that could not have been acquired otherwise. We had each turned resolute, capable of confronting any challenge thrown at us, and the next one took no longer than the following morning to find us. There were people downstairs for us but unable to get past security. Sad that only a certain category was allowed in the lobby. The judgement was based on the attire. Jeans, combat trousers, t-shirts, and trainers were deemed inappropriate unless in the company of a hotel's guest, an official, or pulling up in an expensive vehicle.

Tino and I stepped outside and brought in two. Laura paid for them to join us for breakfast, which they reluctantly accepted. We were unaware of some media presence at Ndôto's launch, and they now wanted to interview and write articles about us. We had to pay for the service. We knew nothing about their companies, but they turned out to be weighty household names.

Just under 36 hours after we had been broadcast, we found a business card and a note at the hotel from one called Zola. He was the head of public relations for *Brassco*, a nationwide brewery. He begged for a meeting the next morning. He had watched the news and was touched. Hence, he offered to fund the drilling of 30 wells in the four most deprived communes of the city, insisting, however, that a third be as close as possible to Ndôto to leave no cracks between the latter and the communities surrounding it.

Laura was already preparing to instruct Rex to free up some cash but had now to put on the brakes to see what would develop with Zola, who asked for the privilege of hosting us at our hotel at the weekend. Monday morning, he introduced us to the company's number one, who had just returned from a neighbouring country the night before. He had been made aware of us from where he was. They presented us with the contract. The boss acknowledged them making a lot of money from the public, so it made sense to give back now that they were in front of a group that shared their vision. That only added pressure to prove that we were worth their trust. We took the paperwork to Zacharie to make sure we were sufficiently covered, and returned it in person two days later with some presents as an expression of our gratitude.

Ndôto had cost us $16,000 to LaSource for 60 metres, plus an additional $8,000 for the extra 40 metres. The solar kit had a price tag of $2,000, while embellishing the exterior claimed $1,000—making it a total of $27,000. We, however, billed Zola $30,000. He wowed us with $50,000 per well, advising the surplus would help meet unforeseen expenses, which he said would be legion. He insisted on always charging at least 50% more if we were to stay in business in the Congo. Quite right!

The lawyer's intervention, for instance, was more frequent and costlier than we had projected. Working on Ndôto, we realised how much we needed him nearby. There was no doubt he deserved what had become a regular remuneration, as he repeatedly came out at short notice, leaving all other cases he had going. Unfortunately, barriers never stopped being erected against us, and only he was sure how to get around them unless we reverted to our protectors, whom we liked no more disturbing all the time, in the interest of their reputation. We feared it being rumoured that they received compensation from us.

Seeking to know the why of Zola's generosity gushed tears out of him. He was unable to find his handkerchief. Laura came to the rescue with a packet of paper ones she bought almost everywhere we went, off kids, because she hated seeing them as young as seven on the side of the streets nagging adults with their products. Expressing gratitude for the tissues, he commented on how we all need one another in life. He tried to force a smile out of himself, but it retracted with more tears rolling out in the middle of saying that "children were permanently at risk because of the lack of water". Then, trying to divert our attention, he opened one of his drawers, looking for something else, and there he found the pack of cloth handkerchiefs he could not locate two minutes earlier.

He elaborated on this over-pricing strategy more than the donation itself, highlighting how even a day's rain could eat into planning and inflict losses, as we would still have to pay workers and bank interests. It amazed us how conscious he was about making a profit, given that this was not part of his work. He had come to Brassco with a degree in marketing, aged 22. Being very clever and hard-working brought about promotion. He was trusted with taking care of the company's image, which included meeting the public's social needs with solutions of significant magnitude. But so far, he had focused on outdoor musical production as this was what his targeted audience enjoyed most.

Because we would be importing supplies to amaze Brassco with quality, Zola highlighted the need to factor in delays. The cost of logistics was a hurdle on its own and unpredictable; he went on lecturing us. However, with his 50% advance payment in our bank account seven days after signing, we afforded the luxury of having Günter's uniquely designed and adapted drilling gears produced for us. The brewer was happy that we complete the first well within six months of committing and the rest six months after that, making it a year-long delivery.

Thus, we allowed ourselves a break, with Laura leading the way, her having come down for just a couple of weeks.

Günter, Jan, Tino, and Themba headed to Asia to oversee the manufacturing of our trailer-mounted rig and to test it sufficiently on the types of soil similar to those in Kinshasa. This rig included a compressor capability, which eliminated the need for a separate unit, shipping, and associated customs fees.

The lack of a compressor was partly why LaSource took four weeks to drill 100 metres. Günter's innovation would achieve this in five hours. At Ndôto, Themba and Tino had taken over from 40 metres to completion, leaving LaSource's workers astounded, else that job would have taken longer to complete. Having our own equipment would have a big advantage in that we would incur only $4,500, all costs put together, which explained our being confident of meeting the deadline with ease, local logistics and weather carefully considered. However, having the right equipment meant not having it easy thereafter.

Greed

Choosing which communes to serve first and where exactly to place Brassco's wells was challenging. We wished we had had nothing to do with this part of the contract. Zola's PR team had shared the news with the media, for they intended to increase sales and walk over their competitors through this community engagement. Therefore, we were swamped with meeting requests from the municipalities' heads of social affairs, who advised us of their needs being greater than those of the rest.

But as far as we were concerned, everyone was in the same boat, and those advocating for themselves were often a bit safer. Some were bolder, to the point of asking for the whole project to come to their commune, thus exposing their greed. The truth was that this scarcity could swallow up any amount of funding if tackled at once, the city over, and defeat whatever mechanism employed if responding to emotions. Because of the proximity of the Commune of Ngaliema to our domicile, we made it a priority to visit its localities to have a feel of their situation.

Analyses from the academic institutions and marketing agencies we had contacted were not worth our time. We knew this the moment we stepped into the first two areas, them being among the most affluent of the city. We were taken to the house of a top man in a telecommunications company. His brother, who worked for the Commune, had arranged the visit, whereas we had approached him to know which neighbourhoods suffered most.

The one-year-old luxury sport SUV in the drive and the two posh saloons in the open garage, together with a beautifully designed massive house, truly had our heads spinning with the gatekeeper letting us in. We were ushered into a lounge, nothing short of a presidential suite in a top-range hotel. However, this was not all that the visit had for us.

We had barely made ourselves comfortable on the leather-rich sofas when a scene that we had not expected to see there suddenly appeared. It was the kind we were already sick and tired of. A line of six girls carrying water hit us *bang* right between the eyes. The lady of the house had just finished telling us she only had three daughters, aged 11, 13, and 15, and no son. They were all at school, hence our not meeting them, this being mid-morning. Those with water on their heads were between 12 and 17. This was their occupation, 6.00 a.m. to 6.00 p.m. to fill up the 2,000-litre tank elevated in the yard every day for all household needs, washing the vehicles, and keeping the garden and its beautiful flowers watered.

"When do they attend school then?" Amy asked.

"There is just not enough time for it," she responded. "Else, we would be without water."

"And how long have they been at your service?"

"Well, that is not how to put it. They are family."

The longest serving joined five years prior. Their mistress replaced them with turning 18, so they could find themselves husbands—the only other thing out there for girls like these. However, she hoped to soften us, saying that she did not take on anyone under 10.

"How do you recruit them?"

"They are a mixture of my relatives and my husband's. We send for them, so their parents do not struggle to feed them."

We were befuddled.

"We give them more than we receive. It is not an easy thing out here to offload someone of their obligations for close to a decade."

This house matched the large salaries we heard people like him were on, despite the country's inability to meet its citizens' basic needs. This being a very elevated location, the land was very much sought after and rendered unaffordable to the ordinary people by the rich, who liked to tower over everyone. Their children were safe from mosquitoes that venture not up there because of the fresh air in places of high altitude. A cheap property there sold for around $1 million. Yet no water out of the tap when I entered the loo, which the couple had already told us, anyway, when trying to justify why they sacrificed the girls. They showed off the comfortable life, in their opinion, they provided for them, especially the flat that was theirs, built for workers, at the back of the sumptuous eight-bed villa.

The husband attempted to win us over, making it clear that he would send his nieces to school if we would place a well at his. His request opposed Zola's wish to see the disadvantaged benefit. The Commune's clerk who brought us there was disappointed that we could not be tricked. We understood not why he failed to see that the project was not intended for a neighbourhood of this type. We suggested our host ask his company to emulate our sponsor, given that his area undoubtedly made his employer a lot of money.

"I would be delighted to work in this area," Tino said, startled by the beauty around.

Meanwhile, a community spirit was evident as the main road, just 200 metres from this house, was in a pitiful state, but the streets inside this neighbourhood contrastingly in mint condition. We wondered how come, and the man who brought us there whispered when the couple stepped out of the living room. These top executives' employers chipped in enough so the Commune's relevant department could give their inner streets special maintenance. This led us to believe that such goodwill could be extended to water provision if sought.

That freed us up to go on using Brassco's sponsorship for the localities buried in ravines in this municipality. They resulted from torrential rains, defacing or eliminating roads over the years and rendering water carrying more shattering. These six girls came several times a day in those valleys to fetch water and bring it up on the hill. One of our drivers asked us not to be shocked that people exploited their impoverished kinsfolks' children like slaves.

Laura sneaked out to meet with the girls with one of our chauffeurs as her interpreter.

"No need, *Tantine*," interrupted the oldest. "We speak French, though not as good as you."

They all giggled while Laura, embarrassed, had tears to wipe off. They had attended school in their villages before landing where we found them. It was sold to them that they were coming to go to better establishments. Now, they only hoped to resume their education when they were released from this slavery, even just to take up some vocational training. Seamstress, baking, gastronomy, and nursing had all crossed their minds, hoping to be of some value in life. Until such time, they read a newspaper a night, splitting the pages between themselves, summed up their findings to each other, and discussed together to keep their little French growing.

The institutions which had given them this foundation were reputable quality boarding schools that attracted wealthy people's kids from Kinshasa. A few pupils from the nearby villages squeezed in too. They were allowed to live at home or in privately arranged close-by accommodations if commuting daily was not possible. But these six were snatched away, like livestock, just before graduating from elementary school. Ironically, their *mum* had imposed on them to only speak French to benefit her household, possibly unaware it was to their advantage.

Gripping On

When drilling in low-level areas, not necessarily where rains had left damages, we quickly had water at depths as little as 20 metres, but we still stuck to 100. Quality confirmed, we wrapped up a station within a week, thanks to our now-established contacts at the testing centre. Out of courtesy and not at their request, we rewarded each of the four staff there with a well in their neighbourhood, as Zola had left the distribution of the wells with us.

The only time he, however, interfered was concerning the implementation of the post-inaugural management programme. His board argued that what we received from them was a donation to the communities, and not a profit-making investment. But they foresaw not the after-delivery state of the wells. We could not do things their way unless they committed to pay an ongoing fee to be relayed to the maintenance team. Such would have to land into our account a year in advance, and we needed them to sign up for 10 years, for we were determined to only build and put our name on what would stand the test of time and provide true value to all stakeholders.

Taking this stand handed us victory. Their accountants produced a costing plan for the combined 30 wells over such a period and compared it with how things would be, for their company, with the population's participation. It got more interesting noticing that a great part of the consumers' contributions would help other communities, thus eliminating the need for Brassco to make extra donations or us begging whomever else to emulate this socially responsible act.

However, just when we thought we had gotten unstuck, some neighbourhoods threatened to boycott Brassco's products and move to competitors who had done nothing to deserve their switching over. They had felt discriminated against. A typical local attitude! It was hard to do something for one person without others feeling displeased and claiming they were also entitled to the same. One had to assist all at once or none.

But there were those who, when properly briefed, bought into our vision, as was proved at parting with the Telecoms executive. He reverted to us to provide water to himself and his community, away from Brassco's account. We seized the moment, especially to help our wish to see *his* girls given the opportunity to return to school. He confessed to being ashamed that a man of his calibre had been living without water on his property. It was an embarrassment shared in his area, as everyone there was a managing director of a company, a business proprietor, a medical doctor, a lawyer, an army general, and so on, all unquestionably with the means to make a difference for themselves and others in the nearby poor sections of their commune. There was just no excuse to have let things be the way they were.

Next to his was a community full of diplomats and government officials, past and present, and their situation was no better. He promised to make contact door-to-door to see if we would tackle the height that had kept everyone in this business away, for water was not available even at 200 metres. But the ordinary locals reassured us of success past 300 metres instead. Anyone who had ignored this empirical knowledge had broken their nose at 80 metres with the sort of rigs that went no deeper. Working in our favour was that there had been no running water up there for years despite the area being piped. Tanks visible high above ground and towering over the three-metre-high brick fence surrounding each property were a permanent embarrassment for the stature of people living in this suburb.

Surprisingly, water catchment was overlooked, despite the large roofs there. The residents feared dirt or bacteria coming down with the first load to spoil the rest of the harvest and cause health issues. Therefore, it was best to keep clear of rainwater altogether. Those who collected this type of water used it only for gardening, car washing, and toilet flushing.

The man had a successful campaign. So, we promised to return once done with Brassco but signed first to avoid the result of our hard work going to those lurking around, although not having the tools that posed a real threat. A $40,000 fee for the initial 60 metres was not a concern to them. The same for the $400 an additional metre. Another reason for their willingness to part with their cash was that the land they had built on broke up easily, making it difficult to keep a hole together, and thus scaring away any drilling company that could have tried to venture up there. At the end of the day, most of these residents did obtain backing from their employers with little effort, so they insisted we just get on with drilling when ready.

But halfway through Brassco's work, inauguration taking place almost every weekend, the City Hall called us up. We were instructed to hang fire on what we were doing and establish 20 wells for various officials in one corner of the capital. The message was that some people were more important than others. Unfortunately, everyone was equal in our eyes, and following the queue was vital.

Being on schedule on Zola's contract still gave us no right to become complacent. And an even better reason to not get distracted was the joy people who had never had water this close manifested at the completion of every borehole. I will long remember the kid who came running to Tino and wrapped his arms around his knees. Then, him looking down at him—because he had not seen the little boy coming—and their eyes meeting, he said, "thank you," and cried.

A woman joined us out of the sparse crowd, revealing that her son got emotional when he pressed the button and water came out. She told him who had made it possible, pointing in our direction. To her surprise, he instinctively took off running, leaving her to watch. He was four!

"He remembers as far as he can being on my back while I struggled to pump water out of a well that seemed to yield none," she said. "Then, with relocation, leaving him behind alone almost the entire day while his siblings attended school, to travel to and from our new source of water. Hence what you have witnessed from him today."

She, too, cried. This alone summed up what that well and the technology thereto fitted meant to even the least of them. Such and many other moments reinforced our determination to see Brassco's communal wells through before moving on, no matter the weight of a new client.

Awful it was that no one argued with the authorities, especially if they were politicians. For that cause, our ministerial contacts asked that we let go of our logic. Fortunately, we had a surplus of equipment in the warehouse, and other 10 sets halfway at sea. Tino and Themba had been busy training a group of 30 people to join our ranks. These already had some knowledge and water drilling experience from other employers, so all they needed was new techniques and instructions about how to use our unique but user-friendly machines.

On this occasion, the good thing about yielding to the leaders was that they took care of getting the regulators to expedite the testing and licensing of our new team members. Therefore, we became partners with the authorities going forward, in that we could count on them if we ever faced administrative delays again. We could not have obtained these guarantees had we not accommodated a degree of flexibility, despite many abusing their power.

We received a further contract from the hands of the same officials to cheer up military and police barracks. The first order was concluded in no time, thanks to our new five teams completing a well a week each. Yet we were to see any money for the job already done. As annoying as it was becoming to keep calling and visiting various departments to find out where our payment was, we stopped all work in progress. That made them come back to us with long-winded stories of administrative problems they were having but that were of no bearing to us.

The new deal was 100 wells, but we did not call Laura for funding. I had reassured her that what came from Zola was sufficient to keep us going, so I was not backpedalling on my words. At one point, she grew worried that I was cleverly getting her out of the business because she saw her role as the investor fading. But I renewed my promise to keep her on as the chairperson and shares entitled her unaltered, whatever we acquired. Above all, our mutual passion for seeing change come to the Congo through the provision of water held us together and stronger, and neither of us would think of ridding of the other for financial gain.

In the meantime, there was only so much room for respect regarding unpaid invoices. So, I pushed the liaison officer at the government's end to honour their commitment, and he got us what was owed on the first contract and a 40% deposit on the second deal. We were able to pay our staff their $350 dollars each per well completed. They earned a fiver per person for every additional metre past the standard 60. A $1,000 bonus was theirs to share for any extra well beyond the monthly threshold of four. This was unheard of in the local market, but to us well-deserved.

No special treatment either but what a family of five needed to live a bit comfortably, it being what we had established an average household size, ignoring those bigger. We also considered what the company earned. To say we taught by example, we had an all-risk insurance policy in place, despite hearing that it was not easy to get paid when accidents occurred. Knowing the business was there to stay, we got beyond the national borders and secured a second and better coverage with a good-faith provider. Likewise, we offered a pension scheme, which had not been around since the early 1970s.

We made sure that our workers' children were in school, if they were of age, and did not overlook those still under 25 who desired to pursue tertiary education or vocational training. Those in rented accommodations were encouraged to relocate where we had installed wells unless there was a plan to install a station near their abode, because it pained us that they should be without water while providing it to others.

Sadly, the suggestion appealed to none or worked not for all. The difficulty in finding new schools for their children, the shortage of houses to rent, and not being interested in relocating were among the long list of reasons we heard from our employees. They flip-flopped on the subject, even when it was apparent their families would be saving money and swapping for bigger and cleaner living quarters. Their fear was more about what would be said of them for going from a not-too-bad suburb to one deemed as indigenous than how they were trying to paint their rejection. The alternative was, therefore, only to drill within the neighbourhoods where they lived.

We asked their communities to get together and come forth with a deposit. They stunned us with the rush with which contributions poured in, showing how much water was needed. Every household gave the minimum required of them, some going without food and together came up with more than enough to cover the cost of a well.

There we were, proud to give our staff 15 stations we had not planned for. But a conflict of interest would arise about who would run these facilities. We intended to keep it the same everywhere: the community leader in charge, with two assistants of their choosing. But our workers had members of their families lined up as though these wells were their own. We had not realised what they were setting up when they suggested these sites: they all belonged to their relatives or people they had been friends with for years.

Greed of this nature was seen throughout our work and seemed to bother no local. But we were not bowing down. That we were able to attract funding somewhat easily was a sign that many people were conscious of the change that could come to them, which could also extend to a change of mentality. This effort was, therefore, worth coupling up with good practice. Regrettably, most of our staff were not on the same page as us. Nonetheless, in keeping with the spirit of this book, which is to enlighten, inspire, and uplift the reader, we will not dwell on our personnel's attitude to want to make these wells theirs.

What we came up with through our first 166 realisations overshadowed the frustration encountered. Put into context, 159,360,000 litres of healthy water became available daily, where there had been none, enough for 2,656,000 people if used responsibly. Industry organisations recommend a minimal usage of 60 litres per person per day.

At this point, we could see more donors and beneficiaries trusting us and ourselves gaining more confidence as our work had long started to speak for us.

7

COURAGE

Eastbound

Brassco handed us further work two months before finishing their initial 30 wells. They wanted us in the Katanga, the Kivu, and the *Province Orientale*, for a combined 100 stations. Any of these three provinces is an average of 2,500 kilometres from Kinshasa. We were allowed to rest as long as needed after concluding in the capital to recharge our batteries before setting up east.

We had not envisioned entering any of these territories, at least not this early, nor had we knowledge of the soil formation there. The first thing that came to mind when Zola broke the news was how to get our equipment across to that part of the country. Roads were not an option. We also wondered what to do regarding hiring new workers, worrying about the time it would take to adapt to more new cultures and getting the locals to warm up to us and vice-versa. This was because the Congo, with its more than 450 tribes, each with its own language and traditions, is among some of the most diverse places on the planet.

The first individuals we turned to in Kinshasa warned us of the rebels' killing of peaceful innocent people like ourselves in the Kivu provinces every day. We considered declining but chose to face the challenge with courage. We had nothing to drive us forward but the first-hand experience of people living without water. More importantly, we did not want to disintegrate the cementing relationship with Brassco, just in case they could turn into long-term partners.

Going that far from what had now been home to us for two years also meant finding trustworthy people to leave the business behind with. We could not afford to lock away the equipment, given the money invested and offers now coming our way wherever we turned. Even tougher was struggling with the idea of making redundant the workers who had proved faithful and established themselves in this business. Not keeping a presence in the capital would also create a gap for a new entrant to reap where they had not sowed—the communal well self-funding proposal being our brainchild, and it was becoming popular.

We had to get our spending right for this new assignment to succeed. But even more significant was finding out beforehand what awaited us. We planned to bring in a further 10 sets of machinery, tools, and materials from our Asia and Europe-based manufacturing partners, all uniquely tweaked to suit our new regions, which had different geological features from what we knew. We could have settled for what we had heard, but we understood the importance of seeing the lay of the land with our own eyes. Therefore, I offered to go and gather the facts myself.

Upon hearing of this plan, a friend I had made at the City Hall thought it best to introduce me to Hilaire, his cousin, who frequented Kisangani and farther north. The NGO he worked for kept him there for a month every quarter. Arranging our first in-person meeting to plan to travel together proved difficult because his journeys beyond Kisangani were not sticking to a schedule. The only grasshopper plane to those remotest villages serviced three provinces. He yearned to come out of the bush as soon as he set foot there, saying he was not enjoying his job. Further trying his patience was switching to a motorcycle for more than 700 kilometres, one way, on trails he often had to make. He settled for this job just to provide for his family.

Therefore, I had a month to spend in the UK before meeting him in Kisangani. My friend talked me into paying for his dad, Albert, to join us. Newly retired, he was well-respected by those who knew him in the capital, thanks to a long human rights activism career and how he carried himself. He was to present me to key people who would help with my investigations, as Hilaire would have only two days with me. It did not bother me to pay for their flights, hotels, food, and per diems, although I was aware that Hilaire would claim back his expenses from his employer.

Blood is Thicker than Water

Time at home went by like it had never happened. I boarded a Nairobi-bound flight at Heathrow. After a four-hour transit in the Kenyan capital, I hopped on a 30-seater that landed at Entebbe in Uganda, where pretty much everyone got off. With only four passengers remaining, I doubted we would ever depart as my watch and boarding pass confirmed we were already three hours behind the scheduled arrival time. No one seemed to care that we were sweating buckets onboard. So, I beckoned a flight attendant when I finally got a glimpse of one and asked if there was a problem.

"Be patient!" she said.

Well, I knew that customer service slacked greatly on these airlines once in Africa. Sometimes, our numerous languages and varying cultures make us come across as being rude when such is rarely our intention. Therefore, I did not seek the meaning of her words at the risk of being considered difficult. This was because, on another trip, I had witnessed a fellow passenger being escorted off the aircraft by the police, falsely accused of having abused the cabin crew, whereas she had inquired about a delay.

The two-engine propeller finally taxied away and lifted off the runway to land in Kisangani five hours later than scheduled. We had come to almost no life on the whole wide apron. There were only two pick-up vehicles, and more airport workers were guiding the plane than the combined crew and passengers onboard. With the engine switching off, ground staff fought over our luggage and pulled them away in a handcart. A person in uniform asked the four of us to follow him, insisting on us staying in line, while behind us followed two armed officers. Lifting my eyes to where I heard someone frantically calling my name, I told myself they could be Albert and Hilaire, for they had confirmed their arrival in Kisangani the day before I left London. Therefore, I waved back.

It took close to three hours to complete entry formalities, despite the only queue being me. My fellow travellers had gotten away quickly. They were locals who made this journey regularly for business, so all airport personnel knew them. It shocked me to hear that my residency permit was limited to Kinshasa. Moreover, I needed an invitation letter from a local company to enter the city. All of which was untrue. As to why on earth they were giving me such a hostile welcome, they highlighted the need to safeguard the population, for it had not been long since Kisangani had come out of war. Hence, I got moved into a private room to face an inquisitor and his assistant, who chipped in whatever entered him into the head, making life miserable for me. But they were unsuccessful in diverting me: I could tell my story sleeping.

The time in transit since landing at Jomo Kenyatta, an hour in the air to Entebbe, three hours waiting in the plane, one hour to reach Kisangani's Bogota Airport, and three hours at the immigration desk, was how things slowed down once back on the African continent. All in all, 12 hours that should not have exceeded five had worn me out and brought the sun to retire, it being past six in the evening—Kisangani is an hour behind Entebbe. In fact, this had taken even longer as I lived two hours from Heathrow, where I needed to be at least three hours before departure. But, I had come prepared to go any extra mile, if required, thanks to understanding the price to pay in order to bring water to my people. Certainly, where the Congo is concerned, for me, *blood is thicker than water!*

My interrogators testing my knowledge of weapons, local current and past rebel groups, and warlords' names led me to realise I had been passed to secret service agents. Troubling them was my going out of Kinshasa to re-enter the country via their airport, refusing to acknowledge that the time in the UK intervened in between. No explanation I provided pleased them, so I kept quiet for a while, unresponsive to probing, pressure, and provocation, even when they menaced me with physical torture.

The only thing breaking my silence was their supervisor opening the door without knocking. Albert was with him. He gave them the address of the hotel Hilaire had booked for the three of us and instructed them to let me go. Albert would reveal to have slipped a $50 note in his hand for him to act as he did. A 40-minute drive to the hotel ensued in a taxi I would not have gotten into had there been another option. The parking lot had only this and a couple of lorries that seemed not to be working. Bookings were made only in person, town-end. They had arrived at 10.00 a.m., it being when I was expected, so this guy earned $40 for each hour he sat there when he hardly made $20 all day on a normal day. But not keeping him would have meant having us walk the 20 kilometres, more than 80% of which were forest-covered and uninhabited.

Detention

Albert had arranged for his high school friend, Claude, to show us around. They had not seen each other in almost five decades. Differing choices of universities and courses of study had separated them. Unusually back then, they had kept in touch via letters and, in recent years, taken advantage of the introduction and multiplicity of mobile phone networks to get in touch regularly. He had kept both Albert and Hilaire busy since their arrival. He was at the hotel within minutes of us arriving and told us about the visits he had planned.

All his eight children were born in Kisangani and were either medical doctors or agronomists, the latter because of the nearby specialised university. However, soon after graduating, they all relocated to other cities with good offers. At 69, he was past retirement age, but even after four decades as a school headmaster, he still had no desire to call it a day. His wife and the mother of all his children had passed on seven years earlier. Therefore, we thought he was rightfully entitled to the company of the younger female, Simone, who appeared at his side. Albert and Hilaire were meeting her for the first time as I was.

I asked to find a place where they served food before the already empty streets got completely deserted, but Claude advised of Simone's cooking. The two of them stepped outside to brief her daughter over the phone. The meal arrived an hour later. It was so delicious that I asked the mother to pass on my appreciation to the teenager who had not stayed. Delivered were containers full of fish and plantains made in a local mashed potato style called *lituma*. The couple ate very little—them eating was only to keep with the tradition to prove that they were not poisoning us. In my gluttony, I went on past where I should have stopped. Sadly, we had overlooked buying water, and everything had shut down for the night. It was past 11. The hotel had also run out and only beer and soft drinks remained.

Well, we all admitted that Simone had beaten us on this occasion, so having her food the following day would give us the chance to show her we ate more. But little did I know that I would be sleeping on the toilet! I also found out that my diarrhoea tablets had their limitations. I had to choose between sticking to the indicated dosage and bearing the consequences of ignoring instructions. On the water side, I had blown up the two bottles I had, so I was in a mess after that.

Another disaster was having only two 10-litre buckets of water in the room, one for flushing the loo and the other for my morning bath. The former I used sparingly, while the latter I dared not touch all night. They were not getting refilled until close to midday, to last me the following 24 hours. I went out to the gatekeeper. It being past two, to him, was like having a laugh. I had to wait for shops to re-open at eight.

Albert and Hilaire had also had trouble with their tummies all night. I was about to ask whether we had been poisoned purposely, as such was the new culture that had come to the Congo with the advent of wars. But that Claude and Simone had eaten with us greatly dispelled my suspicion, although our plates, distributed by Simone, could have been tricked.

We kept quiet about it when they turned up to find out what we wanted to eat on my second night. But, we politely declined, choosing to spend the $50 we paid her at a restaurant where no one knew us. Surprisingly, they found us and joined in. Even the day after Hilaire had gone his way up north, the uninvited duo appeared at the new venue we had discovered and ate with us. Although evident there that they were unmannered, I convinced myself that they were just taking the liberty of someone else paying for them.

Back in my room, Albert and I talked until past one in the morning, as he was leaving for Kinshasa later in the day. Despite the plan to take me places, Claude did not show up to say goodbye, nor was he ever seen again. Franco came to my rescue. He was the fellah in his early thirties that Hilaire had asked to be with me every day when Albert would be gone. Albert knew him in Kinshasa, so he had no concern about leaving me with him. He took me to visit areas in dire need of water. He cost me $30 daily but gave me a lot in return. We scarcely sat down. My flight to the UK was three days away, and I was due in Kinshasa in two weeks.

But there would be a knock on my door the morning after Albert's departure. I thought Franco was early, but it was the night receptionist finishing his shift. A man had stayed at the gate all night asking to speak with me but was denied. He had introduced himself as an immigration officer. Now that it was seven, he insisted on being allowed to see me.

Concerned for my safety, the receptionist asked me not to leave my room or meet the man until Franco arrived. Finally meeting him, he asked that I report to his hierarchy. Instead of waiting for a taxi, Franco called three motorcyclists to get us to a police station, where an army major and his *bodyguard*, a lieutenant, walked us five streets to another building.

"This does not look good, *mon vieux*!" Franco whispered. Twelve years my junior, he was under obligation to call me *old man*. "This is where political detainees are held."

No word from me!

They and I signed in at the gatehouse, where I was asked to hand in my phone and bag but not my wallet. Franco was refused entry and compelled to stand a hundred metres from the compound, with no sight of me nor what the yard looked like. A seven-metre-high wall separated us. In there, it was all inquisitions after inquisitions, morning to evening. The same questions came back repeatedly from different inspectors. Their note-takers wrote by hand, slowly. They tried to put it in my mouth that I had come ahead of a well-trained team to dethrone the regime.

They sent me back to the hotel after dark, with a guard. Franco followed behind. He left me only to go home to his wife and children. The guard slept outside the hotel gate and was not off duty until he had taken me back to his office in the morning. A different man took me back to the hotel at the end of the day and secured the entrance all night to bring me back to his bosses in the morning. Each one of the guards asked for a cigarette, a drink, and food when saying goodnight, but I gave out no penny. I knew the risk of charity being taken as bribing them to escape.

On the second day of what was now clearly my detention, the chief inspector had the opportunity to hear me, and I recognised him as the one who had let me go at the airport. Trying to be polite by greeting him, he ignored me totally, but not pretending to have never seen me before. He asked to see my luggage. So, he sent me back to the hotel, escorted still, and Franco, as faithful as ever, did his best tail tagging. But, because of the impracticality of taking the bags on a motorbike, we waited an hour for a taxi to come by. Sadly, after picking up the bags, the guard refused Franco boarding. He panicked the rest of the day, not knowing for sure whether I was inside the secret service building or not, as it took him about half an hour to find a ride.

Placing the briefcase and the suitcase in front of the person who asked for them, he immediately inquired about the holdall. Before I could even answer, he stated that I had sent it north with Hilaire to deliver money to fuel a certain rebellion they attributed to me. I laughed, and it got documented at his command. He rejected my defence that Hilaire needed it to carry the medications he had for the villagers he was off to visit because the box he had them in was difficult to manage on a motorbike. Hence, they searched my belongings, and I wondered what this was all about. They were restless until they found cash, which they took. Then, the interrogation resumed. All day long, I was allowed no food nor water, citing not wanting to see me kill myself on their premises. How silly, seeing they were killing me by depriving me of these!

Franco finally got hold of Hilaire after several attempts the previous day due to a poor connection further north. Hilaire advised Albert of my nightmare. Feeling a sense of answerability for leaving me behind, he went to his son, Alexandre, at the City Hall, who had introduced us. Alexandre contacted Zacharie, who thought he was pulling his leg until he could not reach me on my UK or Congo number. I had not seen the need to advise him of my going east. Fearing the worst, he immediately went to meet with Tim, a general in the army he had previously introduced me to. Tim had told me to count on him should I have any problem anywhere.

On the third day of my life in the hands of these secret service agents, following the usual cross-examining session, I was told at nine in the evening that I was free to leave town the next day. They still, however, had me guarded that night.

But, once in my room, Franco dialled and handed me the phone. It was Tim. He asked what on earth I was doing out north-east, insisting that this was still not a safe place. Obviously, his notion of *anywhere* when speaking of providing me with protection was limited to Kinshasa, as he had not imagined me venturing out this far.

I explained. Still, he was not happy and asked that I get out of there. He committed Franco to keep him posted, further instructing me to find a way to contact him upon reaching Nairobi. He requested that I leave behind everything confiscated from me, for I was refusing to let them keep my phone, watch, and, more frustratingly, my camera with all the many pictures of the little I had achieved there, as well as those taken out west since coming down.

Albert, Hilaire, and Zacharie were equally relieved to hear my voice. Tim had worked all night with his fellow general who headed a department that worked closely with the secret service to obtain my release and get all the faxes of my so-called confession of the rebellion I was part of shredded. Some people have it so easy lying through their teeth. No wonder they had rejected reading me their notes or letting me read them before signing.

I set off for the airport at noon, in time for the incoming flight that was due in mid-afternoon, just to be informed, when I got there, of a cancellation due to there being not a single passenger coming in. Making it worse was that I was the only person going in the opposite direction. Therefore, the airline deemed it more cost-effective to sacrifice me. But there was a flight from Kinshasa in three hours, returning shortly after that. I pounced into town to get a ticket. The secret service guys had neglected to search me once they had found money in my briefcase. However, this purchase left me only with the equivalent of a two-way taxi-fare.

Imagine my surprise when with my first foot on the staircase, I heard:

"You cannot board, Sir!"

I looked over my shoulder; it was one of the secret service men from the day I arrived, with two armed officers. Two airport management staff tried to intervene but were told to mind their own business. The one in charge of seeing the flight leave on schedule said he was holding the plane back just for me, however, no longer than 15 minutes, trusting the tailwind to level up things. But the response from the one tasked with escorting me back to the terminal was to not waste even a single minute.

Inside, I was told that the very person who had freed me up had requested that I go to see him again. Insisting there was no reason for that, I got passed a phone, and there he was. He complained that he was unaware of me flying to Kinshasa, so I was at fault again. My heart dropped seeing the B727 taxi away and thrust skywards. No vehicle was sent to collect me and the airport-based colonel, so it was my responsibility to pay for the taxi. Fortunately, Franco and the driver who brought us there had not yet left.

"What are you playing at?" was how the man welcomed me back.

By this time, I could care less what they thought about my attitude.

"Am I no longer free to go?"

"Mr. Diamany!" he said. "Why are you causing yourself problems?"

"Which ones?"

"Did you not have a London-Kisangani-London booking?"

"I did!"

"So, how does this undeclared trip to Kinshasa come into play?"

"I called the airline back home and changed my itinerary."

"Please, stop fooling yourself," he said.

In 2010, booking a flight over the phone or from a bedroom was not heard of in the Congo.

"I can either show you my phone or call them right now to revert to the original itinerary, although it would mean paying another $150 in penalties," I said. "Which one do you prefer?"

He claimed to oversee intelligence in all the north-east of the country, yet he was unaware of the cancellation of the incoming flight from Nairobi. I wanted to highlight this ignorance, but held back, knowing it would upset him, which could only make things worse for me. If the airport was a strategic place as he and his subordinates had repeatedly pointed out to me, they should have been informed. The airport staff knew about this an hour before the scheduled take-off time from Nairobi. Unless he just wanted to nag me more.

"Stay away from General Tim," he warned me. "He is dangerous!"

Well! If that was all he wanted to tell me, why wait until now?

But Tim's influence would be further proved when Franco advised him that I was back in the Secret Service's hands. Unable to reach this guy's boss in Kinshasa, he called directly, warning him of repercussions if I was not out of the gate in 10 minutes. I was let to go when the call ended. He looked defeated and powerless.

Pressure mounted for him, as just as I was picking up my luggage, his phone rang again, and it was his own boss. He had just picked up Tim's voicemail, so he reiterated orders with one short sentence and hung up. Those present were confused about who I had suddenly become.

The chief, one of his men, and I got moving to see me out. But I heard a voice I believed to know. It was coming from the corridor. Rushing out of the room, as we were heading out anyway, I had the full view of the back of the person, six metres away.

"Simone!" I exclaimed.

She turned back but did not respond. She slipped into the room closest to her.

"I thought you taught fifth grade at Claude's school," I said before she slammed the door.

At that point, her boss grabbed me on the wrist tightly, making me now feel his military training. He took me back to his office and sternly yelled:

"Shut it! Understand?"

He had me escorted out. Then, Franco and I sped off to the airline, seeking reimbursement or a place on their next flight in two days. I was lucky to be dealing with the man who saw me being refused boarding. He got me a place on the late flight that day with a competitor, out of pity, topping up what was like $35 for me as this transporter was a bit pricier.

"You must run," he said. "The bird lands in 40 minutes, and the road takes 30. Pray for the motorbike not to have a puncture."

He went the extra mile and called the airport to get me checked in remotely. He was not happy for me to stay one more night. Good thing this was a city with no traffic, especially on the airport road. Poor Franco had to dig into his remuneration to pay for the rides, to be reimbursed via a money transfer service. The secret service agents at the airport gathered around me with all sorts of kind words as they saw me going past them. But they were just trying to get a few dollars off me. I gave them none. Besides, I had none left on me. Therefore, I just promised them to soon find out that they had mistaken me for someone I was not, and that there was no need for what they had put me through.

The 170-seater, the biggest commercial aircraft in this nation, took off with me still fuming with anger. However, I was pleased that I could say I had seen Kisangani. Sadly, I had not gotten much response to what had brought me there. I had not visited Brassco's local premises. I thought that this trip was a failure. But, once in the air, therapeutic was the clear view of the Equatorial Forest beneath us—what a beauty! Nonetheless, two hours in the sky was too long to stay awake. When I opened my eyes again, the plane was descending. Kinshasa being two hours behind Kisangani, we still landed at six.

With only a carry-on, I exited the terminal quickly. I would have preferred to stay the night as I was exhausted, but Zacharie, having waited for me all afternoon, talked me into carrying on. Therefore, we proceeded to the ticket sales counter. Two Europe-bound flights were scheduled that evening for half past eight and half past nine. They could not get me a connection to London, but one of them booked me into Paris, suggesting I give them up to boarding time to see what could be done.

Lucky I was to have squeezed into my carry-on some clean clothes I had not had the chance to wear in Kisangani. Zacharie's cousin lived 25 minutes away, so he suggested I shower at hers. The airline agent who checked me in insisted on the risk of missing the flight and warned that reimbursement was not possible, nor was amendment, should that occur. I took the gamble.

But since Zacharie had not given his relative heads up, we came against the harsh reality that the family had already used up their day's supply of water. Hence, he parted with his $10 to purchase 15 litres of bottled water with which to wash myself before sprinting back to the airport, where I was the last person through security, amid my name repeatedly ringing out of the public announcement system, to my embarrassment. The airline staff who sold me the ticket had already panicked enough and given up. What was not their relief to spot me at the end of the long but slowly moving queue, getting on the last bus taking passengers to the plane.

"Here is your connection to London," said one of them.

It was a blank card with a number written thereon by hand. She asked that I proceed straight to their desk in the transit area at *Roissy Charles De Gaulle* upon landing, and there they will print me a boarding pass they could not produce this end.

"You know how to get people worried," her colleague added. "Safe Journey!"

I slept off like a baby, missing meals. The same on the 45-minute stretch between Paris and London. I called Laura to tell her my ordeal. Only one thing came out of her mouth:

"They had no right to that money!"

I wanted to see her face at that moment so she could see my disappointment. Did she expect me to fight them or risk my life for a little over $700? Anyway, this being the first time she had ever been inconsiderate of me, I just wiped off my tears and forgave, although never will I forget. I replaced that money with my own the following day and lied, saying I had found it in a side pocket those guys must have missed. She said nothing.

My time home was nothing of a break. I was there only physically. My mind and heart had remained in Kisangani on the project yet to start. So, I was busy working on contacts.

Customs Clearance

The inexistence of west-to-east roads, coupled with the difficulty of navigating the Congo River, made it worthwhile bringing in our consignments via an eastern link, either via the port of Mombasa in Kenya or through that of Dar-es-Salaam in Tanzania. Our Kinshasa-based customs agents guaranteed us their partners' professionalism at these ports. Their collaboration spanned three decades, without them travelling there even a single time. They had paperwork to back this. We were swayed and opted for Mombasa as my findings in Kisangani included the somewhat abundant traffic coming in with imported goods and going out with timber logs.

They reassured us that the bill of lading was enough to get the containers out and delivered to us in Kisangani. But our presence became necessary after our goods had come off the boat. Doubts had risen amid fears that we could be getting weapons through Kenya, which lived in peace with its neighbours, to fuel wars in the Congo. At least, that was our agents' version of the story. True or not, we could not blame the port as a few years prior, those who had signed a peace deal to jointly govern the country were caught by surprise. Factions of militias were sprouting out, with people becoming unhappy to have been left out of the affairs. Those taking up arms to kill the same people they aimed to govern were sponsored by fellow African countries.

Therefore, Günter, Jan, Themba, Tino, and I curtailed our time off and convened in Nairobi, where we had purchased two SUVs ahead of our arrival. We took the road to Mombasa. Alvin, Amy, and Laura continued resting in the US, with the latter no longer needed on the ground. The Kenyan capital brought back memories of an earlier visit. Katarina and Abhu still lived in the port's region. They asked for the privilege of hosting us for at least two nights, insisting we needed to cool down and pick up a trick or two from them on how to go about clearing our consignments.

They knew their way around because of their regular import activities from the Middle East and exports to various African nations on the east coast. They had no doubt the necessary experience from which to benefit. Of course, some of their instructions made no sense at the time. Nonetheless, we wished we could visit a bit longer because of the conditions they put us in, them having taken care of us way better than we had expected.

Not trusting us to remember their directives, let alone apply them, Katarina got on the road with us to make sure we did not put a foot wrong. Being a bit over 50 kilometres from our destination gave her the opportunity to further lecture Themba and me, as we travelled with her in the same vehicle. She made us stop in a village that was desperate for water. There we visited three farms, all abandoned for this cause. She invited us to set up this close to hers the moment we admitted that the Congo we knew to date was not this bad.

At the port, letting Katarina speak for us aggravated matters. Those in charge deemed her interference disrespectful. For this, they moved us to the back of the queue, causing a week delay. Each day the containers sat at the port cost us thousands of dollars, including fees to move them to make way for the ones behind us. Finally, we got back to the front. But not having import tax exemption occasioned financial bleeding. We should have been able to be reimbursed by sending back any proof that Kenya was not our final destination. Instead, we were told to forget it because that was how customs officers got rich. But we worried not much as Brassco had in advance made up for any unexpected cost, paying us 100% more this time around.

As though the harassment at the port was not enough, securing lorries to deliver our containers to Kisangani turned out to be more of a nightmare than we could have imagined. None of us had given this aspect a thought. We had expected it to be smooth sailing because of the abundant consignments coming through this way.

Matadi was better in that, although it only handled deliveries to Kinshasa, it offered the benefit of the same transporters calling both ends home. There was no problem picking up a haulage company at either end. They charged only one way, for they were in the same country. Mombasa transporters were taking advantage of the absence of the Congolese haulage companies at the port, whereas other regional African countries were there represented.

Scammers

We had overlooked the risk of dealing with people whose official capacity we knew not by no longer involving Katarina. Consequently, we exposed ourselves to three groups of hawkers, promising us haulage for all our loads. They asked for a 40% advance payment. This was $4 a kilometre per vehicle. The road was 2,600 kilometres long. More was also charged for the three overnight stopovers that would have to take place during the journey. We spent a week with the police hoping to apprehend these crooks, while anyone hearing how we had easily fallen into the trap could not help but laugh, irritating us more.

Trusting local beliefs, Katarina lectured us about how these heartless scammers bewitched their targets so they would not resist. We did not argue because we knew not how else to explain the way we had yielded to them. It was ridiculous that even kids under 12 working at the port mocked us. It being a lot of money we had parted with, we were humbled, turned teachable. We lent an ear to whoever came forward with a piece of advice, whether relevant to tracking down these thugs or not.

To gain sympathy, we confessed to having gone with our hearts rather than our heads in getting ourselves to trust our robbers. Our defence was that we did not want to waste more time at the port when help was offered everywhere we turned. But taking shortcuts proved costlier and harder to live with than following verified channels. This second week could have been avoided and saved us the third one we would spend to find genuine transport companies.

Meanwhile, we had become famous because of our multi-ethnic group and were nicknamed the *national team*, implying a European nation's football team. People frequently stopped us for a chat and offered drinks, which led to us recounting our story. Günter and Jan loved the attention, while Tino and Themba wished we were in Kisangani drilling. Finally, one guy made two truck trailers available and convinced two of his mates to chip in one each. Like all others who had turned us down, they feared the rough road in the Congo. But our perseverance, together with their curiosity, earned us their compassion.

Checkpoints

En route to Kisangani, we stopped 30 minutes every three hours, too much in our opinion, as this excluded the time spent at the equally many checkpoints. The plan was to have a full 12-hour break at night, each 650 kilometres, but thrice this changed to a 24-hour rest in the busiest places on this journey. Rather than sleeping in the vehicles, our drivers went away, once in Kenya, another time in Uganda, and lastly, in the Congo. The assistants to each driving companionship were left to look after the cargo.

Control was simple until the Congo. This further east of the country felt different than Kisangani. There was a feeling of unrest, so we scarcely stepped out of the vehicles unless the officers instructed us to. We drove the SUVs ahead of the trucks to avoid dust but slowly enough to keep them in sight in the mirrors. The types of foreign passports we held rarely came this way unless in possession of international peace-keeping permits, a trend in the region and the country over. They caused prolonged delays. More suspicious was having no number plates on the SUVs. The four trailers convoy also raised questions. Refusing to give the officers money gave them the right to park us, so those playing to their tunes could go through after pretending to check their documentation.

Traversing the border also meant the end of the tarred road. It was all moving at a snail's pace from that point on, not exceeding 60 kilometres per hour. Inexperienced driving long distances on a road like this one, we asked the lorries not to go over 40, so we could keep up, for we had now let them take the lead with the road deteriorating the more. But the reduced speed adding an extra two days to the journey would cost us more in wages to the crew and fees to the haulage companies for the time their vehicles remained in our possession.

Heavy rains did beat down over the following two days, making the road swampy and slippery, contributing to our calamity. Overall, the voyage meant to last four days claimed double. This excluded the two-day rest at the destination for the drivers to revitalise before starting their return leg. Until then, we took care of them, except when they wanted beverages and entertainment that all the bars and clubs provided. We told them that water and cable telly sufficed.

I admitted to the assistants how relieved I was when we got out of the port, and they said that others had lost more than we had due to this *know-it-all* attitude. The conversation got so sweet that it slipped out of them that the overnight stopovers were where the drivers had permanent girlfriends. It was their habit to find a reason to stop as we did, as they regularly came this way.

Indebted

In Bunia, the officers imposed an in-depth inspection on us, whereas it should have been a quick one. We had not looked at the paperwork at the Congo's entry point, and it turned out that the seal number recorded was a few digits different from what was on the actual seal. Had we paid attention, we would not have spent more than half an hour there, as the containers had already been thoroughly searched at the border. But having nothing to hide, we let them take all the time needed to complete their job. Consequently, they were stunned by the equipment onboard.

"We, too, are without water here," said the colonel in charge.

He spoke good French. He was young and had made it through the ranks quickly, thanks to the two-year military academy he had had the privilege to attend. But we were surprised to discover that he was equally fluent in English, about which he was very humble, saying it was due to the proximity of this town to Uganda, an English-speaking country. He refused to let us go past them without committing to return to drill there one day. That we had a contract that bound us to only go to Kisangani, Goma, and Bukavu meant nothing to him.

Pointing to the many kiosks lining the road we were travelling on, he indicated that the loud music being played and the dancers and drinkers we could see there were proof that our sponsor needed to invest in the social development of this town. They consumed nothing but Brassco's products, and binging as they did was a sign that they would not have a problem paying for water if it came to them. He took us to pubs, ordering the music to stop so he could address the audience. These were packed, in the middle of the afternoon, with life lovers. He asked them to sign if they liked the idea of having communal wells installed for their population of 350,000.

Being able to take the manual pumping method off their wives' and children's hands got us mobbed. Throwing at least a 500-franc note each into the 200-litre drum cut in half and placed in front of us was to tell us that our proposal had made the cut. Some of them, drunk or conscious of the good having water in their midst would add to their lives, came back twice or thrice, adding to the already full container.

No one entertained the thought of signing on the paper we asked to be brought out. They argued that theirs was a community life. Therefore, what one paid also covered another not present or with nothing to contribute. We were free to go without giving them water but not leaving the money behind. Thought it was a joke, so we just carried on acquainting. Then we were led to a restaurant, undoubtedly the cleanest we had seen since leaving Kampala. They had organised an impressive buffet in our honour. Life was good, but not truly so without access to water.

In fact, the cost of drinking water there was more than that of beverages. Evidently, people in this part of the country were not as poor as the general assumption stipulated. Their water calamity was possibly 10% unaffordability and 90% unavailability. We had come to people with money but begging for water to purchase. Their bottled supply came from Uganda or Kenya, which also resourced themselves from the Middle East and Asia, earning a markup getting it to the Congo.

Our attempt to leave for the hotel was unsuccessful until midnight. All that time, they filled our ears with claims of having wealth under their feet. Therefore, no one travelled through their town without taking some gifts with them. We hoped to be presented with carved wood souvenirs of the type we had bought in Kinshasa, Nairobi, Mombasa, and Kampala, but to our surprise, it was gold dust and nuggets, freshly out of the nearby mines that evening. No one had warned us that we were sitting in a gold market.

A queue formed in front of us, and privileged that we were, everyone else had to wait so we could buy to our satisfaction. It was the first time ever for each one of my guys to come into contact with raw gold, so there they were with their tongues watering like dogs in front of meat that is being grilled. Some of the sellers put together a combined 73 grammes for us to take away free of charge. But we declined both when we could have acquired some three kilogrammes from the hands of a single trader at 40% off spot. The internet worked in their favour as they could now consult the London Bullion Market Association each time they wanted to sell. We had to adhere to the warning our embassies and several NGO workers gave us in Kinshasa to avoid these offers, be it gold, diamonds, coltan, or other minerals. This was because even simply touching these without being licensed, as a non-national, was sanctionable with imprisonment.

In the meantime, two people were tasked with counting the money in the barrel, which came up to the equivalent of $308. They said that we could buy ourselves food or fuel with on our way, but we wished we could give them water in exchange, although too little even for one well. We had everything with us for the job, but getting permits, sorting out a team, and finding a spot to drill on demanded time and would have kept us further behind schedule. It was going to be an early start in the morning, going away grateful for the hospitality received but feeling bad about taking from them, uncertain of when we could give back.

"You better take these people seriously," one of our drivers said as he climbed into his lorry. "This is a gold mine. They will pay you anything for water if you are willing to help."

Two days in and out of rain-filled potholes ensued, the next 700 kilometres still subject to the usual police checks until Kisangani. Saying that we were drained would be an understatement. However, our drivers believed the colonel at Bunia had sent word by phone as he oversaw all the roads in this region. This, because not only were we not held up longer at the barriers, but we were greeted by our names before producing any documents. They opened the tailgate, peeked in, put on new seals, filled in papers, and let us go, nevertheless seemingly discontent for being deprived of getting pennies off us. We gave them sweets when saying goodbye, out of courtesy.

Same Old Story

Our convoy called for even greater curiosity in Kisangani, where a handful of its population of 1.6 million surrounded us within minutes of arriving. Despite being reassured that

Brassco had parking space for our consignment, the only place available was some 30 kilometres further out and in an area I had not previously visited.

"What is the road like?" one of the drivers asked.

"Awful!" answered the manager's secretary.

She was the one who welcomed us. Her boss had not fancied waiting into the evening, it being after seven that we pulled in. It was not safe to travel on such an unlit road at night. Jan started to think about providing electricity to the city, especially when the loud noise of the two close-by waterfalls on the Tshopo River, on the city's north side, attracted us to see them with our own eyes despite it being dark. But we asked that we focus on the water problem at hand.

"Why did you not work your magic to give water to Bunia overnight if you truly have a solution to every problem?" I teased him.

We took ourselves to a convent five kilometres outside the city when we learnt they had a yard big enough for all our vehicles. It turned out that we were the answer to their prayers, for they too needed help. Our two months there rewarded them $25 daily for each container we parked there. Additionally, we gave them a well before they asked, which they saw as super generous of us, especially after learning about the cost to a private customer. Their schools and churches in this city and its surroundings were equally suitable for a third of the allocation we had for the area.

As unfair to others as it may sound, the chasing of permits for individual locations was not something we were keen to take up at that time. This church already had the right to drill on its properties, especially if they would let the communities have access to the water, irrespective of whether they were of their faith or not. They provided us with the persons to oversee the supervision of the stations. These had been in the communities for ages and were known and trusted by the clergy and would have the same consideration from the public coming to draw water.

Since dealing with this institution simplified our job, we could care less that we fell out of favour with the authorities. We had rejected their recommendations of where to drill. They had their own interest at heart, for some of the locations were their own second or third properties or belonged to their relatives. It was the same old story whereby officials sought to fill their own pockets, but we gave them no chance after establishing that the church would serve us better.

Even Brassco found itself powerless to convince the authorities of the communal aspect of this project and that it was not a donation to private individuals. But the locals we hired advised us to make friends with these officials because our security depended on them in the end. They insisted that safety had no price. My ordeal there the first time around came back to mind. For that, 10 wells slipped out of our hands, leaving huge parts of the city craving. We could say that we had given in to bullying, but we had to get moving and face natural problems that awaited.

It rained frequently and abundantly that we hardly put in a full day's work. With nowhere to buy a tent, we resorted to climbing into the vehicles, hoping it would stop raining after a short while, but it was rarely the case. At times, there were hours of continuous heavy showers, terribly loud thunderings, and scary sky-rending lightnings, and as a result, we witnessed inundations that left numerous families homeless. The pumps we had brought to keep the boreholes clear became inefficacious even without it pouring down, for at 20 metres deep water out of the ground was already uncontrollable.

Finally, Günter put together a hangar to hide in. He did it with the four large tents we bought from the owner of the lorries that were abandoned opposite our parking site, which would never be put back in service. He made sure not to obstruct the rig from shooting up. He figured out how to dismantle it when moving sites, and put it back together, losing no more than half a day, thanks also to having two rented lorries from the church handy to transport our tools, rods, pipes, and other materials. Our SUVs towed a trailer-mounted rig each as we decided to be on two sites simultaneously to catch up on lost time.

Alvin and Amy joined us at this point. They had had the bad luck of waiting a week in Nairobi for a connection. Wanting to save money, they had made two separate bookings to reach us, unbeknown they would incur a week-long boarding charge. Two locals I had befriended and I met them at the airport. *My* secret service agents watched without a word. No greeting, no smile, nothing, just like several other times they had now seen me around.

The couple found us on our 13th and 14th installations—a miracle, given all the setbacks. They were keen to add to their tally of experiences, especially with the uniqueness of every location we came to. The soil was favourable on this end; little of it broke as opposed to the sandier and plastic-filled we fought west. This contributed enormously to drilling faster, except when hitting some rocks that Jan's technology picked not up, which was frequent and annoying to those of us new to geological work.

However, Günter's rig was up to effectual, as was Tino's and Themba's gripping of the ground they had come to love. They adored ending every day covered in yellow or red dirt as though out of a gold mine. They missed no chance for a picture that would keep speaking for their time in the Congo long after returning home for good. They made their cameras sweat and were lucky to have memory cards in abundance. Our drivers had turned into photographers and were trusted with taking captivating shots. They were allowed to take some of themselves too, seeing that owning a camera, let alone a digital one, was not part of their culture, even if they could afford one.

Rough

We took a week off between the completion of the 30th well and setting off for Kivu where Dev-Plus we had made a promise to of a possible collaboration in the future had already identified sites on our behalf. My cultural impediment in the northeast and the difficulty sorting out a team of workers influenced our decision to bring them in.

The road worsened every 10 kilometres or so, to the point that the border of Uganda to Kisangani appeared a luxury in comparison. The public had recommended an eastward journey to break off southwards at *Mambasa* (not Mombasa in Kenya), citing a better road. But our drivers had opposed it because it was 340 kilometres longer. Hence, we journeyed 675 kilometres south-eastwards to Goma instead. This was all unpaved and, as expected, scarcely reaching the speed of 20 kilometres an hour.

Stopping for a break and to buy some fruits halfway to our destination, people were relieved we had avoided the rebels' strongholds by not coming via Mambasa. It made us sweat loads, for we had prayed so much for our safety. We could not be more grateful to our drivers to have stood their ground in deciding which road to take.

"They would have tortured you regardless of whether you had something to give them or not," said one of the village men.

"They hide in the bush, away from the army, and ambush merchants to rob them of their goods to replenish themselves," another added. "Sometimes, they even live with the locals who, out of fear, would not reveal them."

Thinking of it, we wondered who would truly find joy in making these charming, seemingly peaceful, open plains and hills a dangerous place, when all we could see was the potential for a real source of income through tourism. All the way, we met or passed lines of adults and children with heavy loads on their heads and backs. Whilst it hurt to be travelling in the luxury of air-conditioned vehicles, despite the rough road, we had since become a bit less sensitive to the harsh lives of these populations than we were at the beginning of this trip.

"Nothing we can do," I said, trying to soothe the lads' sentiment of guilt. "Too many of them for our small automobiles."

I just did not want them to feel like I had brought them this way to solve all the problems that had been there long before we arrived. Nonetheless, even though my forefathers walked such long distances close to a century back, there was just no justification as to why those my age and younger were still doing the same. All in all, what I saw was not making my homecoming a pleasant experience.

When we heard of the rougher road ahead, we hired people out of Kisangani to drive our SUVs, and they turned out more useful. It brought tears to our eyes when they revealed what was happening with this traffic: these were displaced and fleeing armed militias. Often, they said such things to me in Swahili to not scare away the rest—I fluently speak a modest number of five languages and get by in two more. But, although their borrowed French words accidentally gave Günter and Jan hints, they panicked not. The situation was also evident to our non-French speakers, who equally remained resolute to press forward.

"I had easily figured it out," said Themba. "It is just as the media back home describes it."

He had barely finished his words when the next batch we met a couple of kilometres down desperately waved us to stop. They had two children under the age of four lying on the ground, having fainted from the scorching sun. They begged for whatever amount of water we could give. We regretted not having stocked up enough, although it would still have been impossible to meet the demands of their huge group. Left were only three packs of six bottles of 1.5-litre each. We still parted with a pack.

To show we cared, Günter went after the disinterested man who passed us with a baby tied across his chest with a loincloth, the way women do this side of the country. A lady and two other children were trying to keep up with him. We thought he did not want to waste his time seeking what we could not give him. Günter reached out to the baby with his own half-used bottle.

"He will not drink, Sir," said his wife.

The man halted not, nor was he in the mood for a chat.

"My son is dead," he shouted at Günter's insistence.

"What?"

"You heard me."

Günter fell on his knees and wrapped his arms around the man's waist.

"Please, give us a chance," he begged, avoiding looking up to the deceased infant.

The two-year-old had been unwell for a week, then dead for nine hours when the rebels erupted, causing the mourners to flee in all directions. While some grabbed what they could carry, this man only took his son, although without life. He preferred to give him a decent tomb in a village that would give him a place on their way, where he could return one day to pay his respects properly. When we met, they had travelled all night, not knowing if they would see another day.

"Going for good this time," he said.

This was the 19th time they fled in a decade, and they were a village of more than 100 households of eight individuals each on average. They returned each time to burnt houses, missing cattle, goats, sheep, and poultry, and savaged crops. It was not because of the love of their land and birthplace that they always came back. A spring yielding clean water was less than two kilometres from their village, along a stream where their animals drank without needing human help. The other side of their dwellings was a beautiful flat plain offering fertile soil where crops grew in abundance all year around.

We asked where to bury the child, and they mentioned a nearby monastery off our course of travel. We turned around and took the family on board. That day, we learnt what *nearby* was to village people. We journeyed 76 kilometres to lay the boy to rest in the clergies' churchyard at the cost of $200 to us. This included a makeshift coffin, thanks to the on-site furniture workshop. However, this was not until the mother had washed her *son* as when she used to prepare him for bed, humming, and the rest of the family joining in chorus, tears confirming their grief.

Günter had an unused white t-shirt in his suitcase. He wrapped it around the corpse. Jan added his still-boxed perfume to the ceremony, giving the boy a good send-off into eternity. We spent the afternoon going back and forth to bring the rest of that group over for refuge before also putting ourselves up for the night.

Resuming our journey in the morning and some 35 kilometres beyond where we had met the above group, we came across another faction, double the size of the previous. The same cause of migration! A man in his nineties was on a stretcher made of sticks, carried by four younger people. Health issues he had had since his sixties had rendered it impossible for him to walk than had age. His grandsons refused to leave him behind, even ignoring his wish to be buried next to his wife and two sons who had gone ahead of him.

The first thing those bearing him asked of us was water. We gave them two bottles, and the old man opened his eyes for the first time since our meeting when the company said, "thank you," proof that he had been listening but unable to show signs of life. Watching him drink caused a throng of kids to come closer to see if he would leave some. As hard to witness as it was, we parted with a couple more bottles, but unaware of our calling for mothers present to engage in a fight against each other to have their own babies and toddlers served.

"Hopefully, we will not meet the rebels themselves," said Jan as we got going again. "For we know not whether they would let us go about our business."

To that, the driver replied that had it been the rebels, they would not have troubled us, for they did not touch priests or pastors, although nuns had paid the price a few times. That was when we understood why the clergies at Kisangani had convinced Alvin and Amy not to take the road with us. They had made them fly back to Nairobi to connect to Kigali, then to Goma by road. At the time, they had not told us that this safeguarding was because we were about to take one of the most dangerous roads in the region, especially for a female. But, even if they had advised us, we would not have sent such valuable consignments with the drivers. However, to maximise our protection, the church had displayed some signs on our windscreens. We knew not why back then.

"Each of you here is a priest," said one of the drivers. "Should anyone ask."

"Really!" I exclaimed. "What proof do we have?"

My question was not answered until we got to our destination. They brought out the suitcase I had seen a priest place in the SUV I travelled in. It contained a cassock for each one of us and a spare one for Alvin, and what was needed for Amy. The two cardboard boxes a monastery worker had loaded were full of the faith's reading materials.

Shoot!

We were on a job 25 kilometres outside of Goma, with the exterior of two wells being completed, when we noticed people running. Children as young as six were let out of school but could not go home as no one would be there. Amy broke! She stood in the middle of the road and gathered 43, the oldest being just 11, and brought them into our gazebo. They came into her arms with so much ease and haste, trusting her to be a nun or an international NGO worker—the category even kids knew to be able to provide protection in this region. It showed us the extent to which people had grown dependable on foreign presence.

We had parked in the unfenced yard where work was taking place, and the vehicles caught the rebels' attention. They put their guns to our heads, despite having not refused to lie flat on our tummies. To them, we were miners and, therefore, loaded. They pulled the kids out of the gazebo, threatening to take their heads off unless we paid $1,000 per head to save their lives. We gave them close to $3,900, and they freed up four. Then they lined up to execute the remaining they had kept on the ground with their faces down and fired at five like in a movie. Alvin stood in front of those assigned the dirty job, offering himself in lieu.

"Shoot!"

Amy could not look. Her arms seemed to have gotten longer as she tried to cover the frozen 34 who, with those bullets going off, screamed and piled on top of each other. She wanted the next bullet aimed at them to kill her first. This was not the first time these children had come this close to the sound and sight of a gunshot. Unlike me, they were born into this and were growing up with it. A long silence ensued, and the world seemed to have ended.

None of us uttered a word or cried. Tears that had been bathing our faces for the past 10 minutes or so dried up. Salvation would come in the chief-rebel stepping forward and ordering his guys to back up for a moment. He asked for the keys to both SUVs, and Amy signalled the drivers to oblige. They drove off with everything therein: passports, food, clothes, and the $50,000 cash we had hidden underneath different seats. Not sure if they ever discovered this money. I personally hoped someone else found it, even when the vehicles would undergo repair or scrapping as, in the Congo, even the chassis served as a bridge somewhere over an eroded road or a stream.

Gone with them also were the five corpses, in keeping with their strategy to leave no evidence of children dying at their hands. This was how they deceived the patrolling international peacekeepers, who sadly played no other role than that of eyewitnesses; *tourists*, the locals call them. As much as kids mattered, we believed that adults being killed must also stop, but we could not think of how to go about helping with this when our own lives were also at risk. Nonetheless, we would be a bit comforted to find out that our phones, charging from a solar panel in the corner of the yard, had not been spotted. Else we would have been cut off from our families, Brassco, and the rest.

Asking the kids to take courage, one got not up. She was rock solid. We knew she was not with us, but we still put her in the lorry to find the local hospital. No one was there when we arrived. The whole town was deserted. We travelled halfway to Goma, and there it was confirmed she had suffered a heart attack. We were asked to take the body with us and do with as we wished.

"How horrible!" said Günter. "We were trying to help. Is it now our problem?"

We returned with the body, to see if the other kids would know her home. No avail! We kept all of them and the corpse all night. Most of them cried for food. But we had nowhere to get some that night, even if we had money. To add insult to injury, it rained heavily from just after midnight till dawn. Thus, they at least had water to fill up their empty stomachs with, thanks to Günter improvising a catchment off the gazebo. We packed up as many of the youngest as we could in the double cabins of our rented two lorries while the remainder and ourselves *slept* on the top of the work gear in the back.

Coming to ourselves that night, Alvin and Amy offered to fund a new SUV, and Günter and Jan matched that. But I asked them to keep their money. Revenues from Kinshasa enabled us to make these replacements. All I was concerned with at this moment was what to do with the deceased and the surviving 37. The guys working with us warned me of the unlikelihood of finding their parents. This I did not want to share with my partners. They were broken enough already to worry them more.

None wanted Laura to know what had happened to us, but I got on the phone to her with the truth before dawn, which she took very badly, fearing for our lives and was distraught about the children. I also reported to Zola. Brassco's regional executives were cold towards us for coming all the way to do what they believed they could have fulfilled. We buried this 10-year-old without a coffin. Our only help from the police was securing a burial place and coming along to witness what we did with the body.

In the meantime, we had been without food for almost 48 hours, which was hard to see these young ones enduring. Zola had transferred money to us, but it was yet to reach the bank in Goma. Coming to our rescue was a widow aged 85 and four other women in their seventies. They had remained at home with their doors swung open, so the rebels would not think anyone was home. This contrasted with the houses with locked doors, which got kicked in and contents turned upside down out of anger for not finding anyone to kill or anything to take. These five made meals with anything in their houses and allotments—there, veggies are grown right in the yard—and fed *our* children and then us. Congolese women are unique in that they truly possess a mother's heart which makes them give, if they can, without thinking of themselves.

Once the bank served us, we fed our children with the help of these ladies, who again went the extra mile to house them the entire week schools remained closed. When people started to move around town, we took it upon ourselves to locate these kids' homes, with themselves showing us the way. Sadly, among them were three empty houses where neighbours embraced the three children belonging there, crying. They had buried their parents two days after the rebels' visit, them having returned to their bodies lying in their blood. These victims were targeted because of their political affiliations. They used to hide wherever the news of the rebels' coming found them. This time, they were at home, and their neighbours believed someone had sold them.

Four other children's folks had not returned home. From time to time, some people got fed up coming back for the same to happen again, several times a year, so they just threw in the towel, abandoning even those born of them. Hence, orphanages are a booming business in that part of the country. But, despite their multiplicity, they are overcrowded and refusing those turning up with adults.

Hence, many individuals and families were compelled to take in total strangers and just bring them up with their own children.

It was, therefore, not shocking that some of them unable to feed an extra mouth left such children by the roadside. Consequently, some died trodden under the feet of passers-by who showed no mercy but accused them of being sorcerers, simply because of witnessing them, turned beggars, sitting and sleeping in the same spot for months with no protection, yet surviving. Those who stood up for themselves were labelled *shegués* (street kids). These made up close to 60% of those selling or delivering water, as we found out that the water business was not limited only to Kinshasa. They were aware of the enormity of this market and the minimal outlay required to set up, and, above all, it was a blessing in disguise that this opportunity existed, else they would have perished.

Toughening Up

The cost of water to us was not just in terms of money or travail to bring it to the surface. Multi-faceted this operation was, and so were the lessons which came from it. Furthermore, every experience relating to this project toughened us more once we had processed the shock of every story and event lived. Such was the case listening to our 37 children's accounts. Learning that the terror they experienced in our presence had been recurrent throughout their upbringing, we decided not to shun away but fulfil Brassco's work.

Life east was defined by the trauma we had now undergone ourselves. However, the survivors, especially children, knew best how to forgive, at least to trust their words. We could not put ourselves in their shoes or know exactly what it was like to have memories of parents running with them on the back, siblings kidnapped, being subjected to extortion, orphaned, living on the street, or hiding in the forest.

Job was one of those we took home to the parents already buried. He told us how a bunch of men once sexually abused his mum and made his dad watch, tied to a tree in their yard. He and his siblings were also made to stand there and look. This was two years earlier. He was now six, so to tell it as he did meant that the memory of this atrocity would haunt him the rest of his life unless treatment was found and administered.

"I am happy *Maman* has finally gone to rest," he said. "All along, they had meant to kill her but managed not to. Her time was not up then."

That was certainly not what we expected of someone this young. He obviously did not mind growing up without his parents rather than having them alive but continually tortured. The problem was, what chance was there for him to live long when this was all that his environment had to offer? We wanted to stop him from recounting this awful tale, at least not so descriptively. But this being at their tombs, the neighbours who brought us there asked that we bear with him to speak to them as he had not had the chance to say goodbye. We cried more, realising that he had not only mastered his culture but also believed that they saw and heard him.

"Keep an eye on me," he said, struggling to stay on his feet. "I promise to make you proud. I will visit you again if I can remember how to get here. But do not wait for me to come. You are now angels, so come to me whenever I have a difficult time, as I know I will."

My partners and I had rivers of tears gushing out of us as I forced myself to interpret.

"Every day here is just *a difficult time*," one of the neighbours was heard whispering.

Job looked up. It was his turn to let out streams of tears, weeping his lungs out.

"Thank you for coming," he said. "My parents are grateful."

He placed his bottle on his dad's tomb, asked for the one in my hand, and put it on his mum's. Plenty of land in the Congo means no two family members share a tomb.

"Drink sparingly until I bring you more," he concluded.

His four sisters attended other schools. They never made it back home. He and our other kids could have ended up Heaven knows where. Many their age had long been without parents or in displacement camps run by international NGOs, if not refugees beyond national borders. He hoped his sisters were alive somewhere and believed in a reunion one day, although not sure how, or where. We returned to our encampment to figure out a solution for these seven.

Work also resumed slowly, thanks to managing to keep our heads together.

Landscape

A 1,600-metre altitude being standard for that region, we targeted the lowest areas possible, incorporating several reticulations to curtail the number of trips to and from the water source. We had tried this exercise ourselves and concluded that it took a lot out of a person, especially when carrying weight. Even the solar mechanism we put in place, no doubt reliable, did not have the pressure needed to overcome this elevation.

The attempt to keep the cost down was tested, causing us to rethink things to see how many litres of water we could achieve with the 20 wells we had for Goma and the vicinity. Refusing to sway from our goal to make water available closer to people's homes, we consolidated our efforts around delivering it in abundance when we finally found it. Jan believed converting solar power into alternating current would give our system the thrust it lacked, sending water uphill. Hence, he got a design underway, cannibalising a mechanisation with the materials he found in the local market and some imported parts.

His innovation allowed each borehole to feed 10 raised 20,000-litre reservoirs on different levels of the hill. There the houses appeared in a stairway fashion from across the city where we liked to stand to admire the beautiful view on display. This automation sent water up upon a container's content lowering to 5,000 litres, and stopped at 19,000 litres mark, thanks to the sensors therein fitted. Because each tank fed dispensing stations on the level below, we inadvertently prolonged the life of our system as power was required only to send water up, not down, and not when people opened the taps at each station either.

Stored water was also kept clean and free of contamination because of the fitted tight capping. And not negotiable was the disinfecting of the entire system, thanks to having brought with us adequate products to be used in this operation. The frequency of conducting this cleaning was reliant on the weekly results of the testing of the water and the storage units, by the regulators, in the same manner as everywhere we had already established wells.

We prioritised having these scientists become our trusted partners, to tell us only the truth, and never to please us with fake results that could put the consumers at risk. Being trained in this department, Tino had passed his test in Kinshasa and was since licensed to conduct analyses. But the inclusion of an external examiner and letting the government have a role to play in our work gained us more credibility from the public because, despite their desperation, they needed to know that their supplier could be trusted.

We all knew that an unrelenting demand for clean water sources lay in the Congo. However, coming east made the crisis in the capital not worth rumbling about. This side best summed up what water shortage meant in this nation. Not having a heavy-duty drilling company on this end did not help matters. A few firms could have tackled the challenge, but they preferred to use their equipment on minerals prospection because of how manifold the industry paid. But how could we condemn their choice when drilling 100 metres brought them $1 million and that the kind of contract they had, when seeking to determine the deposit of gold in the ground, was 100 wells of this depth per site?

Our realisations spoke volumes; orders—private and corporate alike—dropped in our lap from various sources. We could have gone overboard, charging $40,000 to drill up to 60 metres, knowing there would be no water at that depth. But we were offered double and anything of our choosing for every incremental metre to hitting the bedrock. They feared that not making us an offer hard to resist would see us complete the contract that brought us over and leave because of their difficult terrain.

However, the toughest part of working on this side was not physical but emotional. Managing the trauma sustained because of seeing the brutality with which *our* five kids were killed was the starting point in winning ourselves over to remain determined to make a difference in the lives of the locals. Investing in the Congo demands extreme faith. No logic will do it. It is an adventure not for the faint-hearted. Giving water to those without, whatever the cost to achieve this, became the only way to show we were not numb to their suffering.

The change we were poised to bring to this town was taking place. The multiplicity of organisations and individuals wanting to serve these communities was overwhelming. This delayed our heading to Bukavu, where the idea of facing a similar landscape was frightening, to say the least. But, just when we were in the thick of these new commitments and enjoying the relief each undertaking was bringing, we would discover how malicious the intermediaries we were dealing with were. They asked for a percentage of the funds the moment drilling started.

It mattered not whether these contracts were from commercial enterprises or international non-profit institutions. Someone just believed they were entitled to a beefy portion of the transaction. Earning $8,000 for bringing about the drilling of a well was very enticing to a person who hardly made $6,000 in salary all year. Hence, they made this facilitation a career they undertook diligently, as did an obviously well-connected introducer who brought us 20 pieces of business with supermarkets, hotels, hospitals, schools, neighbourhoods, and more. Overcharging was not our game, nor did his profit-sharing request appeal to us. He was betting on $160,000 and eying more from the $600 he imposed us to demand for every additional metre, whereas we were comfy with $300.

Had we condoned such an illicit arrangement, clean drinkable water being found at 800 metres deep there, this guy and his network would have walked away with $52,400 from every well contract obtained through them. It explained why some people in the region seemed not to experience the poverty that beset the country. Most of them claimed to be mining site owners to cover up their immoral earnings. We needed someone who could take our minds off this disturbing get-rich-quick conversation.

Smart

Gilbert, 28, popped up at one of the sites we worked on. Due to wasting six years of his life in a militia against his will, he was sitting his end of high school exams in a couple of months. He intended to thank us for bringing water into his community. This installation ended his daily struggle to decide whether to draw water 1,300 metres down the hill or consecrate that time to reading his school materials.

"We can solve many problems with water," he said. "This initiative would be best pursued the region over, for people pay for the lack thereof with their lives in our villages."

It sounded like another lecture starting there, but nonetheless just as profitable as most we had been given previously.

"However, nothing will be as efficacious as we would like it to be until we, the Congolese, become conscious that we ought to be the solution to our own problems. We have talked too long and done too little for ourselves. It seems like we have inherited this from the West where a lot is heard of their help to our developing countries but nothing on the ground."

Being at the very centre of the continent, the Congo cannot be overlooked. With a 2,345,010 km² area, it is the second biggest country in Africa after Algeria, since moving up from third place with the splitting of Sudan into two. Having nine neighbours plays an important role for the region, both politically and security-wise, and presents a huge potential for business. Unfortunately, this is a privilege not exploited.

"However, our strength lies best in our capacity, both compatriots and friends who call this nation home, to think positively and synergise," Gilbert insisted. "We have everything to thrive, but not until we are free from the enemy within and the world's envy. Sadly, we leave our gates extremely open to foreign investment geared to exploit us."

We yearned for collaborations and solutions, not accusations and negative pride we depicted in his narrative. Then, he seemed to read our minds and upped his game when we started showing interest in other people standing by and what they were doing.

"A stagnant three percent annual Gross Domestic Product we are subject to seems impossible to overcome," he said. "The lack of production initiatives, natural resources transformation, and a manufacturing culture are all to blame."

He was right! But would not give us the time to interrupt longer. Nonetheless, we were impressed with his knowledge of what could be done to turn the nation's fortune around. His was a very convincing stand. We saw in him one who could have been much further in his education had he not been forced to part with school for years.

"It says all when a land with the potential that only the Congo has its leaders find it normal to import drinking water to respond to demand."

By this time, we had already established that the number of its water reserves alone sufficed to get it out of poverty. So, Gilbert was not teaching us something new there.

"It is, however, true that peace needs to prevail before the rest can normalise."

We concurred. Not much could be achieved with war persisting and the uncertainty of many kids growing into adulthood. But we hoped he understood that it was not our place to provide him with that peace he and the region were so much yearning for. He was very clued-up and exceptionally articulate to know better. So, for what purpose was he plugging in more intriguing statements every time we tried to peel away?

"Please, hire me," he let out.

He was after part-time work so he could meet the cost of Uni, for he hoped to be a mining engineer no matter how long it would take. We gave him more than he begged for when he said his dad had no income to get him into tertiary education. He was so smart and more mature, so we were not going to let the opportunity to earn a little today distract him. Therefore, we made his father a revenue collector over a few stations we went on establishing. He understood the rules. Our collectors were paid way above their maximum daily collection but a month in arrears to prevent embezzlement. They would have fired themselves and left their earnings behind if they failed to deposit the funds collected within 24 hours. With technology, the bank gave us access to online account activities. Hence, we were aware every day of whether the money was in or not.

Partnership

A year had passed since we arrived in Nairobi to start this eastern project, and signs of mental and physical weariness could no longer be ignored. Adding fuel to the fire was that Bukavu, our next planned stop, was 240 kilometres south. The thought of battling another unpaved road alone stripped us of all motivation. We had eight wells to establish there after Goma took up 12 more than its allocation of 20. Katanga's 30 were still intact. However, Lubumbashi, the chief city of the Katanga province, was 1,590 kilometres from where we were, and getting there was a conversation we did not want to hold since we arrived in Goma.

Likewise, none of us entertained the thought of returning to Kisangani by road again, notwithstanding the unused equipment left there. Our drivers strongly advised against flying between Goma and any part of the region. Their reticence was due to the crashes the area was reputed for, mainly because of non-maintenance of the aircraft, but also for adverse weather conditions and the many mountains around, both of which were not met with modern aviation equipment that could detect mountains' highest points when covered by thick mists.

We were a comfortable 15-minute drive to the Rwandan border crossing and a 150-kilometre journey on a tarred road to Kigali, where we had been taking deserved weekend breaks, despite my animosity towards Rwanda that has long been the cause of much sorrow to my country. The first time we went there was to meet the delivery of our new SUVs, together with our own two lorries, as three months of holding onto those we brought to Goma was becoming overly expensive. From Kigali, we could easily be on a flight to Addis Ababa or Nairobi for a connection to almost anywhere in the world.

The killing of the children in our presence, work demands, and exhaustion had brought us close to knuckling under. The only thing restraining us from doing so was not willing to lose Brassco's trust in us. When Zola and his assistant visited four months earlier, we told him openly of our struggles and how we had underestimated the challenges this side of the country. We also advocated the greater need for more than the 40 wells we were given for both Kivu provinces.

Because of people coming forward to pay for water once installed, and just as it was in Kinshasa, he left it with us to decide how many more stations we wanted there. Furthermore, he was happy with our plan to sub-contract any work going forward if only we remained in charge and did not pass responsibility to a third-party. Promises were made to give us a brand-new contract to dot the Katanga with boreholes. That gave us the strength to rise above our limitations and complete eight more wells in Goma, but without Alvin and Amy, who, shattered, headed home.

The city of Bukavu and its surroundings would therefore have the 30 wells that were meant to go to the Katanga. We had a heavy heart leaving the many scattered villages in the area with no water. The fear of militias had had the best of us. The thought of being attacked or losing our new automobiles came to mind many times a day. But we did our best to keep going about our business.

Initially, we focussed on the rich parts of Goma because of the greatness of the instant return on investment noted there and the fact that it gave us an income increase to serve more localities in the future. Water users in this town spent not sparingly. They went for more than the daily minimum volume of 60 litres per person, thanks to their affordability and now having this service nearby. We realised that to match demand, expand, and achieve more, we had to trust someone with the region. Therefore, we gave Dev-Plus some autonomy in Bukavu, with us taking it backstage now that they had seen how we did things with their participation in Goma.

Their countrywide church provided them with trustworthy people to hire, which was a great asset. They satisfactorily completed work with minimal supervision from us, although taking more time to train new teams, in keeping with their practice of not moving workers away from their towns. They were a lifeline that would keep our business going in our absence, making good use of the equipment built to serve more people and not be locked away. Surely, Dev-Plus came in handy in fulfilling our wish to have a permanent presence out east.

We got them to also take over Kisangani and start up Bunia, where we owed those who *hosted* us, especially the officers who had badly begged us not to leave them without water. The trouble would be the heavy investment needed to acquire work lorries for that area. It took close to a year for the project to start paying back, but once both towns had more of our boreholes, cash poured in non-stop; it offered us the opportunity to reach out to nearby villages.

However, this prowess meant not the end of our challenges. We ordered rods, pipes, and other consumables by tonnes and delivered them to our warehouses in these three provinces. Knowing what the roads were like, we felt for our workers who travelled up and down to establish boreholes, although to them, a luxury riding in brand-new automobiles. But to our disappointment, evaluation uncovered their carelessness. No equipment or vehicle was serviced, yet money had been claimed. Consumables taken out did not match the number of the wells completed. The mileage recorded indicated that the lorries had been farther than the assignments reported. As though all that was not enough, one of our drivers caused death to himself and five others. Unopened bottles of beer and empty ones were found in the cabin of the lorry in the ditch wherein it had landed. He had been drinking while driving.

Despite the insurance company providing acceptable compensation, we never felt comfortable thinking that lives were lost while in our service. Dev-Plus learnt from this negligence and tightened up their management to avoid this happening again. On our side, we focused on developing and supplying the equipment that would best respond to local geological structures. This partnership allowed us to go home for extended periods of time.

Timing

Returning to Kinshasa was to further good fortune: we picked up another offer from Zola, taking us to Kenge and its environs and causing the Katanga to wait once more. This was another strong fortress of Brassco's brands, and it pleased us to be within five hours of the capital, where seeing international flights in and out of the Ndjili airport took away the feeling that we were too far from our homes—myself included, to be honest.

Kenge was a town evolving in every aspect of life, with a new type of hotels known as *flat hotels* being the trend. These offered air-conditioned rooms and reliable internet connectivity—a remarkable innovation to any local person. International visitors on short and long-term missions were fewer but outnumbered their national NGO colleagues. Those on government errands, mostly from Kinshasa but also from other parts of the country, added to the ambience, fulfilling contracts such as roadwork and other development engagements. Others were just travelling through and happened to squeeze in a break that made them not want to leave.

Outdoor discos started as early as four in the afternoon and laid out a colourful pre-nightlife decor of Congolese music and socialising. The younger crowd exhibited exquisite moves like we had not seen elsewhere, making it difficult to take our eyes off them. The older generation was rather content to keep warming the seats. They feared sharing a dance floor with their grandchildren, thus sparing themselves the embarrassment of looking outdated and unable to keep up with the speed of today's beat. Music is an enormous part of life in the Congo, and Rumba dominates all other genres. Most people preferred the sidewalk bars, which offered plenty of discounted beer but also well-spiced barbecues.

Local transportation was mostly accomplished on bicycles and motorbikes. But make no mistake: these were people earning a living by taking passengers places. These *vélos* are referred to as *Toleka!* meaning *let*'s *go!* in Lingala, while motorcycles are known as *Wewa!* which is *You!* in Tshiluba, like when trying to catch someone's attention by calling them up: "Hey!" But it had a derogatory connotation over there, meaning that someone earning a living through this method deserved no respect.

Cops directed traffic flow at every main intersection to avoid the few vehicles, increasing bicycles, motorcycles, pushcarts, and foot travellers clashing. School buildings were not just used for learning and graduations but also church services, political events, weddings, birthday parties, and other functions. Being approached with a booking pleased each principal immensely as it helped them top up staff's salaries.

The bureau de change business was the biggest development the country had known in decades, beating even the popularity of the Internet. It had turned some who stood no chance in life rich overnight. Many who had succeeded in this sector had started with as little as $50 in local currency. Their only other assets were a table, a stool, an umbrella, and cardboard with rates written on with charcoal, showing how skint they were to dare invest in a board and chalk. These new wealthy individuals had capitalised on the equivalent of what their peers spent on food, clothing, and even what was to others enough to only *having a good time* with. They had faith in the future and went after it.

Back with us for a brief duration, Laura grew concerned about the piles of banknotes, a-metre high and wide, on tables without special protection. One of the traders said with a smile that nobody would hurt another there. Attempting to do so equalled death by beating, right on the spot and from the hands of all. Besides, they believed to know each other in this town that they were just like one big extended family, despite it being a 42,000-population conurbation.

Shops also changed currencies, alongside their core businesses, due to specialised outlets not coping well with the overwhelming number of customers sending and receiving funds. The long queues there were because most residents relied on their relatives overseas for their everyday living expenses, which had created a dependency the senders wished they had not started. The belief that money grew on trees in the West (Europe and North America) was not an adage in the Congo, and it had long put in deep roots and altered behaviours, sadly not for the better.

The traffic in and out of these premises, without the knowledge of the cause of the havoc, led to think that everything in there was on sale. Most transfers were international. This non-regulated system bypassed and defeated the banks and their high charges. The Congolese diaspora transmitted home over $10 billion dollars a year from the West alone, going back to the mid-nineties. As a result, around 10% commission fee went into unregistered merchants' pockets without paying any tax. The second popular corridor to Kenge was to and from Angola due to many residents on both sides being related. Overall, those abroad relied on the overseas representatives of these shops to support their families in the Congo. However, those with quick thinking, like Alain, found it profitable to stop these wires from crossing borders and get rich.

He approached us as we sat at an open-air pub sipping a drink. Smiling and confident in his voice, he asked if he could join us. He had heard Jan, on the phone with his wife, screaming his lungs out. He was trying to speak over the music blaring from big speakers in every corner that was so loud that it almost tore our eardrums.

"Swiss, right?" he asked Jan in German.

"Someone speaking German here!" Günter exclaimed.

He had barely finished saying so when Alain interjected: "That is a German there!"

His was a fascinating account.

Vision

Alain left Kenge, aged 18, with a government bursary. His parents sold their farm to afford his airfare. Getting together

$1,000 was not a given for everyone in those days. But they had faith he would pay them back one day, despite hearing of many who went away with the help of their family and quickly forgot where they came from. He disappointed them first as he arrived in Finland with no allowance forthcoming. The person who facilitated this favour was receiving the funds back in Kinshasa, and this, for as long as he remained in education and renewed his visa over the six-year period that included a two-year language programme.

He was threatened with course termination, which would have led to deportation. Thankfully, one of his teachers had befriended him from day one upon realising he was too far from home. There was not much African presence in Helsinki back then, let alone on campus. So, he offered him a room at his parents' home. There, his brother would meet Alain and, out of compassion, gave him a twilight position five days a week at the hotel he managed.

Thus, he could afford his expenses and went on to add a two-year master's study and a further couple of years for a doctorate in Economics. A lifetime of education, it seemed like, but he had nothing to rush back home for. Employment with a bank took him places, offering security and satisfaction, but nothing sufficient to meet his larger ambition of helping those in the Congo provide for themselves. He never let go of the idea of having come this way to learn and that it was, by all means, crucial to making an impact back home.

Downsizing and the resultant restructuring stroke on his 22nd anniversary with the bank. At the age of 50, he resisted looking around for a new job. He paid off the mortgage with his redundancy package and handed the rest to his wife, Bernadette, asking her to take care of the family. He headed to Kenge for the first time in 32 years with only two suitcases full of old clothes to keep him going. By then, he had already paid back the family with a replacement farm and helped his siblings get through Uni. Therefore, he was welcomed back, and one of them housed him. He got on with what he had in mind before they could throw him out for not seeing vehicles and other shipments following, as expected of any Europe-based Congolese returning home.

Before leaving for the Congo, he and Bernadette had done some homework not small, and listed over 1,000 families between the countries they had called home in Europe over the years. They obtained these families' commitment to being their money transfer median. Most of these doubled the clientele, for each spouse had their own responsibilities back home. They sent over $2,000 a year each to support their parents and siblings and build themselves retirement houses, although undecided yet on whether to go back or stay.

Anticipating snatching a 10th of the Kenge's business gave him the reason to hurry up before someone else could have the same inspiration and act on it. However, the competition was minimal, and clients begged those going on holiday to take money home for them. Those in Scandinavia used to pass through their compatriots in the Benelux, losing a substantial amount in exchange rates and other costs. But, despite the evident need and the opportunity to put together a more efficient service, fewer imagined this to be something worth best structuring and committing to. They limited themselves to blaming the lack of banking between where they resided and the Congo.

Many in Kinshasa and the nearby provinces of Bandundu and Kongo Central sent money to suppliers in the West to replenish their shops with manufactured and second-hand goods. This was before importing from China took Europe and the rest of the world that supplied Africa by surprise. Alain approached these businesses and obtained their signatures. It was a service much appreciated because of the difficulty of buying foreign currency in the black market, just to hand it to the banks that would otherwise have sold it to them at exaggerated rates. But with fake banknotes going around, the bank was often the first place where they learnt of their misfortune. He was more encouraged when he saw documentation from those interested in his proposal showing that more than $30 million were transacted in the previous two years.

He passed on the good news to Bernadette, who started receiving money from those in the Nordic countries and quickly expanded into other parts of the continent, where she took no time travelling to. On the other end, he collected cash from importers, but served the families of the Europe-based senders with it rather than forwarding it to their suppliers in the West, for she had it covered with what she received. Thus, after a year of business, they had made more than $1 million from this setup and rapidly opened shops of their own in Kenge, Kikwit, Kinshasa, and Matadi, to be known and trusted more. They extended into transportation and property development as their money transfer revenue quadrupled by the end of their fourth year in business.

Astonishingly, Alain fluently spoke Danish, Dutch, English, Finnish, German, Italian, Norwegian, Portuguese, Spanish, and Swedish, besides Lingala, Kikongo, and French.

"I was always on the move," he explained to Günter and Jan who wondered how come he spoke German. "I lived in both your countries for a total of six years during my time with the bank."

It intrigued him that we represented many countries.

"Which NGO are you with?"

"We run our own for-profit," I replied.

"Awesome! It was out of concern for those left behind that I came back."

At the time of our meeting, Bernadette, some of their children, and grandchildren lived in Denmark, which he also affectionately referred to as home and returned to every quarter for a month-long family time and business.

"My next challenge is to kick water penury out of this municipality," he revealed.

My partners and I looked at each other and laughed.

"Trust me, it is possible! I do not have to do it all myself."

"Sorry!" said Laura. "Not disbelieving you at all."

We briefed him on what we had completed to date, making him see that meeting him was not a simple coincidence.

"How can I join you?"

"You tell us," Laura answered.

He offered 20 wells to his birth town. But, as a true businessman, he asked to take charge after completion so he could pay himself and was not joking. He would be a big relief as we no longer fancied lingering around one place. Our previous micro-management approach had hindered us from reaching out to more people. Therefore, coming to Kenge was to vet the terrain and quickly bring in Dev-Plus. But Alain made it easy for us. We only had to get him and the people he would employ organised before trusting him with drilling operations all over the province. Sure, he would not have the time to oversee work in person, but whoever he was to put on the job would be his responsibility, and not ours.

The arrival of Alain's offer did put us under obligation to first convince Brassco to take their allocation elsewhere, despite knowing well why Kenge was of interest to them. They declined. Nonetheless, Alain was chuffed that someone had thought of his town, which gave him the reason to dismiss any idea that we had met by accident. He drummed up the development coming to Kenge on the national radio for his own propaganda. Dev-Plus, unimpressed, came down within 24 hours of the message being aired when they could have phoned. They claimed to have the exclusivity to work for us everywhere. But they had no proof with which to back it up. Those watching were curious to see how we were to sort out our differences.

Dev-Plus refused to lend their manpower to Alain. But he filled up all the positions within a week. Even geologists and engineers popped up simply from word of mouth. And, to our surprise, these were among those wasting time in the streets, dancing in bars, and giving the impression of being uneducated. Many came forward after hearing we were setting up, begging to do any work to get paid. The availability of labour there was due to several graduates returning from the capital to nothing. Hence, a graduate architect, for instance, was farming to put food on the table. But others hoped someone would come to change their fortune, unaware that *hope is never a strategy.*

Not Burning Bridges

Two months into the Kenge job and with six wells embellished, we travelled to the city of Kikwit, some 300 kilometres beyond Kenge and home to 450,000 people. The purpose of the visit was to figure out what to do with Alain's investment. He was pushing to solidify his partnership with us by moving his interest to the parts of the province not yet taken up by Brassco. Having gifted Kenge with 30 boreholes, there was just no room left for Alain's cash there. How sweet to see donations and investment fighting over the opportunity to give people water! Nothing wrong with his enthusiasm being the result of knowing the profits that could be his. We, too, wanted him.

We were forced to curtail our visit when we failed to get hold of our staff in Kenge for over 24 hours. Of course, we wanted the report for the day, but not as much as we were worried for their safety, as we sensed something was wrong when both team leaders failed to pick up.

But 60 kilometres to Kenge, my phone rang. It was Zacharie! The court in Kinshasa had contacted him as he was down as our counsel. The police had just waited for us to be away to call on our crew and escort them to their station. They interrogated, physically tortured, and made them stand all night. They were denied the use of the phone, leaving us frustrated for not connecting.

Once in Kenge, we first stopped where we could inquire from those who could have witnessed our workers being taken away. Amy was in tears hearing of the brutality with which these were led away. The police asked that we report in the capital before our people could be let out, the caution Zacharie had paid there to regain their freedom coming to naught. We lost another day thinking that the matter could be resolved locally. Worse, we were not allowed to see or speak to them as the commander had taken a day's leave.

Meanwhile, the population gathered at the police station upon our arrival, unaware it was to our detriment. They had started to enjoy having water, so they did not take this interference well. Zacharie's persistence resulted in Kinshasa ordering the release of our staff two days after we returned from Kikwit. However, we were still expected in the capital. It took the remainder of the day to find fuel for the 270 kilometres ahead due to avoiding roadside vendors as some added water to their stock to maximise profits.

Leaving a bit after 7.00 p.m. caused us to miss entering the capital before midnight. So, we slept in the cars, at the borderline separating Kinshasa and the Bandundu, waiting for the gate to re-open at 6.00 a.m. This was Menkao, a rural community on the N1 Highway. The need for the barrier, 44 kilometres to the Ndjili airport, which in turn is 23 kilometres to the city centre, was to prevent the rebels from entering the capital at night.

Also contributing to our not making it on time was spending a couple of hours where two lorries had collided. Each had only a single headlight and, consequently, left each driver guessing the whereabouts of the offside of the other vehicle. Neither was driveable after that. So, the passengers got busy unloading to be able to push them to the side. We lent a hand in the hope of speeding up the process and making a passage for ourselves. Thankfully, despite this being the only road connecting to the capital from Kenge, there was almost no traffic. But what was not our surprise to find out that the vehicle coming from Kinshasa had nothing onboard but bottled water.

In Kinshasa, it took a month to deal with the magistrates. They were not in a rush. We were not allowed to carry out any drilling at all, leaving to doubt our dream of giving water to more people would come to fruition. That Dev-Plus had asked to drop the charges two days after filing was of no interest to those now with a case of their own against us. Inciting the locals to insurgence was harshly punishable. We fought hard to prove our innocence for the uproar that had taken place in Kenge, to the point that a more experienced and costly lawyer was hired. But we sacked him when he preferred bribing that the clerks chasing us around throughout the proceedings suggested.

This evil was the work of Dev-Plus' manager whose apology came too late. He had misled his leaders who were now prepared to do anything to regain our business. Not wanting to start all over securing a new partner, with the Kivu and the Province *Orientale* already in their hands and on track, we deemed it wise not to burn bridges. Hence, we left those regions with them while Alain managed the Bandundu. But the public that had been following the saga closely saw in us a soft touch for having anything, going forward, to do with Dev-Plus. But they knew not what it had taken us to swallow our pride.

Kenge welcomed us back like we had won them something of national gratification, worrying us of being seen as claiming to have defeated the authorities. Surprisingly, the police wasted no energy in dispersing those busy chanting, "water win!" no end. They left them alone until they were tired. We resumed work, fulfilling Brassco's contract to the satisfaction of all.

In just a short while, water penury became a distant past, to the point that even vehicles stopping by on their way to and from Kinshasa had free drinking water. Therefore, we reached out to a few villages within reasonable distances of Kenge, despite their contribution not permitting us to recuperate the investment within a decade. But the larger communities indirectly made up for the shortfall. What remained of these villages was only to commit to fully fund their wells' maintenance once completed and handed to them.

Alternative Funding

Determined not to perpetuate dependency, we taught the villages increasingly coming forward for water how working together funded a communal well. Their contribution needed not always be monetary. Often nothing we said added up. But we were not a charitable organisation. We had to be bold. Therefore, we found ourselves being torn between sticking to promoting self-reliance and giving way to their definition of humanity. This was a difficult equation to solve, but we eventually got around to helping three villages within a seven-kilometre radius of each other take care of their destiny where there was no hope.

They had found the courage to accomplish something extraordinary after noticing our frequent travels on the highway and learnt of what we were doing in communities beyond theirs. Therefore, they sent out exactly 20 of their residents to block our way while cruising at 60 kilometres per hour because twice we had only waved and passed. In our mind, they were after a lift or intending to sell us something.

Their motive was a journey to and from the source of water that took half a day a trip and left them with no time for anything else. Children, with school some 14 kilometres away, were not spared either. Even lands favourable to growing staple foods were 12 kilometres in the forest. Hence, their overall productivity was undercut by 90%, making it difficult to realise a sustainable income or for children to hope for an educational life beyond what their parents had achieved.

Therefore, asking them to pay for drilling would be like rubbing salt in the wound. But we had no other way of answering their plea to favour them over everyone else. The turning point was Alvin advising that he could get them to sponsor themselves if what he had noticed there was what he thought it was. A certain chilli plant was found in almost every yard we entered.

"It is growing abundantly but unwanted," said his interlocutor.

Alvin laughed, keeping it comical and friendly, as it had been since our coming off the N1, because of the jokes they were telling, thrilled to have foreigners visit their village. He had contacts in the Middle East at a company that was part of the value chain producing analgesic solutions. They extracted the very high-grade capsaicin contained in this type of chilli, and then supplied it to manufacturers of dermal patches, nasal spray, ointment, pepper spray, tear gas, and many other chemical and medicinal products to be input into a global distribution network.

The village chief made 2,000 acres of land available, and people got their worn-out hoes and machetes out. We ignored their demand for a *motivation* arguing that this was for their own good, else we would go our way. It was best to see how willing and committed to changing their own fate they were. So, realising we could not be influenced, they got in line and did not disappoint.

All we asked of each one of them was eight hours of their time a week, from as young as 16. This was not a problem as most of the younger ones preferred being bent down tilling the earth over going to school because of the distance involved. However, I must admit that their neglect of classroom learning was also partly because of the illiteracy culture the older generations had passed down. They had no one to emulate. The only way out of this had been going away, although in doing so, some had ended up slaves to rich kinfolks who gave them no chance for education.

To our surprise, some adults responded more than we expected, putting in 30 hours minimum. In the meantime, they struggled to believe that thousands of dollars could come out of a commodity as ordinary as their chilli, let alone would it improve their lives. Harvesting was every three to four months. But with only a small portion of the field tilled and labour being manual, we only shipped out a single 40-foot container of dried chillies the first year. Samples sent over beforehand were confirmed to be among the world's top and much-in-demand quality. Thus we found ourselves under pressure for bigger regular deliveries.

It was, therefore, imperative to chip in a couple of tractors at that point, with all the needed accessories, to veer away from farming by hand. This attracted more workers in the process as it meant that tasks were rendered simpler. We had used humans only to gauge their desire to lift themselves out of poverty, while we came in to form a support line, and by no means were we tolerant of relying solely on physical labour in this technological age.

Agronomy being taught to *licence* (five years of Uni), a pair of graduates with field experience came by easily. They were to study and prepare the land to increase production volumes, adhering to our buyers' request to keep the soil natural so the chilli could maintain its high-grade chemicals. But they were short of ideas until the village's notables revealed that some specific animals' waste served as fertilisers.

These animals were domestically raised in abundance there, as well as in nearby locations. The downfall, though, was that what had all along been useless and cumbersome suddenly gained commercial value. Within a few months of buying, we provoked rarity, and its cost went through the roof. We could not say what the owners of these animals were doing with this substance before we manifested interest. Our accountants demanded an explanation as to why we were paying for it in the first place. But we were not going to be distracted. We knew, nonetheless, that our suppliers would come out worse if buying from them was to come to a halt.

We became skeptical as to why only this manure worked. Therefore, we went on to experiment with other animals' waste on a separate portion of the same field. We wanted to cut down the cost, have more choices, and discover something to teach the locals. This was done in connivance with our agronomists, who thought of their ancestors' knowledge as archaic. They were not at ease with the elders' advice for the simplest reason that it was not taught at Uni. We produced huge volumes of the chilli, but the feedback from the Middle East was to stick to the first area, insisting on the lesser quality the new patch had yielded. Hearing so, we never revealed to them what we had done.

Going back to the rich animals' waste and using the machinery in our possession to full capacity helped us harvest 65 times more. The resulting income funded more wells than the participating population needed. We allocated the surplus to farming sprinkling, fishery ponds, and care for the animals and poultry we got them to raise more. The money from the chilli also permitted the plan to build a couple of schools for these three villages, a modest medical clinic, and solar power stations to light up these villages. All this was an opportunity for some to enjoy structured jobs and regular salaries.

A proper market infrastructure came to them, and businesses that once operated only in cities found it beneficial to set up in the area that had now turned semi-rural. This development caused an exodus from other villages. A decade later, the 70,000 population we first found there swelled into an administrative territory of more than 250,000 inhabitants. We envisaged connecting this district with 22 kilometres of asphalted road to facilitate goods transportation to the central village and the N1, and having houses replace muddy huts.

It was amazing to see lives changing quickly by turning to export rather than trying to build the economy with imports that not all ordinary people had the means for. The key was finding ways to stop leaving substantial profits in the value chain abroad. For example, consuming processed tinned tomato paste, not manufactured in the Congo, only enriched overseas-based manufacturers, whereas eating locally grown tomato fruits kept every penny in the country. Water produced plentifully on and for the farms allowed us to accelerate our chilli production, as well as many other products of daily necessity, tomatoes included.

With this humble achievement, *our* villages started to weigh on the provincial scale, and the authorities found every excuse to drop by. They asked us to tap into other localities. But, away from them, we wondered what was restricting them from doing so themselves. The answer was simple: the Congolese love white-collar jobs more than getting their hands dirty. We had our own hurdle of problems to sort out, so we pushed their flatteries aside.

Much money was wasted on the first shipment using air cargo. That stopped with harvesting hundreds of tonnes. Sure, pulling the consignment to the port took time, especially with no vehicles of our own to accommodate 20 containers each time. But it still was overall a more economical strategy. Air transportation was not furthering our aim as no Congolese airline delivered to any international destination, let alone ours. In contrast, those drivers at our service were all nationals. Paying them for the 1,000-kilometre round trip benefited the nation in terms of employment and tax contributions.

Starting with One

We faced problems soon after permission to function as a farming cooperative was granted. The trouble arose when we entered a location 97 kilometres from our first chilli farm. Some people were not happy with the success of those we were just helping along to fight for themselves. Therefore, three folks in their forties pulled up in a nice SUV—a sign that someone had made it in life in the Congo. They called two of those tilling the earth to the side. They questioned why we had subjected them to manual work if we were investors and had their welfare at heart. Pretty much everyone was talked out of it.

Hence, our first production in this new location was realised with the village chief alone. Even his own and extended family, constituting a quarter of the 180 we had gathered, deserted him. A week-long negotiating with all, begging them to give our initiative a chance, failed. But he refused to let the whole thing end there, because he knew it had worked where he had gone to see the change that had taken place with his own eyes. He bent down with a hoe many hours a day, updating us of the development every Saturday morning, at the same time of nine o'clock, unfailingly. He told no porky-pies.

"On my own still," we heard each time. "But, making progress."

We could not see what to hope for from his sole efforts when several containers were needed. However, our disinterested tone of voice did not deter him. We warmed up to him again only six months later and visited because of his persistence. He had managed 11 acres, and the earliest parts of his work were ready for harvest. This was away from where he and the group had started, to avoid them claiming the right to a portion of his production.

"I am Adam!"

All along, we had been calling him *Chef* (French for chief), which was how he had introduced himself when we first met, and everyone called him the same. It was the same in all villages, offices, and so on. People are fond of titles, honour, and recognition in the Congo, so we just went with what pleased them. We wanted to know how he got this far on his own.

"I always count on myself."

Growing up, his mates were welcome to join him in farming, fetching water, hiking, kicking a ball, but he always started without them. He believed he was named *Adam* for a reason, besides being his parents' firstborn. The first child, if a boy, is customarily called so in the Congo, to signify that life has started and that the future weight of the family lies on such's shoulders. But for us, it was great to learn that even a single person was worth investing in if it would benefit the community.

Those who got off the boat had nothing better to go to but still did. They stayed at home, under the trees, playing cards and other games all day long, whereas it was only that wasted time we had asked of them, and of course, their energy. Short-sighted and giving in to negative influence, they missed out on the first harvest's rewards. One thing we regretted was the inability to deny them access to the clean water resulting from Adam's sweat. Besides, we had before decided to make it accessible to all.

"Jealousy is a big killer to us," revealed he.

The guys who had created dissension were politicians seeking followers and glory. Elections were looming. They preferred us to go through them, so they could claim the project and earn voices at the poll. Too bad they had resorted to intimidation rather than approaching us with their intentions. We gave them a kick in the teeth when they later came asking to play a part. Regarding the workers, we were glad to have not forced anyone. This was how we proceeded wherever we went, letting people join us of their own free will and choice, which sat well with their belief that even God forces no one to obey Him. All we did was make them aware of how to participate and tap into untouched resources around them.

Ask!

Churches play a crucial part in everyday life of the Congolese. In general, there is a place of worship for every couple of streets in any major city. This was why one of the prominent ones had 800 congregations in Kinshasa alone, despite not being the largest. We were introduced to its four chief representatives, who oversaw the four districts of the capital. Asking about the problems their members faced, they answered with those of a spiritual nature. They reassured us of the blessings that awaited those who endured today's challenges on the other side of life. But further probing led to admitting that unemployment and hunger caused some to stray. Consequently, non-believers who would have converted hesitated, seeing those inside were not better off.

"If these two curses could be brought under control, as overcoming them might be impossible, people would live a more pious life," stated one of these leaders.

Inquiring how they measured the welfare of their faithful, the answer was the paying of alms or not. We believed to have understood what that implied. But it was not until we mentioned water scarcity that they confessed it to be another scourge that held their development back and that it was just as disastrous as we already knew. They asked to join our fight for the sake of the communities where their churches were established when they heard what we were up to.

"I have been drinking more soft drinks than water for a long time now," said one of them. "Quality natural water has become rare."

He could not have rendered our task any easier with his statement. And roles seemed to have been reversed, with the four men elaborating how the basis of their ministry consisted of caring for their believers' wellbeing and never limiting to faith building.

"Our people thirst spiritually, but even greatly temporally," another pointed out. "We all need water to nourish our bodies with."

Therefore, they committed to instructing the individual congregational pastors under their stewardship to invite their members to provide for the communities in need. No one in attendance doubted a moment that water was life when their ministers addressed them. They got the message across using nearly every reference to water in the Bible. A vow was made to shine through this act of sacrifice. An assembly with an audience of 1,500 people plus funded a communal well in full, despite coming in that Sunday unaware of this call. The remaining groups within this denomination donated, together, enough to drill 13 wells.

Another church with over 4,000 worshippers in its branches weekly surpassed itself. Its main sanctuary was built to welcome only a third of the 600 plus congregating there, but the rest refused to stay at home. They occupied the sidewalk and part of the road, bringing their own chairs and blocking pedestrians and vehicles, to listen to the all-day-long sermon via loudspeakers and large screens placed outside. Hot weather could not prevail. Even torrential rains pouring down failed to win over their commitment to stay put. Our visit made the pastor realise the significance of having water on-site, for their premises had never had any and consequently no toilets. But they had no space to drill on. The building filled up all the parcel.

Contrary to the reputation the pastor over this branch had earned himself as being greedy, because of his love for luxury cars and expensive suits and jewellery, he called for funds out of pure concern for this locality's residents he knew little of, except those who frequented his church. A big basket got in front of the pulpit. Adoration hit the roof, musicians competed with singers, dancers took to the floor, and *all was well in the kingdom*. They sang their hearts out, convinced that angels applauded in heaven. Alms time, every Sunday, is an opportunity to exhibit new dance moves and compete with fellow worshippers, justifying that dancing started in heaven. A second basket also filled up within minutes of being brought out as more believers lined up still. Wealthy members honoured their promise to donate more away from the cameras, whereas we had come over with warnings not to expect anything from this pastor.

Where it is necessary to display faith, churchgoers in the Congo can be counted on anytime. They worry not about what to eat when they get home. This congregation paid us $20,000 to give water to this neighbourhood that had learnt to live with the noise of its music. Many of these donors had nothing to do with this area, apart for being there only on Sunday and midweek, for they came from every corner of the city. They confessed to being drawn to their leader's power to heal, provide good luck for marriage, overcome a barren womb, give the luck to find employment, business success, and other miracles. Hence, their wallets emptied with him announcing that whoso contributed would run out of room for what they will receive in return.

Giving Back

The beneficiaries funded a well for the next community, and it went on like a snowball, each community refusing to remain indebted, although morally feeling never capable of paying back enough. Soon, we found ourselves unable to keep up with how quickly all these responded. We thought it unwise to hold onto their money, not knowing when we would get administrative clearance for each location, besides the difficulty of training a team to put on the job. But they would not hang fire.

Growth caught us by surprise, and even more the ever-surging challenges. The regulators were right; the long blocks of terraced houses left no room to drill on, let alone where to install a water station with multiple taps. The front door to each dwelling was right on the street, while the tiny backyard had long been developed with an extension to the point that even children had no playground. The narrow streets, unable to let two cars pass each other, were asphalted and unsuitable for our work.

Shockingly, some religious institutions with unused space rejected our undertaking because donors were their rivals, citing the risk of helping a competitor to the top with being seen as saviours. With that, we wondered where fair play would be found if it did not exist among the clergies. This rivalry extended to schools when affiliated with differing faiths. Where we were successful was with state-owned ones. They did not mind where sponsorship came from but set out strict rules. These included allowing only a limited number of drawers on site each time so learners were not distracted, which was understandable.

Thankfully, we had the wherewithal to secure some room. The money raised helped to acquire a couple of end-of-terrace properties and join their driveways when the chance to realise even a single well in this congested area looked bleak. One of these purchases was next to the previously mentioned church that had raised funds for us. We included multiple toilets and shower rooms in our construction and drinking dispenser taps to be used only by this church, giving access to its members through a passage between their property and ours. They appreciated our thoughtfulness, but still refused to be paid back. Hence, they contributed hundreds of dollars monthly to use these facilities, which came in handy to employ a cleaner, for some of these worshippers spent entire weeks locked up in this church fasting and praying.

Acquiring properties to drill on sadly did not work everywhere. This was more to do with owners not willing to relocate, no matter how reasonable our offer. Many were born and bred in these 1950s constructions they had now inherited jointly with their siblings from their parents. It was, therefore, difficult for co-owners to agree to sell off and move on with their separate lives, especially as most still clung to the middle-class status these suburbs once had.

However, the majority of those now owning these properties were not associated with this social status, long gone, as it was attributed to the white-collar jobs those for whom these houses were built held, seeing they had regular salaries that afforded them a mortgage. The original owners also enjoyed being second, in order of importance and in the public's eyes, to the colonisers who lived downtown. But the unyielding heirs were greatly unemployed, even with university degrees. Fortunately, soliciting elsewhere somehow compensated for our failure to give water to more people in these neighbourhoods we were to leave behind.

Saying No

National and international NGOs also came under pressure to do something after contemplating the residents doing their best and underfunded institutions going beyond the call of duty to give people water. It made no sense to advocate for complex matters such as democracy, human rights, and the like while ignoring a crisis as tangible as water shortage in the life of the populations they were defending. When we came knocking, their spontaneous reaction proved that funds were available and only needed to be applied for. Sadly, some governmental officials saw our cooperation with these entities as hiding something that could be detrimental to the regime in place if not intercepted early.

They came up with time-consuming procedures that restricted us from receiving donations. We were required to receive payments minus up to 60% through intermediary organisations. Supposedly, these deductions would be redistributed to institutions like ours, and it was not the donors' place, nor ours, to know who the fortuitous beneficiaries were. Even worse was forcing that we go to drill over 1,000 kilometres away, in remote villages with little population, far from the capital for which we had sought and obtained the said funding.

Our declining to sign exposed them. By then, we felt at home and cared not what anyone thought of us, for we were certain to have broken no written law. We fought back by informing the donors and the media of what we thought was happening. Those with powers over the government agency playing this dirty game investigated, and when the money could not be traced, the culprits were picked up. We were warned to wait for retaliation, so we did amid seeking to form new partnerships.

A People Determined

Truly, nothing can stop a people determined to take their own destiny in hands. This was the case with the many middle-class households who placed orders for themselves, offering cash in advance. But quite often, would see their applications turned down by the authorities. Among the reasons given was that their properties were multi-family occupancy or had little room for our equipment to operate on, rejecting our feasibility study and ability to squeeze in without endangering anyone. The concern over the noise level in the proximity of children was also a scapegoat, as our machines were all soundproof enabled. Günter had seen far ahead in his design process. Health and Safety being of utmost priority to us, he had come up with a rig that produced fewer decibels than the industry minimum for anyone within 75 metres of the undertaking.

While denying this category of customers water seemed unacceptable, the officials remained relentless. The downside turned to the fear of the owners being tempted to serve their neighbours without any insurance policy. Hilarious! This argument was pushed aside as such a protection culture never existed there. The temptation to turn into a commercial activity was next. That, too, was just out of order as a myriad of small-sized businesses operated without any licence.

Regardless of red tape, our small team of direct marketers had already started to make an impact. They yearned to prove they could do better for themselves and their families if given a chance, especially with a product that kind of sells itself. They were busy encouraging communities to form groups to contribute so we could install communal wells for them. Where possible, that could be extended to sub-delivery stations that would permit most families to have water almost on their doorstep. However, this aggressive sort of squeezy approach would encounter further barriers. The involved civil engineering work, although not of great magnitude, was not well seen by the authorities.

But, a big crowd of children, youth, and adults gathered several times a week at the Commune to demand water. They saw no risk in having a well accommodating two, four, or six streets through a pipe deep enough in the ground from one property abreast into the next street. We intended to cut down the monetary participation per household and avoid any surplus out of a borehole sitting there unused.

Streets in our targeted areas were straight and made up of 200 to 500 compounds each. Due to perpendicular roads not intervening until every 25 plots, our piping would avoid people going around a long way to get to a station. Several boreholes would be the answer to our mission to let no one walk more than five minutes to bring water home. Hence, the administrators painted themselves in the corner with their refusal, for the public retracted not.

Seek!

Some churches we worked with received donations of clothes, food, medications, and the like from their overseas headquarters or counterparts. Others were simply not in the know of what was available and where. We brought up the subject, and Alvin and Amy helped them put together applications as they used to during their time in South Asia and West Africa. Tino also knew his way around this avenue because he had similar experiences in Peru.

We got these ecclesiastical leaders to set up email accounts and briefed them on how to use the list of thousands of religious institutions the world over that we presented to them. Our overseas marketing associates, specialising in establishing fundraising contacts for non-profits, had dressed this up for us. The outcome was noteworthy, and in the event of funds not being awarded, promises were received, or alternative leads came back with messages of encouragement acknowledging the giving of water to people as a cause worth every effort. All this was good to our ears and disappointing only to these potential partners as they were not trained to handle rejection. But, as much as we wanted to help them secure funding, we spent not all our time attending to them, for there were many others to reach out to, the need for donations being general.

Apart from very few top-end private schools, no other learning establishments had water or toilets. The average size was 1,000 students per school. They could not afford the resulting monthly bills where there was a connection. Pupils had a history of being unruly, so no principal fancied running the risk on their behalf. The SWC joked not when it came to billing. Therefore, with over 100 schools on our radar, we engineered a plan with a few delegates, including principals, teachers, learners, and parents. The conclusion was to have parents pay for drilling beforehand to avoid disappointment.

They had a year-long notice to contribute a $10 a year per student. Failure to comply would result in their child losing their place the following year—good news for stand-byers. But they were more supportive because this arrangement included toilets and showers, an innovation they looked forward to having in their children's lives. They were happy to pay a further $3 a quarter towards maintenance and repairs. This also covered the provision of tissues, hand sanitiser, and dryers when these facilities were operational.

However, we would waste three months disputing over ongoing management, which the principals wanted left to them. To put this into context, these negotiations did cost us each, on our side, at least four hours a week and more for each delegate from the 24 pilot schools from the 24 communes of the capital that sent us three representatives each. This was because they changed infrequent and overcrowded buses three or four times to reach the meeting place. Students attended only the first session. We stood our ground and had the support of the parents who, away from the headmasters, insisted we give not in. They were convinced these facilities would look undesirable a month after handover if left in the headmasters' hands.

Partnering with schools in this manner was also not attained without going through opposition from the municipal leaders who were on a mission to discourage us. They suddenly appeared to be protective of the parents, contrary to what we had all heard from the latter. Apparently, we were overwhelming families with expenses. They pointed out the average salary in Kinshasa as though we were not informed. But the question of affordability was addressed at the beginning, and these parents had brushed off our leniency with the first sentence in that direction coming out of Amy's mouth. All they wanted at this point was a healthy learning environment for their children.

Not winning, our detractors chose to unnecessarily prolong their granting of approval by two months, whereas the schools contacted had already signed, materials were ordered, and contractors hired. Parents were on schedule with contributions, so they expected not their children to be without toilets on their return from the summer holiday. They insisted we impress their children with a quality they had never seen before. We obliged, seeing some of them would go without food to keep their children's places. But just when we were thinking we were home and dry, those at the ministry of education decided to give themselves a role to play in this process.

They brought in architects with a design as stout as though erecting a high-rise in lieu of the simple structure the schools had already accepted. There was a work progress monitoring committee put together without consulting us. But each parent threatened to back out, and, fearing bad press, the officials retracted before we could challenge their audacity.

We would hit the same brick wall when it came to hospitals which likewise experienced serious sanitary problems. About 95% of all medical institutions in the capital had no toilets for either in-patients or out-patients, and needless to mention showers. This was because of the same old cause: water deficiency. Yet, again, we did not understand why someone was not taking the initiative to discuss things with the stakeholders. Concerned, we started with smaller clinics rather than discriminating against them because of their inability to fund a well and sanitary facilities. We agreed on a repayment plan despite the fact that it would take longer to recoup our investment.

This approach was more inclined towards helping rather than getting rich. We were conscious even of those who came to see their interned relatives with the intention to stay longer but were having to curtail their visits. The disadvantage of our *Good Samaritan* attitude was how most of them, once served, dodged settling their accounts. We heard of patients not paying their bills, dwindling numbers, the priority to update medical equipment, and more. The only thing not mentioned was how that affected us as a business.

Staff at these hospitals did a great job, together with patients and visitors joining in. They placed boxes, although not secured, at the receptions and in other parts of the buildings, with a message to "contribute if you agree that having water, toilets, and showers will help improve the service" they provided. They operated under the burden of a heavy volume of patients, many of whom were hospitalised for long periods. These were discharged daily to meet their needs outside and be re-admitted by the end of the day. Workers also sought refuge in the neighbourhood because of the state of the *staff-only* facilities. Yet the management needed to be reminded of where they had come from. But we were nowhere near being discouraged. There were other people and the risks they lived with calling for our attention, sadly suffering terrible losses for some of them.

Insurance

In Kinshasa, living standards between communities vary tremendously. I grew tired of explaining the same things repeatedly to my friends as this contrast kept staring at them wherever they looked. Rich urban areas with enviable luxurious houses were extremely opposed to the less desirable suburbs. Gombe and a small part of the Commune of Limeté fell under the first category and gave the impression of being a different city. They were what my colleagues wished the entire country was like, given its immense natural resources they had long heard of and had now had the opportunity to witness in some parts of the country.

These beautiful areas were constructed before the nation's independence and for state officials. Some neighbourhoods started to invite themselves into this bourgeoisie in the 1980s owing to property development taking centre stage. They erected multi-storey buildings when no room to construct on was not found. Planning permission applied not to them if they were friends with or related to someone in government. The absence of sewage, water, and electricity bothered not the proud owners the moment they had the money and could find a tiny piece of land for the villas of their dreams. Nonetheless, the narrow and unpaved streets in these neighbourhoods told how these individuals were forcing matters.

A status-seeking mindset led them to anarchically occupy public parks, sporting grounds, local markets, and more, thanks to having access to someone in administration. They were unyielding to the idea of missing out on claiming appurtenance to what is nicknamed the *Republic of Gombe*. Constructors under instructions to build in an indescribably unruly manner obliged, provided they were paid for their labour. All this made it difficult for water piping to take place without causing great damage to these properties.

This was why we would stand, one day, in front of a totally burnt-down four-floor building in one of these parts of the *new Gombe*, unable to find answers to our questions. This unfortunate edifice sat on a portion of what was a recreational park until five years back. When construction was completed, people endorsed it, advocating it enhanced the neighbourhood, failing to think of when others would follow suit; which they did, eventually, and it took not long for the green to disappear.

We read about this fire in the newspaper without knowing we would pass by this site two days later. Over 20 businesses, including a pharmacy, a dentist's, an optician's, a general medical practice, a restaurant, a mini supermarket, a dry-cleaner's, and others, had nothing left of them but ashes. Gladly, no one had died. Only one fire engine had turned up, three hours late, to fight smoke, whereas we had read the City Hall praising the firemen for putting out the fire. Nonetheless, it seemed unthinkable that a city of 15 million relied on two engines, which were insufficient even for the original *Republic of Gombe* when it had 50,000 residents.

That day, by the way, one of the engines had chosen not to start. And, as though that was not enough, the one that got there had less than a quarter of its 1,000-litre tank full. With no water from the tap, even the onlookers could not help but improvise themselves as firefighters with what they had bought to drink on their way to and from their various engagements, although having no impact.

We learnt with sadness that those who lost their businesses, and the owner of this property, would not get any compensation. They were among those who had no faith in the country's poorly regulated insurance industry. The only provider was state-owned and good only at taking payments. A policy with this firm was no different from having none, as many had found out.

The lack of water having aggravated this disaster, we offered the City Administration to drill and install 100 fire hydrants in commercial centres out of our pocket. We further promised to expand all over the city and bring in fire engines if they would charge local businesses a few pennies to pay us back. We were to start with 10 to monitor the incoming repayment for six months before proceeding with the remainder. They asked to check with the hierarchy.

The total offered under this arrangement was to be completed within a year. We were to collect 50% of this levy for a year and reinvest it in more stations, with nothing coming to us as profits. The other half would be used to remunerate the people the authorities would employ in this department. However, the expected approval was delayed and finally not granted. We sought to see those making such a poor decision to explain the good this project would do, and they told us that buildings catching fire was much rarer than in the West.

All this led us to seek our own insurance coverage from a neighbouring country, so that should anything go wrong we would not suffer a total loss. But thinking of doing the country disservice, especially if everyone followed suit to buy insurance policies from outside of the Congo, we approached the central government with suggestions of how the city could be prepared to fight fires if they happen. But we should have listened to Zacharie when he advised us not to come to the government with solutions, for they would often turn a blind eye. His counsel was to stick to private clients and leave the authorities alone where possible.

Fire Hydrants

We were surprised when the same City Hall decision-makers introduced us to a property developer, leaving us to wonder if they truly believed there was no need for hydrants when they said that he would like to hear about our proposal. He handed us 27 houses across the city before we could give him enough details about our service. We heard of the big lesson he had learnt in a not-distant past, and dreaded fire could strike again anytime. He lived with guilt for losing one of his plots but said no more. Then, other people revealed to us that he was the owner of the building that had burnt down in the new Gombe.

Knowing how fresh this incident still was, we asked him for 30% advance payment to show our sympathy and the rest in installments. He would pay the balance within five years by increasing his tenants' rent. They would not complain, for they, too, had butterflies in their stomachs since that other incident. By now, time passed quickly, as opposed to when we first came over, and everything seemed to be standing still, and people asked us to have patience. Five years never sounded to our ears like an eternity again. Now we were at ease entering into long-term business relationships and trusting pretty much everyone we met.

Three months after signing, fire broke out at a house four doors from one of the addresses this man had decided we start at. This was right in the middle of the over-populated Commune of Bandal, and it was a 15-room flat hotel that had smoke and flames coming out of it. A block of six terraced houses would have been destroyed that day. But the street gathered in front of our customer's house, begging for the use of his hydrant. They were grateful that the head of the house was in, for she kept it locked and took the key with her when out, this being new to her.

We officially entered a new business sector that day, providing fire hydrants to flat hotels throughout Kinshasa. Eyewitnesses campaigned on our behalf, knowing it could save them too one day. Another customer base formed around restaurants through the same witnesses of how the availability of water and a hydrant had avoided a catastrophe. Hence, we also returned to the hospitals where we had previously drilled with this complementary service. A new culture was shaping up, and more commercial and corporate entities we reached out to opted to have a well and hydrant on their sites and donate the same to less privileged neighbourhoods.

However, we could not get rid of the guilt of not assisting the less-privileged municipalities that heavily relied on kerosene lamps. They also cooked with wood fire indoors when it rained. Both not only filled their children's lungs with smoke but were fatal. We did not have to go far to see the danger with which they lived. Our trajectory led to a site whereon we had completed a well eight months earlier, and we sought to see how it was faring. Among those who came to meet us was a 13-year-old asking whether we remembered Charles.

"I was with him, and he spoke to you all the time," he said.

After a few descriptions, as everyone had been talking to us all the time on that site, as well as everywhere we had been since coming to the Congo, Charles came to mind. He was 12 and stayed rooted to the spot, watching work developing, with a particular interest, and this being on his path to school, he ended up playing hooky. He continually asked questions about us and the drilling processes as they were happening. Each time we made him leave for school, he obeyed, but just to reappear a moment later. I got to know a bit more about him and his family.

His father made a living as a *Kadhafi*. This is what the Congolese call one who sells fuel at the roadside (in reference to Gaddafi's Libya's immense oil production). He was out selling throughout the day, six days a week, else he would struggle to provide for his five children and their mother. Charles and his 10-year-old brother helped Sundays, so their dad could rest. When he needed to order more supply midweek, his wife stepped in, braving the sun with their two youngest in her lap.

One night a customer knocked on the door at about 10. He took the time to chat with Charles as though he needed to get the boy's sympathy. He had run out of fuel up the main road. This was a cab driver at the end of his shift. The warning light was not working; the car had choked and halted in the middle of the road. Tired after a long day in the sun, Kadhafi, listening from his bed, ordered his eldest, who was revising his lessons, to serve the customer who handed in his jerrycan for five litres of unleaded. No grid connection in this suburb. It was believed that Charles had opened the barrel with the lamp in his other hand in the usual manner, for it was frequent that people called this late for fuel. But this time, a blaze went off.

All that both parents had time for was just to lift their sleeping youngest two and jump out, escaping before the flames blocked off the doorway. The father only caught sight of the back of the guy outside, already in the street, calling for help before disappearing for good to avoid any liability. Charles and his other two siblings were incinerated with the house and seven barrels full of unleaded, two more with diesel, and another with paraffin—their only stock. Any cash they had was in the house—no bank account.

There was nothing the neighbours and all others who came out in their numbers could do. They stood far enough, grateful there were survivors. Thankful they also were that this was a commune where everyone built their own house to their taste. That this one was detached and single-family occupancy was a blessing. Else more lives would have been claimed. The watching crowd's pain intensified because of the absence of a nearby water source, although this was a fire no one could extinguish.

We could not leave that spot without offering a fire hydrant in Charles' memory. Many gathered had never seen one before, so we repeatedly had to explain what it was all about because of the size of the crowd that surrounded us within minutes of parking. We would not be surprised when a later visit led to the discovery that this hydrant was now replenishing lorries full of drums to deliver to more remote areas that paid good money for the supply. The excuse given us was that the other well we had placed up the road was insufficient to meet demand. All it took was only for the family to sell the property and move on for the new owner to yield to pressure.

Sand

As much as people were buying into this preparedness concept, our biggest difficulty remained where to place these hydrants. The lack of urban planning had left no room for anything like this to be incorporated later in this never done growing mega-city. Not even a business could come up with a corner of its property big enough to accommodate both a borehole and the fixing of a fire hydrant onto it. Yet, the danger was permanently staring at the defenceless population. While we explored the options, we came across a local bakery that employed over 40 people. One of these sent for her niece, aged 17. Her face was so terribly scarred that we could not look twice.

"What happened?" Amy asked.

"Water!" replied the auntie.

Until three years prior, Sandrine was very beautiful. Everyone with a son had asked her parents to keep her for him—just the way the Congolese compliment someone with a pretty daughter or the girl herself; the same goes for a boy with good manners. But, because the family could not afford charcoal to boil drinking water, they used dry sticks they cut off dying trees near their home. One day, Sandrine was blowing into the fire to keep it going. But the wind suddenly invited itself to the party, causing the flames to come out sidewise where she knelt and catch her long curly hair extensions.

She could not see a thing by the time she pulled back and got off her knees. She screamed as loud as she could, and when the nearest neighbours arrived, her clothes were burning already. With no water nearby, they dragged her into the street to quench the fire off her body with the sand.

She was in the hospital for five months but remained the way she was brought to us. Fixing her required advanced cosmetic surgery, overseas. Her father drove buses and earned little. The mother was a stay-at-home spouse. Hence, his company, having done what they could during her hospitalisation, she was sent home to live with her scars. Since her release, she had not looked in a mirror, for when she last did at her discharge, she cried, asking why she was being rushed out in this condition. But the doctor pointed out the need to count herself lucky to be able to see again.

She had not returned to school since her first attempt that had ended with all her colleagues deserting the classroom. Every time she went out, most children who saw her ran away.

"Her burns could have been lesser had water been available," said her auntie. "Sand is not that effective fighting fire, but we are grateful it was there. But even better, we could not have been where we are now had we not had to boil our water to turn it potable."

Feeling that we had to help, we started to accept speaking engagements which corporations in Kinshasa had been approaching us with for a while now but we had no time for. They wanted their staff to know why their companies were busy funding water drilling irrespective of whether it was where they, the employees, lived or not. We asked that Sandrine be present everywhere we committed, so she was proof of the multi-faceted danger waiting to strike families because of the lack of healthy drinking water. We passed all donations from these events to her for her cosmetic surgery. Sometimes we delegated our public relations officer to represent us at these events. But only when we, ourselves, attended did we secure new contracts, which increased our chances of giving more people water and work. There, I understood the impact my partners' presence had.

But, unbeknown to us, undercover agents were keeping tabs on us. One of them would reveal this to us out of compassion and fear of seeing the good work to help people take their destiny into their own hands stop. He knew we had nothing to hide. We truly cared about the people, and it was bringing us supporters both seen and unseen. Our journey was just commencing.

8

SUCCESS STORIES

Water-carrying become School

We loved the east side of Kinshasa because of the success previously registered there. The land was low in altitude and knew little erosion. Despite being among the most poverty-stricken of the capital and water-denied, the population of the Tshangu District was notably hard-working. They remained exceptionally welcoming, especially to the non-nationals. Their opinion, however, was that foreigners were interested only in the downtown. Hence their appreciation for those who reached out to them.

Coming off the boulevard, we followed a wide sandy road until, some four kilometres on, the first car got stuck in the mud. The four-wheel-drive mode needed to be applied. Günter and I stepped out to engage the external traction knobs, but a helpful crowd had already surrounded both vehicles and beaten us to it. They trusted their strength more than Japanese engineering. They got us unstuck and asked for money. We laughed with them, then obliged.

Next on our road was a local market where those with stalls by the roadside waved in the customary amicable manner known of the Congolese. This was how they got vehicles to stop and look at what they offered. Amy and Laura asked for a brief stop. They were fond of the chubby tasty bananas, mangoes, oranges, pineapples, and other fruits the country produced and pretty much lived on these since we arrived. They were taking advantage of the low prices these sold at. It pained them that what was unsold was binned as it meant a loss of both profits and capital. They returned an hour later with baskets full and new acquaintances helping with the loads.

Among these was Clara, whom they had closely watched bringing down a heavy basin of water with the help of two ladies at a restaurant at the other end of the market. They instinctively inquired why she was not in school. Laura had hoped she would speak some French, but she spoke not even Lingala for others to facilitate communication. Therefore, they brought her to me in the direction opposite her water source, delaying her. They believed my Swahili would get her story out of her.

"This is my school, Papa!"

"Your school!" I exclaimed. "How old are you?"

"Twelve!"

"Then, how about classroom learning like all children your age?"

Amy and Laura asked to meet her parents, but she did not give us her address. Instead, she revealed where to find her mum, Beth. After which she disappeared into the market in a rush; she had wasted her valuable time talking to us. We doubted she had even taken us seriously about seeing her mother, and she likely thought we would not cross paths again.

But, five hours later, she appeared again, along a different road. She had difficulty walking with the weight on her head. This was because of the fear of spilling some of the water, which would have demanded more trips to fill up at her delivery point. There were signs of tiredness all over her—it was nearing the end of a day-long shift. She was on 400 litres daily, using this 40-litre basin. Arms stretched to the limit and sprung as wide as she could, she just managed to grip the container's edge.

This was her Monday to Saturday, covering three kilometres each way, each leg of the journey requiring 45 minutes, her day starting at five, while those her age attended school. Amy and Laura vowed to do something about it, saying else they would have failed their mission to the Congo. Hence, we called on Beth at the convent where she worked and arranged to go over to her house on Sunday. She was lucky to have one day off a week, a blessing many in a housekeeping job had not.

"Clara has known nothing but grief all her life," the mother told us, sobbing.

Theirs was a small dwelling. Amy and Laura yearned to be indoors to best understand this family's situation, and the drizzling rain's timely starting saved us from being seen as going too far. The room wherein we sat was everything— lounge, kitchen, storage, and more. Eight of us and them two crammed in there, knee-touching, left no room to move around. No table but two chairs. Luckily, there were enough yellow 25-litre jerrycans for us to sit on. Only one other equally sized chamber was in view. It was the bedroom.

Unfortunately, the complicity between the weather and us would cause Beth the embarrassment we had not anticipated: the roof let in drops that landed on our heads.

We adjusted ourselves a few times amid Beth's apologies. But Amy wrapped her up with her arms while Laura pressed Clara against her bosom. Alvin rushed out his camera to capture the moment.

"We are here for you," Amy reassured them. "Not what you have."

Nothing about this felt uncommon to either Themba or me. He was confident the love there displayed would help heal whatever hurt had been inflicted if they would give us a chance. He was referring to how his people gained some dignity when the world joined their fight to say no to Apartheid. What we heard that day was so painful that we wished someone was pulling our leg.

Nicolas was married to Beth, and they had three children: Jeff, Emma, and Robert. Together, they were a very happy family and loved each other to bits. He taught secondary school some 25 kilometres away. A colleague had offered to put him up to come home only at the weekend, but he preferred to come back to his family every night. Luckily, he had a bicycle he rode on a sandy road. Many walked it and often farther than him, so he never complained.

Beth was a midwife who had learnt the trade from her mum. She earned a living helping bring children into the world in five villages in a 56-kilometre radius area. She did this from the age of 14. These occupations afforded Beth and Nicolas a nicer house than most people in their village, although running water and electricity were unheard of there. Kids who were supposed to attend school from age six were delayed by a couple of years as the distance to be walked was some eight kilometres away, going through a forest and up and down a mountain.

A boat trip with children rowing themselves provided a shortcut to school but was not a good choice as bad weather resulted in disappearances. When lucky, bodies were discovered further down the river. The latter, at least, gave families the certainty of knowing what happened to their children and burying them with decency. Nevertheless, losing a loved one was very hard to take in. But, it was not only the river that killed.

One day, Nicolas had just returned from work and put his bicycle in the shed when two men stood in the doorway and ordered him to come with them. He only had time to ask why when they forced their way into the house. They pushed him from behind with their guns. He was powerless before weapons, especially in this region where murdering had become the language of force the previous five years. The only other thing he managed to utter was:

"*Maman*," he said to his wife, "I will be okay. Just look after the children and yourself. But, if anything...go with *Carlos* or *Clara*."

Beth was 27 weeks pregnant.

They quickly covered his mouth with a dirty scarf hastily coming off bushy hair that had possibly not seen water in who knows how long. She knew what he meant. Their rural life gave no means of telling whether it would be a boy or a girl. Jeff was seven; Emma five; Robert three; and the mother only 22. This was 1998 and at the peak of the war that savaged the eastern part of the Congo and escalated west. Nicolas' absence was hard to live with, and life never the same.

Five Becomes Two

The four of them were starting to come to grips with the reality of their fatherless home. It had taken seven years for his absence to sink in. But a boy, looking nothing more than nine, unknown to them, entered their front yard at the going down of the sun one day. He timidly advanced towards the door and asked Jeff and Robert to follow him. Not because he was unarmed that they told him to get lost, but because they had their hearts stitched together and were ready to die rather than surrender easily to bullying and recruitment into a rebellion group. It only took the recruiter a whistle to move to the next level.

Three impatient but ready-for-action adults emerged from the back of the already deserted hut across the road. They reiterated the order, which the boys again vehemently refused to execute. The intolerant, heartless leader commanded the other two to pull the trigger, and the brothers straightaway lay in a growing pool of blood with holes in their chests and their heads. Beth and the girls had not had the time to close their eyes, let alone look away. She knew what was coming the second that instruction was uttered.

The next minute, 12-year-old Emma was grabbed by the wrist and brutally taken away to compensate for failing to secure new recruits. She was made to carry an AK-47 on her head before even stepping out of the compound. The mother shielded her seven-year-old away, firmly covering her mouth with her adult's hand to avoid her calling for help, although no one would have come out. The village knew that interfering in a case like this meant dying in someone else's place. Clara herself, despite her age, had before seen someone pay with their life for trying to get involved—she was not stupid to make such a mistake.

The following morning, Clara, with no voice left to cry and tears having dried up, helped Beth lower the boys into the ground in their backyard. They had wrapped them in the jute bags that, until then, contained the little provisions of beans and rice that remained. Not surprising that the village was already half-empty. Whoever could find refuge elsewhere in the previous decade had not wasted time thinking things would improve. Therefore, it was only the two of them at the burial. The brothers' wrongdoing was being born male, a requisite criterion to be forced into a rebellion they knew not what it stood for nor supported. Their age counted not. Likewise, a girl was a sought-after prey for reasons surely obvious and not needing detailing here.

Jeff and Robert had broken a rule to be observed without question—they had undermined the assailants' powers. The kid who called on them needed not to have turned up with a rifle nor dressed head to toe in military uniform. The beret on his head, too big a size, gave him authority. No doubt his masters had snatched him from only God knows where, for no one straight in their mind could have let their child be on this errand. Turning up at Beth's, his only weapon was a stick still fresh and indicating that it had been cut off somewhere not too long before his arrival.

He had brought a couple of buggy army tops that he threw at the boys before opening his mouth, but they had landed on the floor as Jeff brushed them off. These child soldiers came with threats and the language geared to do the trick. Anyone in the region knew too well that wherever a *kadogo* (*little one* in Swahili but during these war years a *child-soldier*) appeared, there was always an adult bearing a loaded weapon out of sight, and most times undercover. Sending them in this manner was how they built them up. However, Beth's sons cared less at this point in their lives. Their dad's disappearance was getting them angrier the older they got.

The family resided in a small village, about 30 kilometres from Beni, a city that was compelled to live with atrocities and the ubiquitous raping of its females greater than registered malaria cases. Peaceful and promising sons and daughters of this area continued to be taken away from their loved ones or killed. They always had a permanent knot in their stomachs, going to bed unsure who would still be around in the morning. Daytime was even scarier and more restrictive as it was best to stay at home together in the hope that they would go as a bundle if death came. Going farming or drawing water was riskier. A week hardly went by without these ignoble acts being committed on children and adults, depending on whom the rebels desired.

The Cost of Water

Until then, Beth had managed to keep her girls safe, never allowing them to go fetching water because of her own experience of falling into the hands of bad men. She gambled going out to fulfil her midwifery responsibilities until insecurity deepened. She was made to pay for her courage and desire to serve others and provide for her family. Soon, she resorted to an allotment within a reasonable distance of her home when she was caught and abused day after day. But there, too, those determined to erase the female population from the face of this region still found her.

Unfortunately, there was no way to suppress the need for water in the household. Therefore, she did put her children before her safety. What she endured on the way to and from drawing water before and after her husband's abduction could make volumes of books. However, she could not tell even the tiniest part without stirring up the ever-fresh and unbearable pain that was hers. She had also found it worthless to keep informing Nicolas that "it happened again" whilst he was around or when speaking to him after he was already gone, as though present. Their communication took place in the corner of the compound, away from the children, late at night. When we heard a bit of what she had been through, saying that she had suffered too much was still an understatement.

She had nonetheless faced her challenges head-on, coming out in the open to the oppressors to bring water home. Life had become too stressful that she and Clara preferred not losing sight of each other. When she first took the road to the water source three days after the killing of her sons, neither of them was certain to see each other again. They had used the last drop the day before, so she had no choice. That day, she entertained committing suicide and would have done so while gone, had there been someone else to care for Clara and give her the chance to live into adulthood.

Clara always plunged into solitude, even in front of her mum. She could not get her siblings out of her head. Her situation deteriorated each time the mother went for water or food. Depression, over there, is referred to as a headache and expected to go away on its own. Her cure was, somehow, forcing it upon herself that Jeff and Robert were now free from the fear of being enrolled into rebellion by force anytime or being killed. However, it remained agonising not knowing where Emma was, let alone guessing what she could be going through that moment in time. Beth was no better herself, but knew how to conceal it to not further affect her daughter.

From as young as four, Clara had learnt that females were unsafe in the village and beyond. Mothers, Beth included, had come under the obligation to lecture their daughters about this rampant evil, ignoring the culture that had long prohibited them from holding a sex education conversation with their children, regardless of the latter's age. Only at puberty was an extended family member or a trusted person from the community appointed to deliver the truth of what was going on with their body. This tradition weighed less in the face of a reality as harsh as that which besieged them. To conserve the respect due to them, females revealed not that they were raped, not even to each other, because of shame. Not being discreet saw their spouses no longer come near them, and if unmarried, chances of being taken to wife dimmed. Males' pride and customs there supersede the fact that the victim was not at fault.

The last nail in the coffin was when Beth returned home the day before with no water but in tears, because *it had happened again.* The writing on the wall was becoming thicker. She feared her daughter to be next. Hence, three weeks after losing her children, she told Clara they would visit a relative in Beni. The youngster was not at ease with the journey because of what she had heard of the town (*the capital of rape* was what the *International Community* called it, mocking our women's suffering rather than siding with us). True, their destination was not favourable to women, but neither was the place they were about to turn their back on.

She suggested to her mother to go to Kinshasa instead, despite not having any knowledge of where that was from where they stood, nor what it would take to get there. Beth did not want to put her off, saying they had no money for such a trip and that it was over 2,300 kilometres away, which would require an eternity on foot, especially at a seven-year-old's pace. But rather, she smiled, fighting back tears, and said that, "Maybe one day."

"I do not want to come back here," Clara insisted at being denied taking all her clothes with her.

A Shared Dream

At that point, Clara vividly remembered the dream she had had the night before and announced it to her mum: she had seen her dad even though she only knew him through a couple of pictures that were in the house. He was with Jeff and Robert and had instructed her to ask her mother to take her to Kinshasa. She, too, had had a similar dream that same night but withheld it from her, and instead, she just wept. That instant, she believed her daughter's future to be in the capital.

Beth looked in the corner where she kept provisions, and there was enough only for two more days. No water! Grounded by the fear of falling one more time to the aggressors she now imagined everywhere, she thought it best to surrender on her way into exile (in her own country) than succumb in her backyard. Even dying of want was better happening elsewhere.

They took off with only what they had on, leaving behind whatever little possessions they could have carried on their heads. They did not want the fewer still resisting village population to know they were throwing in the towel. They took the road, their hearts in their mouths, ready to meet those they were fleeing from halfway, should falling be all that was prescribed for them. It was a mentally arduous journey that seemed longer than it was, and so physically tough for the daughter that she ended up on her mum's back most of the road.

Once in Beni, they first asked for food and a floor patch at the priests' and got neither. They went next door to the nuns, changing their tactic, offering domestic service before asking for room, and got both. Beth, it turned out, was an excellent cook, unknown even to herself. She impressed and got better every day, coming up with various new recipes. She had no more condiments than what she had always had back home or what everyone else had at the convent.

Her secret was not thinking beforehand of what she would do but just mixing up the ingredients, accidentally producing tastes that wowed both the nuns and their visitors. Soon, she began to write down how she made every meal, so she could reproduce it when asked for the same. The nuns set up a restaurant when they realised that Beth could make them money. Her cuisine brought in more revenue than the beers they had been selling. News travelled to the point that those working in proximity started lunching there. Soon the place was refusing people due to limited seating, leading to a takeaway service, a practice not new to the Congolese.

Beth also did laundry by hand as there was no washing machine there. Good for her that she had never heard of one before. Together with ironing, to the immense satisfaction of the nuns, saw her being required next door where the priests, who had previously rejected her, knew not that honey was better past the entrance to the hive. They had certainly turned her away based on her appearance. The fact that she also had a child with her had given the impression of a beggar. But whatever had crossed the priests' mind so as not to even give her a trial was no longer important; Beth had taken the chance presented to her and proved that it is bad to judge a book by its cover.

As a result, she gave the priests only what was left of her time, although not limiting herself to working only in daylight as the notion of unsociable hours was not part of her vocabulary.

At this point, Beth wanted her daughter to be able to withstand the hardship of life should anything happen to her. Therefore, she trained her up and left the mopping of the floor to her. Clara had no choice but straightaway to be of help. She cheerfully took responsibility and worked all day long, humming like her mum. The clergy watched in admiration, while the child labour taking place on their premises meant nothing to them. The nuns and priests paid them enough to get north to Mambasa when a vehicle with room passed their way. There, they used the same approach as in Beni to obtain sustenance.

Seven months after leaving their village, Beth and Clara were in Kisangani, a much larger city. They easily got hired to fetch water for relatively rich families, a job many locals avoided taking up due to pride and the resulting aching. But the monastery and the convent remained their main places of work to not disappoint Beni's and Mambasa's clergies who had recommended them.

Well, 18 months of hard work later, they found themselves with $1,200 in savings. This was enough for a one-way flight to Kinshasa at $350 each, and ID cards, vaccinations (as though going abroad), airport taxes at $50 each, and $400 for rent. Beth hoped to find work upon arrival. She did not want to have to worry about food once there. They had never starved again since they were allowed at the nuns' in Beni. Therefore, she did not want to let go of the comfort now discovered.

But Clara, suddenly revealing her fear of flying, asked if the journey could be made another way. Travelling on the Congo River at $25 each was considered. The cost of paperwork and getting someone to secure them a place on the boat required an equal amount. The mother had always been frugal, but she discussed the expenditure with her daughter, despite her not being even 10 years of age yet. She was taking this opportunity to teach her to budget. For her, they were partners in that they had earned this cash together.

Kisangani was gracious to them. They were never short of referrals and offers. However, it still posed a threat because, a few years prior, this was a battlefield to two African countries—Rwanda and Uganda—fighting over the control of the province's abundant mineral resources. The peace experienced was precarious and not promising to get better. Acquainted with unrest, they could tell they were yet far from safety. But Clara was enjoying making friends. These came to her at the monastery for a game of netball, and she, too, went to theirs. She had discovered what it was like being a child and started talking less about getting to Kinshasa. Nevertheless, the mother was not relinquishing her grip on Nicolas' instructions.

Hence, taking travel agents literally, they made the mistake of coming off work early. They purchased tickets two days before the announced departure date, unaware that no one did so until the anchor was at the harbour. They said goodbye to their employers at the end of what was to them their last shift. They, too, wished them well, some giving them clothes and food for the journey. However, the boat from the capital would get delayed by two months because of breaking down several times on its way to them. No one had cared to tell the waiting crowd all this time.

Every night, all passengers were told to be ready in the morning, saying the boat would turn around and head back upon arrival. But no one could see all the merchandise waiting to be loaded taking less than two days with the lifting done manually. Nonetheless, mother and daughter, too, were on their feet. The delay made them homeless. They had to start buying food with some of the money they had vowed to spend only in Kinshasa. Where they used to work would not have them back. So, Beth went into town looking for work while Clara remained glued to the spot to keep an eye on their possessions.

Having secured a new place to supply water to, she reconsidered bringing in Clara to earn more while they could. This required trusting someone with their belongings. A young couple appealed to them. They had become acquainted while waiting for the boat together. Sadly, all they needed was some space to disappear with everything. Enquiring around, something Beth had not thought of doing previously, revealed that these were not travellers but merchants. They had been spending days and nights at the port to get hold of incoming manufactured goods and resell them on the quay to fellow traders not prepared to sleep outside. Luckily, Beth had been carrying all the money with her wherever she went.

What they made on this new job was not enough for more than a meal. The only way to make more was to be gone from dawn to dusk. It was a long distance between the source of water and their delivery point and then to the port, where they continued to sleep rough. They could not go on like this after two months. Many passengers had booked themselves on other boats and gone. However, doing so meant losing the fares they had already paid for the boat that was yet to show up. With money so tight, they could not afford to spend any they had saved.

Sailing Off

Beth survived the panic over thinking of losing the money in her handbag to thieving that was prevalent in and all around the port. When the boat finally docked, they sadly found themselves battling to find room onboard due to over-booking. They were asked to wait for the same to come back, *maybe in six months this time*. At this, Clara broke. Her mum struggled to hold back her own tears. Therefore, they put themselves on the next boat available a week later.

A journey said to take seven days turned into four months because of stopping pretty much along every town and village. They spent days in some places and weeks in others, letting people off and taking more with their merchandise despite having left Kisangani full. Everyone aimed to earn more selling in Kinshasa, so the captain had a good reason to leave no one behind. Breaking down was as frequent as jamming on the numerous sand isles not visible to the naked eye, this being the dry season. Hitting carcases of sunken ships and other obstacles was recurrent, as the boat was not equipped with navigation gadgets and the river had not been dredged.

Travelling in this manner, though saving money, came at a cost as all that time, illnesses, deaths, stealing, and other dreadful events occurred. Contagious bugs almost decimated everyone a couple of times. However, when they passed, survivors resumed keeping merry, drinking, eating, celebrating birthdays, new births, and witnessing weddings. Churches also formed, with converts taking care of the improvised preachers. People sold and bought in a market set up to rip off others of the little they had.

Men travelling without their families became too friendly with Beth, as they did with other women; single or married, it mattered not. In the Congo, dating, cohabiting, being engaged, and marriage, all has the same meaning. Even answering to flirting with a smile to be polite is considered agreeable to a husband-and-wife relationship. Beth was *lucky* in that she received eight proposals, despite her admirers knowing no more than her name and that with her was her daughter.

"I wished they could have had a bit of sympathy," said Beth. "But how could I blame them? They were not aware of what I had been through in my life. Nonetheless, the last thing I wanted was a man nagging me in the name of how they felt about me."

Advice Seeking

Not knowing anybody in Kinshasa, Beth asked fellow passengers that had become like family what she should do. They recommended that she and Clara come off with them at Maluku, the port before the end of the line. This is the farthest commune east of the capital and 70 kilometres from the Kingabwa Terminal. Its semi-rural nature offered a cheaper cost of living. However, the captain decided to go past this scheduled and in-demand stop, upsetting more than half of the travellers who, in response, proffered verbal abuse in his direction, more than Clara had ever heard, to the point that Beth could not look at her until they had calmed down.

Funnily enough, eight kilometres to Kingabwa, the boat stood still in the middle of the river for two long days, making passengers more furious. This time, word that there was no access to the dock was received. Hundreds of ships were disorderly parked while loading and unloading took place on humans' backs and heads, cutting through several other barges to get onboard or on land. Those at the quay made money daily, even when their vessels were broken down or were never to run again. They paid less monthly to the authority and earned more serving as footbridges. The captain had in this an excuse to pretend to be saving his passengers money.

Many canoes approached the boat as soon as people saw it to sell food and water to the hungry and dehydrated onboard. They had run out for days already, and those coming to their rescue knew it. The river water was dangerous to drink. Those who gave the impression of being immune were nonetheless not without knowing of the consequences to follow, often not much later.

There was a fee to come near the boat. Some travellers, in turn, sold at a premium as buyers climbed in to get hold of dried fish, bush meat, palm oil, and other products ahead of their competitors. Amid all this havoc, it became hard to tell who was winning and who was losing. This is how the Congo works. Beth wished life had not taken her out of her village where humanity and mutual respect once were the norms.

The way she recounted these proceedings led to think of the captain as getting rich cunningly. But the money received helped to pay a boat owner at the dock to use his position for a few days. The real solution to this problem was to create additional ports and give the government more income. The authority not tapping into this opportunity, independent operators started to open private ports all along the river. These were not authorised to welcome the public, but no one cared. Sheer demand made people do things as they pleased. Besides, it was quick and less hassle to deal there than at Kingabwa, where police officers fed themselves out of the poor travellers.

The only difficulty at these ports was that the berth was never deep enough for mid-sized boats. Additionally, when the inspectors turned up, they fined not the port owners or the vessel captains. Now that was unheard of that the service provider went unpunished, but we would find out later that the regulators, the port owners, and the captains were all one band. Passengers were just victims who paid these fines to get their goods and themselves off the boats. Finding something that works without causing a headache in the Congo is rare, but this is how the locals become resilient enough to face life's challenges when no other nation would have survived.

In Town

Coming off the boat, Beth and Clara lost sight of those with whom they were supposed to stick. This was due to the mayhem that suddenly happened to get cargo off the barges. So, they headed into the Kingabwa suburb, asking for a place to rent. Their poor Lingala got them fewer responses, none of which were helpful. Kinshasa natives look down on their outsider compatriots. They derogatorily call them *movila* (villager) or *mowuta* (newcomer).

A budget hotel was not inexpensive to them, especially with the uncertainty ahead, and, mind me, it would have been Beth's first time setting foot in a hotel to ask. Good that she did not dare, else she would have been ripped off. So, they stayed three nights at the port, with hundreds of other travellers waiting to depart to the Bandundu, Equateur, or Kasai, all forming *a Kingabwa* of their own. It was to them two a repeat of their situation at the Kisangani port.

Help came from one who took them where to get transportation towards Maluku. Going south instead, her mission ended with getting them on the right bus. Five minutes on, the mother confided herself again to someone she sat next to. This one counselled her to stay clear of anything west of the Ndjili river, just as she had heard before, and, where possible, to even go beyond the airport to make her money last.

Her advisor's destination was Mpasa, and Beth did not need to be persuaded to come with her. She made room for them in her modest dwelling and provided them with food for a week, both free of charge, while helping them find a place of their own. This was without rushing them, to avoid them forking out more than they should. They were glad to have talked to her because of the affordable rent there and the produce from the nearby farms. Mpasa being the beginning of the city, supplies out of the Bandundu further helped their tight budget hold up well.

Having landed with a little over $900 afforded them a six-month agreement tenancy, at $50 a month for nothing with which to impress anyone. They also paid a $300 deposit. However, they struggled to understand why it was equal to the advance payment, unaware that every landlord in the capital made their own rules. Nevertheless, they had

$300 left. This was a huge sum for the commune they had come to, irrespective of whether one had a job. The two of them could get by with this money for six months. They counted themselves lucky for this and when thinking they could have been dead by now had they remained rooted out east.

Contrast

The city welcomed Beth and Clara to a stark contrast. Fetching water was safer, in their opinion, reasonably distant, and most importantly, no travelling through the woods. No need to accompany girls to and from the sources of water. It was shocking, however, that people in this suburb carried water to put food on the table, given that the capital was sold to them as where everyone had it easy. They had to resign from their plan to provide cooking and housekeeping services. No family in this area could afford their skills, no matter how little they tried to charge. Having no other options made it simple for them to go with the flow.

Many laughed at Beth's claim of being a midwife because of her inability to write, read, or speak French. Being literate in Swahili counted not. The truth about her ability to deliver babies was now held only by her, and that alone sufficed for her to believe she could acquire other useful skills in the future; so, she remained confident. Her attitude was that the capital belonged to everyone and gave all a chance, although not an equal one. Therefore, she let go of midwifery, for no hospital could take her on without being licensed, even if someone could endorse her.

High rates of unemployment forced even men to settle for water delivery. As a *movila,* she was paid less than the locals who could negotiate. Holding down a customer was also hard at the beginning. Bosses spoke very fast and liked not to repeat themselves. Out of fear of being yelled at, she pretended to grasp what she was told. Hence, she got fired at least twice every week, during her first month, for no other reason than getting the instructions wrong.

Being out of work repeatedly and not letting their savings run low saw Clara lend a hand. She had more chances to find a job and keep it longer than her mum out of pity for a kid. At nine, she picked up the language naturally, and integration ensued. She was the sole provider each time Beth was out of work. The latter gave us these details in her defence as to why Clara, now 12 and having lived in Kinshasa close to two and half years, was yet to enrol in school—this being what had brought us to them.

Lethal

Sure, they were grateful for getting paid, but water remained a weapon in Beth's mind because of how going after it had turned against her out east. It kept bringing back the bad memories of how unthoughtful men harmed girls and women on their way to and from fetching water. Kinshasa had put a smile on her face but never dried up her tears. She tried her best not to sadden her daughter anymore. For that, she often cried out of her sight because she had vowed to help her get the best out of the new society in which she was now growing up. Clara, too, wished she did not have to be on water duty for the same reasons as her mother.

"This used to be a peaceful country," she said like someone much older would. "Then an international conspiracy was imposed on us, executed by our fellow Africans, costing more lives than what is reported."

At first, we thought it was the usual tagline played on us until her narration deepened. Each one of us was on the brink of tears. Given her age, she could not have come up with such a poignant account unless it was part of her. Losing family members and being forced to run from violence had left her bleeding. The fight going on inside her made it difficult to enjoy life. We asked her to put the past behind her. But what *past* does a child have? We just did not know how else to word it.

"Bringing water home was lethal to us females," she carried on relating. "Our males were killed protecting us."

She pleaded for many but to those with no say over how the *world* is governed. We could have listened to her for hours, but as heart-breaking as what we already knew to be true was, we tried to divert the conversation into something less pinching.

Beth told us of how, even before her teenage years, she journeyed in the bush to bath in the river, birds over her head singing along with her, alone and unworried. If a male happened to be coming down, he would call out from a distance, out of sight, to see whether there was any female down there and if it was appropriate for him to attend. Where a woman was bathing, she would answer with a warning to hold on and proceed only when she would say so. That alone summed up how a male revered a female. It was a tradition observed not only in the villages. There, the woman in question would not be touched nor made to feel threatened.

"Gladly, some still hold fast to these values," she said. "Those that stray are manipulated."

However, what she said was not the world Clara identified herself with. Her upbringing constantly reminded her to trust nobody, which was hard to demand of a child.

Trampoline

Kinshasa offered children the freedom to do what they liked, leading at times to bad choices that later proved hard to correct. Beth instead picked up where she left off in Kisangani. She did not surrender her parental role of instilling in her daughter the values with which herself grew up. This is because she was aware of the evil found back east not being limited only to a war zone. But she struggled seeing other people's children turning up for school where she worked and not hers. The nun in charge had said there was no room for Clara, whereas working at the convent entitled her daughter to a place. The reason given was that she had come mid-year. However, even the passing of one pupil a month into the new school year still earned her no enrolment.

Sadly, each attempt was made with Clara present. Her mum thought that her looking the administrators in the eyes would soften their hearts. But they addressed her directly as though she was an adult and with no feelings that could get hurt. No diplomacy whatsoever! They justified their denial by how attending with six-year-olds would not make a pleasant learning environment. They worried that her juniors would be distracted by her age. All of which made her sob right there, but still unmoved they were.

"At least I know why," Clara said. "It has helped me stop dreaming of school and concentrate on water as best as I can. Who knows where it will lead?"

As much as it was hard hearing of her grieving, the real problem was that she had never attended school. At the same time, was it bad that she was shielded, or was it best to privilege school at all costs? Who on earth would not have protected their daughter like Beth had in the name of formal education?

"We took interest in you because of the water you had on your head," said Amy. "We saw you carrying your weight the best you could."

Clara was only one of the many of her generation back in her village and most parts of the three north-eastern provinces of the Congo to have not tasted of education, this, because of the violence towards females that was going around and had already lasted too long. Hence a high level of illiteracy will weigh on the country for many decades to come. Truly demoralising sitting with a 12-year-old who could not write or read her name, as we found out when Laura handed her a piece of paper and a pen. Yet she was eloquent and to the point whenever she opened her mouth. She needed no help structuring her sentences. The only downfall in sharing her thoughts was that my interpretation was not equal to it.

Her boldness was proof of one with no fear for the life ahead. She considered not herself lesser than those in school, although making it known that she carried a wound that bled every time she saw others in school uniform. But, she believed that fetching water for people was her trampoline to somewhere better. It made us wonder what she was seeing that we could not see for her.

"God has not yet said His last word about me," she said.

For the time being, Clara kept busy, unlike many adults who complained about pretty much everything. She carried out her tasks effectively and with a smile; many wanted her to work for them. Earning the equivalent of $5 a day for eight to 10 hours was a magnificent thing. This was more than what she made in Kisangani, the city she jokingly said to have provided her with the necessary training in preparation for what she was now accomplishing.

Rescue

Günter told his wife, Anna, of Clara that night, and she decided that he should not return to Munich until she was in school. This was extremely difficult to achieve seeing the shortage in school numbers, coupled with her entry-level. However, rather than limiting ourselves to these obstacles, we added to our eventful schedule the task of shopping around. Nothing came up as her age had increased since the first time she was rejected. No one we approached wanted to know.

Anna was having none of it. She was tormented by the horrible feeling of having a girl going through life without formal education in this modern-day. On our end, the reality was a mould we knew not how to break. A female missing out on this front was a non-event to anyone in this culture, especially where a poor family was concerned. We tried hard to break what we were facing into pieces, but it was not just sitting well with Anna. We wished she was present to see herself what she was asking of us. Fortunately, every night was a good time for us, in our beds, to ponder new ways to overcome this challenge.

Sharing thoughts at breakfast, we realised that we had become too reliant on ourselves. We now believed we were sufficiently acquainted with the area and the culture. Therefore, we no longer wanted to bother those who had helped us on other occasions. But it was necessary to put our pride aside one more time. So, we went back to Jacques, who was now a friend. He had been checking on us from time to time and twice had fed us at a posh restaurant way out of his area, spending more than he would have for himself. He and Laura had kept a live wire about his school expansion plans. Therefore, he brought along his budget needs.

His figures were exquisite, but nothing in writing. It was all recited to Laura and came out effortlessly. To him, it was just a normal conversation between friends. She took notes, however, struggling to buy into it because there was no business plan to refer to later. Her doubts were due to seeing it all through the lens of a twice Uni graduate with years of business and investment experience. Also, having formed partnerships involving big sums across the globe rendered any participation in this proposal pointless.

Jacques humbly confessed that his education included none of the diagrams, graphs, compelling write-up, and more that Laura was seeking. He offered to hire someone to conform if it would help because he had never seen, let alone produced, such a document, especially with her asking him to keep it between 40 and 50 pages. Upon hearing so, she agreed to fill in any gaps in his story instead of letting someone else manipulate his thoughts and inadvertently distort his vision which, as narrated, she deemed flawless. It was not her habit to let a third party influence her qualifying as a potential partner.

It turned out that Jacques had a waiting list of unemployed teachers he could make happy with a job offer. He also had a huge number of kids hoping for a place. But Laura was first going to check with her office back in Cali, although the investment could come out of her pocket and not necessarily her corporation. However, Clara being the focal point, he suggested hiring two of these teachers to educate her at home, on a one-on-one basis, to make up for the lost ground.

Very pleased with his forward-thinking, Anna committed. Instead of $100 monthly to each teacher, she offered to send $3,000, so there was no worry about keeping her student taught over the next 10 months. This way, schoolbooks were also covered. Clara would have lessons in the morning while drawing water in the afternoon, for we thought it best not to brutally alter who she was. Also, we did not want to strip her of the financial freedom she had developed. But rather than spending all that money on her alone, Amy offered to meet Anna halfway if she agreed to let in four additional kids in the same situation.

The configuration was complete within five hours of Jacques putting out a board outside his school. This was due to the steep number of children waiting. Too many parents came sprinting, but neither of the duo was flexible. They feared drifting away from what they had in mind. They wanted a class small enough for the girls to benefit greatly.

Coming timely was Laura creeping in, paying for the class to move to the priests' events hall that was not used until five o'clock in the afternoon during the week. Jacques' licence covered this arrangement as an extension of his school; however, not without the usual complications of getting approvals from the authorities.

Breaking the Mould

Amy, Anna, and Laura were set to confront the cultural ideology that limited a girl to being groomed to become a wife, keep the house in order, and rear children, at the expense of education and employment. Even before their involvement, Clara was curious as to why her upbringing had to differ from that of a boy, even away from the village. But wondering was as far as she went. She knew that people praising her for being very helpful to her mum was in keeping with this tradition, so she always responded with a smile to be polite. She hid her longing for school well, putting on a beatific countenance to avoid it being taken that she appreciated not the opportunity given to her to earn money; else, she would have seen herself no longer getting work.

It surprised her not when most she drew water for came across as unsupportive of her new schedule. But, having discovered what it was like to be a pupil, there was no looking back. She replaced her income shortfall with the increasing joy emanating from her new pursuit in life and the intellectual brilliance coming to light about her. Congratulatory messages stimulated more performance. These were from the teachers and Jacques who followed the development closely—to the point of sitting in the classroom occasionally.

Clara wanted her new status made public by wearing a uniform. Therefore, she approached Jacques with the subject after her teachers had said no. He was not in favour at first either but gave in when she followed up with the argument that it would boost their morale. The proof was in the pudding: their grades, although already good, got better. She aimed to prove to those who knew her that she was now in school. Compliments of how pretty she looked in that attire were just appearance, whereas she hoped they would mention how good it was for her to be in education. Nevertheless, she was not ready to be run down. For once, she was full of hope for the future.

Talking of outlook, she radiated positivity all day long, even with water on her head and despite her bare feet burning in the hot sand. This was all down to the confidence that her situation was now about to be transformed. She was, nonetheless, aware of the need to keep doing this, for the time being, so she could put food on the table and have a roof over her head. Her change in fortune made her more conscious of others her age and younger, with no one to pull them out to safety. She believed many to be smarter than her—a great sign of humility learnt early in life. She saw them whenever she had her uniform on, with water on their heads, and she hurt.

"I dream of rooting up for children when I grow up," she told us. "To pay back, that is."

"Very unselfish of you, young lady," Amy whispered as though Clara understood English.

Anna heard of what she projected and sent a postcard for us to relay.

"Clara, every day is an opportunity to work towards your dream."

She hung it up in the lounge. She read it every morning before going out, and before bed. Hence, each time, she felt like getting closer to her goal when it was but a child's wish expressed without ample details of what it required. It was nonetheless exciting thinking of a future different from the calamity she had known. This was why she worked hard on her education.

Little by little, her special group was introduced to the mainstream class of their age for civic education, geography, history, physical education, and other general knowledge lessons. Despite no vacant seating in the classroom, all therein still welcomed them. They were briefed in advance of their situation. Therefore, everyone offered to have them at their desk, in three rather than in two they were used to. Thus, being spoiled with choices, they moved places daily to keep everyone happy and show gratitude to all for facilitating their integration.

The many friends Clara made at school filled in the gap in her life. They were all to her like her own sisters, this being a girls-only institution. But all of them combined still made not up for the void Emma had left in her life. It pained her that she did not have her mum's permission to share her sister's story with anyone. Beth feared Clara becoming ostracised. It was also intended to help put this ignoble situation behind them, though difficult, no matter how hard they tried. The future was on their mind, and so was the reminder of what led to them coming west.

"Everyone here also has their fair share of problems," Beth often said to Clara. "Had we known this beforehand, I doubt we would have brought ourselves to safety."

That was in reference to how children were more disobedient to their parents than back in their village. Drunkenness, the use of illegal drugs, knife-related crimes, corruption, unemployment, and traffic jams causing parents to be away from their families all day long were just a few of what people dealt with day and night, and it drove her nuts. Her consolation was that her daughter was still young to know all the negative aspects of the society that had become theirs.

"Take not your eyes off the ball no matter what," Beth always said, referring to schoolwork.

Misuse

Stella, Jan's wife, back in Switzerland, worked for an international NGO that catered to girls and women worldwide through partners in the recipients' countries. They provided access to medical treatment, emotional therapy, teenage pregnancy prevention, promoted family planning, and more. Therefore, she asked that we visit their corresponding organisations in Kinshasa, register Beth and Clara, and pass their case numbers to her.

She wanted to secure funding for the children who had lost a parent or both. This assistance was limited to a selected area of the city so that the impact could be visible. Clara's commune ticked all the boxes because of the many orphans living on the street and just outside the two barracks there. Their fathers had perished in war, so they were kicked out, but they refused to leave the place they called home. They had chosen to shame the authorities with their presence. Some of these victims were babies in their mothers' arms.

Our contacts would be an eye-opener into how these NGOs functioned. The beneficiaries received very little if anything at all. A couple of these organisations had over $10 million coming to them annually to change lives. Their accounts for the previous five years revealed that this sum was always used up. Sadly, their main expenditures were huge salaries, luxury housing, new cars every two years, and air-conditioned offices. Even work laptops with a good

Internet connection were used for socialising and entertainment during working hours.

They thrived only at cementing the beneficiaries' dependency on donations. The same individuals had been on their books for years, with delivery partners doing all they could to show that the fictitious victims needed treatment and were far from recovering from their problems.

Irritated by our curiosity, these representatives counter-attacked rather than simply dismissing us. They pointed out that we were at fault for leaving Clara to work part-time. They viewed us as partners in crime with those who paid her to furnish them with water. We explained that teens elsewhere babysat or did other light chores for pocket money. We would have wanted to see her do the same had there been a market for such. But we had no doubt we had created her the balance needed to slowly get on track. A sudden change in her routines could have been nothing short of a treatment badly administered.

Another NGO blamed us for helping only five kids when we could have taken up at least 10 times that number with the same investment. But our approach was still better than their building of a large school in an isolated rural community with only 16 households. They had expected over 800 children from multiple scattered villages to walk some 30 kilometres to attend.

That was where we left our intellectual conflict at, them having found a scapegoat to not support Clara with the sponsorship Stella could not directly get to us. A copy of the communication addressed to her headquarters outlining the Congolese side's rejection read that "Clara was earning money". This was their local policy, but not of a concern at the source of funding. Gladly, we depended not on either of these parties to keep her moving forward.

Jacques' teachers were doing a good job for *our* five. Their first year covered only calculus and learning to write and read their own vocabularies, which they had picked up quickly and surprisingly only with the challenges any new starter would have had. They had come on the course already familiar with counting money, and Lingala, as spoken in Kinshasa, being full of French words, came in handy. The following year was structured to match the first year of secondary school, however focusing on Arithmetic and pushing up French, with Geography and History taught in a storytelling fashion. With that, their world was widening and becoming exciting.

Thanks to the intensity of the programme, they spoke fluent French by the end of year three. This was achieved with Stella chipping in two additional teachers to compensate for her disappointment about getting them the funding she had in mind. She also sent over computers and reading materials donated by schools on her end. It did help a great deal with conversational French, demanding of the girls two extra hours every afternoon, consequently further shrinking Clara's water business. At 15, they joined their peers full-time as sophomores, beaming confidently and showing no sign of coming from behind. They were, in fact, ahead in many ways. They understood the course materials and completed their assignments without supervision.

Doppelgangers

Year five saw Clara move to a different site, joining Jacques' newly formed vocational nursing school, which Laura had funded to give as many girls as possible a chance for a career. She was two weeks late coming due to picking up malaria. The seat reserved for her was next to Julie, to whom she bore an uncanny resemblance. Inattention persisted in the classroom from that moment onwards as students failed to take their eyes off these two for long. The teacher was forced to pause to help everyone's curiosity, his own included.

"Are you related?"

They were nothing short of identical twins. Therefore, no one believed them when they shrugged their shoulders. They got called to the front, and, with school uniforms, they were different only in hairstyle. The teacher made four students close their eyes and asked the girls to speak, taking turns, and each time their colleagues guessed wrong who had just spoken, for by now, it was no longer possible to tell that Clara was a *mowuta*. Only their records dispelled the possibility of them being twins. Julie was three months older than Clara.

They took it to their parents, who saw no point in following up.

"Humans, we each have someone in the world who looks like us," Beth said. "And, I know not of mine or your dad's relative living here. Must be pure coincidence."

Then came the end of the school year. Each student was invited to come forward with their parents to collect their results when called. Clara was top of the class, and Beth, insecure still in front of the crowds, timidly walked up with her. Julie's dad was in the audience. His and Beth's eyes met with her and her daughter turning back to acknowledge the applauses given to Clara. While his wife covered her mouth with her hand to contain herself, he and Beth instantly and vividly recalled a past they never wished to relive.

Beth moved not an inch. Her eyes remained on Bernard way past the clapping. Clara tried to pull her, to help the principal who had twice politely asked her to return to her seat, to no avail. He, therefore, called for another round of applause, assuming she was emotionally overcome by the 93% her daughter had achieved. But she fainted! She was rushed to the closest medical centre, on someone's back, there being no ambulance or anyone driving. Thanks to the nurses on duty, she went home the next day.

The girls' paths did not cross over the summer. Twelve kilometres separated them. Their senior year would see them graduate as assistant nurses. It was geared to keep them less in the classroom and more training in hospitals. Parents were obligated to meet with staff at the beginning of the final year. Beth was determined to face Bernard, but he was a no-show. Esther had asked him to let her handle the matter in a gentlewomanly manner.

"Is she mine?" was how she approached Beth after the meeting.

They both broke.

"Do not worry!" Esther said, now with her arms around Beth.

This only caused more streams of tears out of them both. They found a place under a large tree a couple of hundred metres away from the school.

"My husband would not harm anyone," said she. "Let me tell you about him."

The Cause

Bernard was an astute student who left his village out west and worked hard selling anything he could find to pay for Uni until he graduated with two civil engineering degrees. He had a job with a company everyone envied, a car, a house, and other benefits. He met and got married to Esther. Everything was what he had dreamt of, and he was really thriving. Three years later, an even bigger opportunity took him to another level. Off east he went as a director over a project to last not less than half a decade.

For that, he would have to relocate his family. He preceded her to prepare for her coming in four months. She had just told him that she was a month pregnant with their number one and would not entertain the idea of giving birth without him present.

He hardly stayed in one place in his new assignment, as he had a small window to familiarise himself with every district manager and the vast area under his jurisdiction. He travelled many kilometres daily with an assistant and a driver. One day, they fell into a trap laid by the rebels who had spotted them in towns and villages he was soon to link up with telephone masts. They made them carry supplies on their heads and draw water from rivers under secure escort. Their vehicle became the chief rebel's.

A week later, they were separated into three groups, going in different directions. Bernard's headed south. It was there that his battalion would meet a lady with water. Her speed was short of any escape. With the first person grabbing her while the others waited, she let out that she had the killing disease. Sadly, it was a known trick; an attempt to put these evil men off. This was because many had resolved to die of a knife or a bullet rather than live with remorse, as they most of the time killed whoever played this game on them. But her fate would be different. The aggressors chose to let her go die away from them but not alone.

Bernard got placed on the altar out of anger. Any resistance would have been met with a gunshot. Preferring not to succumb to the latter, he did as instructed, hoping for heavenly intervention when he would be infected. Until then, he had yet some time of servitude ahead of him. He cooked, did laundry, and more for his capturers. They taught him how to fire a gun but never gave him his own—they did not have enough even for themselves. Two months later, they trusted him to go fetch water some 700 metres down the hill, believing they had a clear view of the valley from where they camped. But he knew he would not have another chance.

He followed the river until he came to a bend, where it narrowed down and made crossing nothing for someone who grew up bathing in the Atlantic. By then, he had already heard being called exasperatedly and three bullets crackling to force a change of mind. He needed no one to tell him which outcome returning or being apprehended would have. Therefore, he ran non-stop, without knowing where he was headed or where exactly he was. The sunset made it impossible to place the four cardinal points.

He kept going for as long as his brain functioned, paying no attention to how tired he felt. He had the impression of riding on the back of an invisible horse. The wet clothes dried on, thanks to the warmth running generated. At dawn, he would realise he had been heading south-westwards, whereas he had hoped to be going towards the Ugandan border to seek refuge. At least, he could now come back on himself south-eastwards to reach Butembo, which was part of his work area.

There, he found out about his replacement—a man he had worked with in Kinshasa. The local manager refused to give him a lift to what he still considered his office and housing in Goma. A message from the capital confirmed his dismissal, and he was being sued for misconduct, embezzlement of the company's funds, and misappropriation of the vehicle. They were not interested in hearing his side of the story.

Next was phoning his family with the help of someone off the street, those once his subordinates having turned him their backs to the point of not allowing him even a two-minute call from their handsets. Hearing his voice was a relief for Esther, but she was furious at the same time. When she finally gave him a moment, she just asked him to wait for the instructions to pick up the money she was going to wire through a money transfer network. This was all that was left in the savings. He caught land transportation to Goma and was in Kinshasa within a week, thanks to the frequency of cargo flights between the two cities.

* * *

"Do not come near me," he said when she tried to join him on the couch that night.

First thing in the morning, she took him to be tested. He rejected the negative results given. By this time, he was already conditioned beyond belief by the statement of the woman out east. He attended four times in two months just to be told the same. Then, he returned to his employer but was not even allowed past the gatekeeper. Fortunately, a friend in the government got him hired.

"Which one of us do you blame?" Beth asked.

Nicolas had also not been near her in the three years preceding Clara's birth when she first fell victim four months after giving birth to their third child. This explained why the gap between them was longer than the two-year pattern established in adding to their family, like most couples they knew. What happened between Beth and Bernard was only one of the many times she had suffered at the hands of the assailants. More than once, it was up to a dozen men lined up. When it first occurred, she begged them to kill her, rather than becoming worthless in her husband's eyes and all who could find out.

But even coming to Kisangani, she never bothered to take the test. She preferred the virus to take her away in its own due time if she ever was infected. She was one of too many females who feared being served with the bad news.

Taking No Chance

"What did she say?" was how Bernard welcomed his wife home.

She could not find the right words to summarise her two-hour-long conversation with Beth. Tears were pouring down his face because of not knowing where he stood. They both had hoped it was a simple case of resemblance between the girls, despite Esther going out that morning with him reaffirming this was the lady in question.

"I am now a mother of six," she finally replied. "Clara was what her husband had asked that she be called despite knowing it was not his. Sadly, he did not see her. He might have died what could have been your death."

Esther called Clara hers in line with the tradition. Polygamy is part of this society. So, there are several cases where a man would come home with children born of him elsewhere. His legal wife would open not just her house to rear them with those born of their union but also her heart to love them the best she can. So, she put it in Bernard's head that this innocent and their children would be second cousins until they each turned 20.

"Do I really have to accept this paternity?"

"Well, we will then need to have her DNA done without her knowledge," she replied. "But you, Beth, and I know it is pointless. She already has two mothers. And I do not think Nicolas would have had a problem with the four of us sharing her. He is certainly happy they have found us. This woman has already gone through a lot, so we must not add to her sorrow."

The couple arranged to meet with Beth during school hours to iron out things between adults, away from the kids. The results of the test could not have been closer and clearer. They had to keep Bernard's spell out east away from the children's knowledge as they had to this point done, especially with Clara having already told her classmates where she was born.

"Otherwise, we would have questions to answer earlier than we plan to," said Esther. "Kids these days are better at piecing the puzzle together than we were in our days."

The girls broke the news to their mates, who were glad two individuals had not defeated the entire school. However, Bernard and Esther were not doing well putting together a statement bold enough to convince their extended families when bringing Clara to light. There was no relative she could have been attributed to that these were unaware of.

Meanwhile, the reunion was turning into a thorn in the side for Beth. She was not coping well with seeing her daughter being grafted into another family, on top of how dealing with Bernard was waking up the devils in her. Furthermore, it concerned her how she would need to reveal to Clara that the image she had in her head was not her biological father. Of all the three adults, Esther was the one who remained optimistic that all the pieces would fit together in the end. She was the oil in the engine and trying hard to make the situation feel normal, although very far from it.

They made boundaries early in this new configuration: Bernard was not to be found alone with Beth. That imposed on him, he found an excuse to keep away from both mother and daughter as he had anyway previously expressed reluctance regarding being part of Clara's life. Therefore, when it leaked out to her mum that this was due to having limited finances, Beth uncovered her brighter side. The last four years had taken a new turn for her.

Stretching

Beth could not bring the household revenue back to what it used to be when Clara no longer drew water full-time. She had to stretch herself anew and more. This led to realising that what had all along seemed like the limit was no more than a breakable glass ceiling. Their first challenge under this new structure was letting go of having three meals a day they had become accustomed to. Breakfast came off the list, and before long, they were on a single meal. It did not bother them as they had known worse in the past. Besides, they were aware of their neighbours eating only once every two days. Her priority had shifted to Clara's future, so she was prepared to leave no stone unturned in her quest for her daughter's success.

This included coming to us and asking for funding, this time for herself. For the shy person she was, this approach indeed took her out of her comfort zone. Among her gifts were being creative and self-motivated. Her friendly personality made it easy to get on with pretty much anyone she met. She had some experience using a sewing machine since the age of nine but was unable to pursue a seamstress' career when she was given in marriage. Her firstborn's quick arrival further distanced her from her dream. She turned to midwifery, where she was not needed every day so she could still have time for her growing family. Both her grandmothers and her mother were midwives, so she picked up the skills almost naturally.

Her situation now seemed more favourable to give tailoring another go. But she was yet to touch an electric machine, as development had caused the kind she was trained on to disappear. She just happened to have a strong feeling that tailoring would better provide for her and her daughter if only she could overcome her fear of electricity feeding this sewing machine.

Beth enrolled on a course with money from Amy, Anna, and Laura, who took no time responding. All she did to win their hearts was bring banknotes to the value of $1,000 to the two present. Not many people saved this much in this nation, and it was unheard of for one earning a living in the manner she did. Only she and her daughter, knowing they had done it before, never doubted for a minute they could save up again. She could have paid for the training with this sum, but that was not what it was for. She did put it aside for their sustenance. This sufficed to cover at least 10 months. That way, she could focus on her learning, which included long hours in the workshop and facing a difficult transport system, leaving no room for another job.

Her going after learning demonstrated a great sense of responsibility for someone who earned not much, especially given her very humble background. She had to revert to her daughter being the lone provider, supplying water into the early evening, as she at least had four hours to spare after school. But, despite having no other options, she did not take the money until the ladies had agreed to be repaid. She was already morally indebted to them for what they were doing for Clara and wanted not to be an extra burden.

Rewards

Returning to school gave Beth the confidence to see the future as a battle she could win. Her outlook and transformation amassed her many friends in the process. Those in her neighbourhood started to fight over her when she projected the image of one doing well for herself. They wanted to know what was new in her life and how they could join in. But being out of the door long before dawn and not back until after dark was not a sacrifice any of them would make.

Beth was rediscovering happiness because of doing what she loved; she looked forward to every day. She was certain to be in control of her life going forward, imagining nothing but success, for she had found out that winning commenced with adopting a positive mentality. She understood that dreams had to be followed up with actions. This often meant starting all over a few times, and that courage was permanently a requisite.

Clara equally walked with her chin up, optimistic about life, progressively drifting away from the horrible past for which she was not responsible, despite the scars she carried. Her mum's rebirth had triggered her own. She came off the burden of supplying water. Both back to it occasionally was to provide for the elderly and the incapacitated near their home, free of charge. Beth was instilling in her daughter charity, without which themselves could not have been where they now were. What they had received from Amy, Anna, and Laura was an example of the help that had come to them at crucial moments. Therefore, she felt it right to keep the light burning.

Our biggest satisfaction was seeing these two following their hearts and fearing no obstacle, especially Clara, who was more exposed to the influence of others. Hence, we stood not in her way when she decided to take nursing, despite Amy sensing she might be suitable for a law degree study. She loved interacting with her classmates and asking questions that demanded taking time to answer. Beth also, three weeks into her course, while chatting away with two of her colleagues, let slip that she was able to make clothes already.

"How can that be when all we are at now is cutting papers?" asked one of them.

The conversation moved in the classroom. What sounded like a joke raised serious interest.

"A seamstress is a dreamer," the teacher told the class. "But action must ensue."

She wanted them to know that they were artists. Therefore, she asked them to imagine something and then project ways of bringing it to life. Next was making sure it was sellable. It had to go on someone's body to see what credits it would get from the beholders. A good or bad rating is all a step forward and to be taken cheerfully.

"Fear has no place in this profession."

There was some fabric to play with that day. So, the teacher asked Beth to come up with a design, and she obliged. She first drew it on the board and explained how the pieces would fit together. To the surprise of all, she made the machine sing like a musical instrument.

"Did you not say that you had never touched an electric one before?" a colleague interrupted.

Well, the loan from the ladies had a surplus that she invested in this brand and model the moment she had sight of it in the workshop on the induction day. She practiced in the evening, going to bed late every night, and all day at the weekend. Hence, she was ahead of her mates. She knew what she wanted from this course. Therefore, she did not wait for all the learning to be given but self-taught herself as much as possible.

It took her four hours to complete a sample for the teacher, who put it on and walked to the principal and her colleagues. They all not only complimented her but rushed out to see the creator. They desired the same. The person who taught marketing advised of its potential to sell. This being Friday, she gave the students the homework to return on Monday with a plan to make money out of Beth's garment if it was duplicated.

Whereas everyone brought back an average of six pages of written words, most of which making little sense, Beth returned with $342 in cash. She had spent her Saturday canvassing on her street, door-to-door. The teacher had sufficiently elaborated practical marketing principles, which had registered into her head. Among these were the notion of someone's natural market and proactive ways to make oneself a place therein. The advantage of having classes taught in Lingala and other national languages, if outside of the capital, although filled with French words, is that lessons incorporate local realities and proverbs. In this manner, students like Beth and her colleagues, most of them having never graduated from elementary school, learnt very quickly.

Her street consisted of 600 compounds of 25 metres by 25 each. It was straight and as sandy as a beach. Walking it felt like going backwards. Every step buried the foot deep; it took time to bring it out and deploy the other. The wearing of flip-flops burned feet. Those with an income to afford themselves proper shoes or trainers picked up a lot of sand to the point that their experience was worse than that of the former category. Hence, one can imagine what Beth's day was like. But she spared no effort.

Starting at #89, hers being #87, she walked on to #599 with no one placing an order. However, because each woman there liked what she wore and the sample she showed them, both made from the same fabric, she was encouraged to cross over to #600 and work in reverse. This side was hit-and-miss until #2, getting the $2-dollar deposit she demanded per order, advising that the balance of $3 would be needed on delivery. She offered them eight swatches and designs to choose from. Then she measured them up as all orders were *MTM* (made-to-measure). Back to her side of the street, there was nothing from #1 to #85.

Her instinctive attitude could have been that her neighbours at #85 and #89 were not supportive. But she had faith that they, and everyone else who did not commit on this occasion, would buy when the need would be there. Ending her day with 171 customers, including her own order, to bring herself luck, a 28.5% of her street, was not bad business, even to her untrained mind.

What she learnt most from this exercise stayed with her longer. It had crossed her mind several times to quit by the time she reached #299. She was trying to talk herself out of going to the rest of the addresses, reasoning that nobody would order when they could buy *prêt-à-porter* in town. Besides, a few of these families knew her and could not tell when she had become a dressmaker. An even more compelling voice told her to stick to water drawing as it had always worked for her. Further was the fear of selling and the reality that it was hard to create interest in someone, in contrast to people needing water daily. But she ordered all these negative influences out of her head when she remembered how difficult it was to land her first water contract out east and also in the capital.

It mattered little what people thought when a teacher's statement came to mind:

"Legwork is crucial to sales, and the latter the heartbeat of a business."

Given the width of each parcel and perpendicular roads intervening every 10 plots, Beth had walked over 15 kilometres to bring back that deposit. She was left aching but believed in it bearing fruit as, in the future, customers would be coming to her more than her going after them.

Chuffed, she aimed higher, nonetheless not dismissing that most purchases from her street were out of emotion, compassion, and even curiosity. People noted her courage and liked that she was fighting to lift herself out of her less privileged situation, although their own was not much better. She was aware of how tough it would get when she would move into areas where she was not known. However, nothing was going to make her tone down. She did not hide her ambitions.

"How many more pieces before I am a millionaire?" she asked during a finance class.

Her colleagues laughed, but it did not bother her as she was the only one out of them already in business. She anticipated getting more sales from each one of the five streets on either side of hers. The teacher wrote 171 x 10 x 5 =? on the board, and Beth could not come up with the answer. Someone else resolved the equation for her.

"Oh, thanks! A long way to go then; but will get there one day."

In her support, all 10 in the room, including the teacher, signed for a shirt. They loved the classy fabric she brought them the following week and chose a single design from the few they described and that she drew on the board. She charged a premium for not meeting her *MOQ* (Minimum Order Quantity) of 50 pieces per group. Even those struggling to part with a fiver paid 40% and the rest two months later.

A month in the workshop, from 8.00 a.m. to 6.00 p.m., Thursday, Friday, and Saturday, she completed the orders from her street and class with the help of two colleagues. This was counted as their practice. After all the expenses, including paying these two a tenner each per day worked, Beth enjoyed 20% earnings. She also gave them each a shirt, free of charge. This fulfilment gave her a spring in the step. The noise of her prowess reached the principal, who asked her to organise a uniform for the school, for they did not have one.

She shared what she had in mind, and the principal and the four students called in to participate in the design agreed to have the uniform in conservative but beautiful colours. They went for a shirt and a skirt, and a tunic for the workshop. Her ability to listen to others paid off when she turned up with the samples. The entire establishment loved it, and she bagged a three-set order from each of the 550 attending. The 30 staff members also enlisted for an attire for each workday of the week, unfortunately passing the cost to the students the following year, in tuition. This institution expanded to 1,500 students in three years thanks to the visibility the uniform created.

Witnessing all this, we asked ourselves, "What were all these students doing before they were enrolled?" We also wondered, "How many more are still missing out on being formally educated or trained for a profession?"

The school went on to offer full vocational programmes, leading to employment or Uni, and was forced to turn away many applicants yearly. Meanwhile, Beth was getting richer because the school refused to take anything from her business, even though the uniform was sold on-site, and she used the workshop at no cost. For the principal, her work promoting the school and giving students practice time and wages was a way of paying back.

She became their ambassador, speaking in disadvantaged suburbs to help recruit school dropouts, so they were not inundated only with those from near the school as it was not in a poor area. Her story as one who, until *yesterday,* drew water for a living was captivating. It contributed to the school opening three new centres, as many saw themselves in her and yearned to emulate her. Likewise, she was always willing to help.

Giving Back

Beth's achievement gave her the confidence to approach more families, time permitting, making those long walks as though she still was cash-strapped. Both streets on either side of hers led to 419 individuals signing up, following her timidly selling them the idea of Christmas presents. That gave her the courage to revert to her own street and sell more than the first time there, thanks to most households having many children.

This activity would extend to New Year's, and Easter clothes, which kids in the Congo customarily receive during these seasons in place of imported toys. Beth put a lot of work into retention, visiting these families when she could, to see if her apparel lived up to their expectations. These efforts generated orders of more than 3,000 sets within a five-kilometre radius of her home. Everyone was proud of the business they saw coming out of the ground. The selling point was seeing what she wore sit well on her silhouette, for she no longer put on any dress unless it was the work of her own hands.

A lot of bravery went into landing these contracts, for she worried those she approached could mistake her for a beggar. But knowing that her life hung onto a passion turning into a career was sufficient to accept any misconception of her by any. As any salesperson would acknowledge, her skills propped her up in desperate times. Boosting her morale was looking back at how far she had come. Then, thinking that if she had got where she now was, she could get farther with a little added determination, all fears evaporated. She did show up for herself every day.

Beth surprised the children whose parents ordered clothes for these three festive seasons with free outfits on their birthdays. This was for up to 12-year-olds. She delivered them herself. Hence her day started at six in the morning. No child had a good day if out on their birthday ahead of their gift arriving. This was about who Beth had become to them than the package. Turning 13 was not something they looked forward to anymore.

With children attending school wherever they could be admitted, Beth's beneficiaries spread the word among their peers and extended families—and who would not want a freebie on their birthday? Therefore, soon orders were coming in from all over her commune. But, it became impossible to personally be all over the place at the same time. Thus, she delegated and turned up here and there, which still thrilled many and always attracted new customers.

Her generosity earned her a name change to that of *Tantine Beth* (Auntie Beth) over the neighbourhood, initiated by the youngest. The popularity that ensued forced her to make blue-and-white public school uniforms. Seeing what she was becoming, Laura briefed her on the necessity of visual branding. She was about to impose on Beth her new appellation, but a prompting came to bring her to the table.

"Pole-Pole," Beth said.

This is Swahili and simply means *slowly*. But, unsure it really brought out what was inside her head, she asked Laura to bear with her while she experimented with how it resonated if changed to *Kidogo-Kidogo* (little-by-little), as to say step-by-step. This, in turn, being two syllables longer, she thought it could be difficult for non-Swahili speakers to pronounce.

It was good to see her getting her head around it, disagreeing and then agreeing with herself, unconsciously proving that hidden in her was an analytical mind. She took a week to decide and convinced herself that Kinshasa deserved some recognition for the chance it had given her. Therefore, there could be nothing better than opting for a Lingala slogan. She leaned towards *Muke-Muke*, which is *Kidogo-Kidogo*, to remind herself of how coming to the capital was achieved by taking multiple small steps. Waiting for an NGO or angels to airlift them to safety might have had a different outcome.

The Name

The new name still required to align properly with the local mentality and beyond, for Beth was aware of the division tribal diversity caused. She was thinking out of the box and envisaging her business reaching out to other provinces sooner or later. Therefore, she did not want to rebrand when entering each one of the main four linguistic regions of the Congo. A quick thinker, she picked on how the French language unified this nation. Hence, she went for *Petit-à-Petit…!* It being *Muke-Muke* sat well with children, for it was found in a recital that was part of their early elementary school textbooks.

Laura further pointed out the need for a logo, explaining that Beth was the image associated with her business. But she seemed to have it all figured out. That recital indicated that a bird never constructed its nest with all the materials readily present. Therefore, a bird with a piece of grass on its beak and adding it to a partly completed nest best conveyed the message. The name was placed under the image in a semi-circle, leaving the public to finish the sentence with *"l"oiseau fait son nid"* (the bird builds its nest) each time they read *"Petit-à-Petit…!"*

It was all fun but equally a reminder to keep moving forward no matter how small the steps they were making in life. It was an effective marketing tool that incited children to get their parents to buy them only Tantine Beth's products.

She was delighted when Laura surprised her with labels, packaging, and other promotional materials like school notebooks and pens with her branding on. These came with machines, so she could brand them in-house after that and save both time and money. However, brand awareness caught her unprepared to handle increasing demand.

She kept her feet on the ground thanks to Laura serving as her mentor. She had to step in when she sensed that growth was starting to cause an imbalance in Beth's life, leaving her with no time for herself. She needed someone to help her learn how to manage workload and equally success. None of us was as well qualified as Laura, who had been prosperous since her mid-twenties. It was somewhat inconvenient with her being around only when she could squeeze in a week to be with us in the Congo. Thankfully, video conferencing was already on the scene, although full of caprices on the Congolese side.

By this time, Beth had the funds to acquire an additional machine to put embroideries on clothes to keep up with the trend. The same machine also helped place school names and logos on children's tops. This set her apart from competitors who were unaware of her sneaking into their backyards. She made safeguarding every customer already gained a priority, thus guarateeing repeated business.

All this hard work pushed up her market share and reputation as customers acknowledged she had them at heart. With that, her work brought in a high enough income to allow some extravagance, although saving remained her leitmotiv and expansion her pursuit. Progress was further occasioned by making uniforms for over 30,000 pupils throughout her district. Private schools were lucrative accounts, for parents who sent children there had some money to play with.

What Goes Around, Comes Around!

Beth's way into the private school sector started with her generosity—giving before receiving. Her next-door neighbour had just passed away after a short illness. He was survived by his stay-at-home wife and their two children, seven and nine. She noticed them not going to school since the burial, which had been two weeks. The fees due at the end of the previous month were unpaid. Beth's heart sank. She knew what it was like to have a child not attending school.

Instead of being vengeful, because this was one of the families that had never purchased from her, she took them to school the next morning. Their mum was left wondering by what magic she was going to get them readmitted. She forked out $100 a head for that quarter. The children asked why she was doing this, but she just took the receipts and bid them, "See you later!"

I was furious with her as she related this to us, questioning how on earth she could get involved when Clara's schooling still depended on others and herself owing for her own training. I could not share this with my partners, fearing they, too, might be unimpressed. But she was not yet done testing my patience.

She had witnessed the admission clerk rebuking these two for the tattiness of their uniform, which she had also noticed. Therefore, she ran to town and purchased the fabrics with which their uniform was made. That evening, she measured them up and produced a replica over the weekend, despite it being compulsory to wear only what the school sold. It was necessary to prevent the establishment from finding out that the boys had taken their money elsewhere. But her perfectionism betrayed her as she had corrected the other supplier's inattention to quality. Her neighbour was called in to say where such a high quality had come from rather than telling her off. Beth was in. This was five months to the end of the school year.

She delivered the samples. The embroidering of the logo sealed the divorce between the school and its long-standing purveyor. She further made more sets for her neighbour's children so that they could look neater and more refreshed than their colleagues. Their teachers awarded them the uniform cleanness prize monthly until the end of that year.

Beth's resolve to win this institution as a reference was evidenced in how she meticulously tailored every piece. The laying of the buttons, stitching spacing, sizing, fitting, fabric quality, ironing, folding, and packaging all spoke highly of her professionalism. She had outclassed the previous vendor in every aspect and contributed to the dismissing of any lurking contender. Hence, from that moment on, she did not rest on her laurels because of witnessing how a decade-long loyalty had vanished in front of a valuable alternative.

Therefore, instead of the 720 sets the former contractor sold, Beth's offer was double but at the same price as her predecessor's. This was her response when the disposed firm tried to come back with improved quality. She was keen to put a foot in the door, so she understood that some sacrifice had to be made, however, not at the expense of a healthy profit margin. This told how merciless some suppliers were when it came to charging their customers.

Realising what she had got in return, I apologised for having jumped the gun. She would not have obtained this contract had she been selfish and ignored her neighbour's suffering.

"The younger child's uniform was in its third year," she said. "His brother had used it for two years, thanks to their mother going for a size bigger."

I interpreted all of this for my partners. Unlike me, they had been nodding long before getting to the part that changed my attitude.

Going forward, Beth received orders from future customers a year in advance. With that, her delivery was ready by summer, which was three months ahead of school resuming. Her preserved relationships with the nuns and priests facilitated her entry into most schools of their faith. And seeing her evolving, they claimed to have contributed hugely to who she was becoming. They believed her confidence emanated from their convents; else, she would not have made herself a place in Kinshasa. All of which she accepted for evident reasons. She lost nothing in letting them have the glory. Besides, she was not one to fight over something of no significance.

Nonetheless, Beth went from them humbled and grateful because of hearing one of the nuns revealing that she had always prayed for her since leaving them. She wished the city to be kind to Beth and each one of her efforts to yield a hundredfold. The two of them were very close during her time there. She visited her and Clara several times at home to let them know they were not alone. Yet, she knew no more about them than that they had fled the general insecurity situation out east. The nun in charge of personnel also disclosed how she had struggled to replace her. No one she gave a chance to came close to her in timekeeping, cooking, housekeeping, gardening, or anything else. She had hired and fired more than she could count.

Patience

Church-affiliated public schools displayed Beth's products on their premises so parents could contact her directly as rules to not be involved in trading applied to them. Soon, she was dressing the clergies throughout the capital, starting where she used to be employed. It was proof that relationships are worth privileging over remuneration. She would have missed the opportunity to gain these invaluable referrals had she not borne with patience the peanuts they paid her at the first convent in Beni and thereafter.

"I would be a liar if I pretended to have known, at the time, what working for the nuns would lead to," she said, humbled.

They told their congregations overseas how Beth sponsored children with books and donated meals to their malnutrition centres. As a result, orders poured in from neighbouring countries, giving her the means to extend her charitable actions. She planned to return to where her relationship with the clergies started, taking her products to them in person to say thank you. But she would be beaten to it with pictures of the Beni and Kisangani clergies in her clothes presented to her, when she was requested to attend the end of the school year event at her last employer's. She was shown to both students and parents as a role model.

Such belief in her, coupled with her staunchness, led to competitors pushing their boundaries. Amid this, she learnt that one had to spend money to make money. She responded to those who imported quality goods by investing in local manpower. And, despite nothing being smooth sailing, more than 200 individuals worked for her on three sites by the end of her fifth year of trading. A top-notch downtown shop of her own, targeting non-nationals, unintentionally took her products beyond Africa.

This was how a diplomat at the end of her service asked for exclusivity to market Beth's line all over Western Europe. Thus, in no time, she was bringing Beth prizes from festivals held in cities with a remarkable African presence. At these events, not only Africans turned up in her clothes, but all who had a connection with the continent. Others also purchased out of curiosity or in support upon hearing of the story behind the brand.

This partner had served her country in six African nations spanning 18 years, and the idea of going home to no new overseas assignment traumatised her. All other times, she was made aware of where she was next headed before the end of a mission. Back home, she would be a civil servant with no benefits compared to what she had abroad. She had always admired the Congolese's love for clothes. Her three years there were spent getting to know the people, and, where appropriate, she dressed as colourfully as them. Therefore, meeting Beth was an opportunity to keep ties with the country she started calling *home.*

Through this relationship, Beth would travel to Europe for the first time, ahead of other African nations. A bad dream woke her up in the middle of the flight, and she screamed out for help when she realised she was not in a car. Her embarrassment increased with lights coming back on and people turning to look at her. She shyly admitted to her compatriots on either side of her seat that she was new to this mode of transportation.

"You will get used to it," said one, as though predicting the future.

Back home, local businesses ordered uniforms because of Beth's rebate on bulk purchases. She won price wars, thanks to Laura introducing her to having fabrics mass-produced for her in less developed countries. The pieces were also cut there and came ready for sewing. This strategy helped to achieve 70% savings on raw materials and cut production time by 60%. Cheap labour in the country meant she had a competitive advantage over importers of end-products. Refusing to complete garments abroad was not out of patriotism but understanding where in the process profits lay. And to which if one showed the Congolese savings, then such is guaranteed loyalty.

But she was not winning all the time. Sometimes she lost or had no control over issues arising, and all were part of the learning curve. One such lesson happened when she was compelled to pay a huge sum in taxes twice because the agents who called to collect cash disappeared with it. Her own staff also did the same. To stop it from happening again, she decided to pay through her bank, despite opposition from the authorities that hers was not a big entity to do so. But soon, they would acknowledge her transparency and grant her relevant rebates. She still donated all these refunds towards road maintenance, erosion fighting, and stagnant rainwater removal close to where her businesses were based.

Advocacy

Beth went on to be solicited to speak at schools and other venues to build up fellow females to stand up for themselves. She wanted them to dissipate the ideology that said that not much could come out of women, whatever the level of education they could attain. It had to change. Her story of leaving the village with only what was on her back and succeeding wherever she set foot was awakening. Being seen as an agent of development became a label she could not rid herself of.

"We are in this together," she replied to the honour. "If I am perceived as doing any good, it is because you, this city, welcomed me with open arms first."

She was referring to all who helped her with advice, room, food, work, kindness, business, and more. Then she would highlight her commitment to see girls come off the burden of carrying water and being able to overcome illiteracy. Only the word *rape* was painful to pronounce when attempting to spell out as clearly as she could that *it must stop*, because she still hurt.

"No one, males included, is safe until all females are," she always ended, implying that the world would be extinct without women. Therefore, they are to be protected, whatever the cost.

This explained her acute interest in the welfare of the children where she lived and worked; for she employed many mothers. To that end, she remunerated her employees decently. However, those who knew nothing of her journey did not appreciate her asking them to work extra or learn to budget. She had developed a strong belief in merit and took every opportunity to instil the same in others. Hence most fulfilling to her was not seeing a garment coming off a production line but knowing that those who made it would meet their family obligations, and as a result, their daughters, and also sons, would be safe.

Distance Learning

Committed to teaching by example, Beth was not satisfied with where she was in her life. She placed more demands on herself, making small steps that moved her forward. She filled up her secondary school education gap taking private

French lessons and soon reading every evening. Starting with an hour, she soon found herself with four hours a day to dedicate to learning, thanks to being her own boss.

The Congo offered no distance learning nor a programme that suited her busy life. So, Beth was off to Europe thrice a year, four weeks each time. She had enrolled at an establishment that allowed her to study away, visit the campus for a few in-person lectures, and sit exams. Three years on saw her complete a bachelor's degree in Business. A further two-year granted her a Master of Business Administration with an emphasis on Entrepreneurship. She was 42 by then.

Rather than accepting praise for the progress in her life, she always mentioned Laura, who talked her into this academic pursuit. She was also ever grateful to Amy, Anna, and Stella, who believed in her and gave their matchless support. The latter two visited her every time she was over to lift her up and revise materials and assignments with her, seeing they both were postgraduates themselves.

From there onwards, Beth was liberated from the inadequacy she felt in front of those who were educated. In fact, she was now fighting to remain low-key. Her colleagues, working for big corporations, and the teachers thought it was their place to instil in her the charisma that comes with one studying for or having an MBA. Furthermore, they tried to talk her into having an attitude that showed off her business success. But she had a different view. Staying with a host family in Europe helped her pick up the equality culture. There was no reverting to how people lived back home, where the rich looked down on those with less, which was the way towards which her colleagues were unknowingly steering her.

How nice that, when she received her MBA, she had been banking more than $450,000 in net profits annually for three years. She donated a 10th of it to good causes and reinvested half of the remainder to employ more people. What she got in return were ever-increasing orders. Her products were sold in 26 outlets in the country. She was running a vocational school of her own. This educational initiative extended east to the nearby Bandundu province. In total, she accommodated 780 learners in various disciplines and helped with their entry into the labour market as much as she could, including hiring some herself.

However, the fight against illiteracy remained her focus, drawing in as many women and girls as possible. She did not need to make much effort recruiting, for there were too many longing for a place. Therefore, they came in quickly wherever she opened. Equally, many were after the free uniform she offered—they left before even setting foot in the classroom. These were in their late twenties and above and considered themselves past school age.

Funnily enough, the following year saw them registering anew, using different names and even dates of birth, at which point an ID check was introduced. But this left many genuine candidates unable to enrol because an ID card was not produced until every five years, when elections were due.

This was a big disadvantage to anyone turning 18 in between and desiring to enrol. Consequently, numbers dropped sharply. Beth was compelled to let go of the uniform.

The uniform attracted crowds because it consisted of the normal female adult's attire in the Congo. She gave them two sets of wax fabrics. The choice of wax was due to most students being mothers, and the culture being that they were to dress modestly. Each six-yard gave each woman two loincloth pieces and a matching top. Having no uniform did improve retention as only those intending to learn came forward. Yet there was still not enough room for those sincerely looking to learn.

Abandoning the uniform was also beneficial because many hated being identified as secondary school students, as this was the level at this vocational institution. Worse was the general public's perception of these students as failures and illiterates.

Many victims of this misconception, the city over, were left to deal with deep anxiety and depression. Beth paid for the medical costs of 12 of such patients. She wished she could do more. They were dying in the street, rejected even by their own. Gladly, she went on getting sponsors from the organisations her Uni colleagues reached out to on her behalf. She was invited to talk about her journey, business, and humanitarian efforts each time she made it to Europe.

"When did you really step up to the mark?" an attendee asked.

"The moment I started to give to those who had lesser than me," she answered.

D-Day

A few weeks prior to Beth's graduation, she gave in to Bernard reminding her of his colleague who had a sister with a degree and would do any work if it paid. She was reluctant to employ those over-qualified, seeing all she could offer was shop floor work. Besides, the candidate lived 30 kilometres from the factory. Public transportation was chaotic. However, he came under more pressure because he had said that the owner was a cousin.

Beth called in Amy, Alvin, and me that day to see if we would instead have an admin role within our water business for the candidate. By this time, she was a non-executive partner of ours in Kinshasa. Esther was also present, in keeping with never leaving her husband and Beth alone.

The door opened, and Alvin and I stood up to welcome the two ladies. Esther remained seated. I pulled up Bernard, who seemed to not get it.

"Is it Joe?" asked one of them the moment she stepped into the room.

"Lydie!" I exclaimed.

Alvin and Amy were equally shocked but uttered nothing besides a less genuine smile. Lydie started to explain, but I insisted that we return to that later, away from the meeting. Intrigued, Bernard asked where the two of us knew each other.

"We all know her!" Amy pounced.

Lydie was embarrassed, realising who else was present.

"Very sorry!" she said. "But wait!"

She went into the bag over her shoulder and handed me an envelope the three of us recognised instantly. The hotel's receptionist had let us help ourselves to a bunch. It was still sealed, just like 11 years earlier. Not only was it the exact amount, but it was also the same three banknotes. I had marked every bill we gave to someone with a hardly noticeable black ink dot, just in case they came back accusing us of giving them fake bills, which is common in the Congo with any foreign currency. Inside was also Amy's handwritten thank-you note. It was as though some tricks were being played on us. Breaking the silence was the beautiful young lady with Lydie, leaping and screaming at the appearance of Beth, who, until this point, was not in the room yet.

"Mama! Mama! Mama!"

She hugged Beth, giving her no chance to see who it was, for she was taller than Beth. But blood spoke!

"Mungu Wangu!" (My God!)

That was the only thing she said. They did not let go of the hug, but when they did, at Esther's insistence, Beth appeared without life, *again*. We sat her on the couch and brought the portable air-conditioner closer. Opening her eyes, she kept them on the young lady who had not taken hers off her all this time either. They embraced anew, crying, realising that this was real.

"Clara…ni dada! Clara…ni dada!" (…it is your big sister!)

Workers who could come off production crowded the doorway, fighting for a glimpse of what was going on inside the room. It was the first time they heard that Clara, all along known to them as the boss' only child, had an older sister. For those of us familiar with the story of this family, we did not hold back our tears. However, we wondered who could have been the architect of this scenario.

Heaven-sent

Lydie's father had been acquainted with a certain girl at the hotel where he worked. She confided in him that she was taken by force from her family out east. She was a slave to a rebel who would become a government dignitary. It broke his heart to see a man of 66 years abusing a 12-year-old. He helped her escape, consequently deserting his employment and nightly finding refuge in another part of the city. He hid until the nation's first elections in over three decades removed this man and his partners from the political arena. No one knew where they went.

Hence, a year later, when we met Lydie, she was uncomfortable at this hotel. The memory of what Emma, now *her* sister, had gone through was still fresh and made her want to throw up. This was why she did not desire our money. She had kept her eyes open in the hope of bumping into us and just handing it back to us without a word. But, not having a business at the time, she did not know under which name we operated or if we were still around. Checking us out at that address was a no-go for her.

She could not say how that day, out of her few handbags, she had picked up the one with our envelope in it, seeing she had parked it when she had lost any hope of our paths meeting again. Well, they did, resulting in the now 25-year-old Emma reuniting with her mother. She would be saddened, however, to hear that she had to wait a bit to hug her sister she had not seen in 13 years. Beth calling out to Clara had given her the impression that she was within reach, whereas she was in her second year of a bachelor's in Canada.

"How did she get there?" Emma asked, surprised.

"You fill me in first," replied Beth, frenetically sobbing.

Lydie's parents were heaven-sent. They had done all they could to care for Emma for nine years amid sending her to school. Lydie helped, too, when she started earning money. Now 40 and with a family of her own, she wanted Emma to be employed so she could look after herself. This was not because she considered her a burden but to not leave her parents' work half complete. She referred to her as the only inheritance her dad and mum had left her, alongside her blood siblings. Lydie had shared with Emma whatever little the family had from the day her father brought her home. Hence, Beth took in not only Emma but also Lydie, her husband, and their three children.

Sadly, Beth's desire to honour Lydie's parents with nice tombstones could not be materialised. Their burial place had since got new occupants. Big houses belonging to the rich and famous had emerged there within a year of the government declaring the cemetery full and no longer to be used. When Lydie took Beth and us to visit, it was the first time she had ever returned there since those houses started to come out of the ground. Hence, she, her husband, and Emma could only guess which homes sat on top of her parents' graves, hesitantly pointing their fingers from the street at a few.

In the Congo, the living fight over dwellings with the dead if they cannot get along sharing. Often, priests and pastors get called in to settle disputes. There were some beautiful buildings empty and awaiting mediation. We were told that kitchen utensils, for instance, were left out, and food was missing from fridges and cupboards, clearly indicating that someone had helped themselves at night. Several times, residents had heard a party going on in the house past midnight, people cooking, eating, and talking while all the household had retired. When that was heard, no one dared to interrupt.

"So, why not leave?" Jan asked.

"Well, good question," Lydie said. "I wish I knew what to answer."

The Penny Dropped

Bernard and Esther dropped in at Beth's workplace frequently, despite having rejected the opportunity to work for her to avoid any risk of one crossing the line. Emma inquired about this closeness, and her mum always said they were family. But this would change with Julie coming out of the arrival gate at the Geneva airport a month after Emma's emergence. Beth had flown Julie, her parents, and Lydie in to join her and her daughters for her graduation.

Emma's suspicion went through the roof. Her mum pulled her aside and told her things as they were; she was already an adult. Julie had also found out just four months earlier—her 20th birthday *treat*! Emma was dead quiet for about 10 minutes until Beth begged her to speak again.

"I heard you talking to Dad. You were crying. I was awake."

She was only five at the time but had not forgotten what was said that night. Only her own ordeal at the hands of several men, and finally by this one who shamelessly showed her off to everyone as his wife, made her, to some extent, ignore the pain of knowing the circumstances of her sister's birth. Nevertheless, she was comforted to know that where there was still life, there was hope. Dwelling on what had already occurred could only be detrimental and hinder any progress they, as a family, now so badly needed.

"*Papa* appeared to us," Beth informed her. "I feel his presence here. Your brothers' too."

Emma broke!

Clara caught up with them and snatched her out of Beth's arms, leading her away for a sisterly time. It had been less than 36 hours since she had joined them, but ahead of Julie and the others. Teeth gritting, Emma looked back at her mother, with compassion. Towards Clara, she put on a positive spin to the moment as they walked forward; the truth was just too hard to swallow. Amid telling each other good things, the two sisters unintentionally crept into life back east.

"It was not her fault," she said. "We are lucky to have her alive. I know you are picking up a new culture where you are, but half-siblings is not part of our vocabulary."

"What do you mean?"

"Oh! Mum has not told you yet?"

"Let me explain," said a gentle voice behind them.

They were unaware of Beth closely following behind. She made no sound as she was barefoot and enjoying the pavement along *Lac Léman* that warm evening at that end of Montreux. She requested that they return to the hotel to face Clara. It pained her to go through the details again, with even more tears than when she spoke with Emma who knew what it was like to be a victim of rape. The guilt Beth felt was more because she had long withheld the truth from Clara, who had always been with her. The three of them embraced and cried more. Overcome, they fell asleep without saying goodnight to each other, let alone calling the other rooms for this purpose.

Waking up, it was past eight in the morning.

"We cannot change the past," Beth pleaded. "We have the whole future ahead of us."

Alvin, Amy, Laura, and I landed the following day. Anna, Günter, Jan, and Stella joined us at our hotel at noon before meeting up with Beth's group for some visits the two brothers-in-law and their wives had organised.

Two days later, the graduation gave us the opportunity to appreciate how valued Beth was. Because of how she was introduced at the ceremony, not only the audience gave her a well-deserved standing ovation, but speaking invites competed for a slot in her already full diary for the rest of that year and beyond. Her story, though hard to relate, had turned sweet and inspiring—no longer to be ashamed of this side of the world. It was since referred to as a *victory over evil*. Many believed she had gone through this to be able to help others.

It was to all present—colleagues, recruiters, other organisations, and individuals—a unique product the world needed to pay for and learn from also. They took notes as she spoke. No institution could have taught her best how to keep her feet on the ground the way her experience had. She had come to this Uni with tried-and-tested knowledge that contributed a lot to her classes. She was well respected because once she had accepted to speak at an event, even before realising she would be needed in the Congo, she never went back on her word. We, too, knew this of her.

Coming to pay back Amy, Anna, and Laura within one year, and them declining and asking her to re-invest that money for another person to have work, she did just that. She returned every year to show who had benefited. When there was a need for charity, she used the savings from this account and reported accordingly.

Outbreak

While driving to her factory with the radio on one day, Beth heard of a cholera outbreak in the Kongo Central and the government's plea for help. She knew too well that poor sanitation exacerbated the general health situation in the country, but this epidemic was quickly exterminating the province. This case was of special interest to her as children were concerned. Since getting Clara to safety, she had always wanted all others to be given a chance to grow into adulthood and to be able to take care of themselves from there onwards. So, she booked me return flights out of London with her own money when I confirmed my availability.

According to the news, those most affected were the neighbourhoods with minimal hygienic facilities and where access to drinking water was beyond retardation. The town of Tshela was on the brink of disappearing. She was pierced to the heart hearing that the cause of this plague was the consumption of contaminated water, whilst knowing we had a solution.

We waited a week in Kinshasa to get the necessary permits to distribute chlorine. The supplier would tell us that a further seven-day period was needed to release the 10,000 litres we had paid for. There was a problem letting a buyer with no history in the field have access to such a huge volume because lives were involved. Soon we discovered that the true cause of the delay was because the seller was busy shopping around for supply, as no one held this kind of stock. In the meantime, people had already been dying for more than three weeks.

Arriving in Matadi, 330 kilometres to the west, this being within the province, we had a feel of the unpardonable killer. Anyone who consumed or touched this water did not escape. Infants led the way. But, as though we had not wasted enough time, the officials decided we hang around a further week before driving the remaining 180 kilometres to our destination. Additional permits were required to operate in Tshela. Fortunately, we had been through all this before, so it was not patience that we lacked. It only hurt thinking that someone could be dying that minute.

Once there, word of mouth caught us by surprise. Every household needed at least five litres to get by. They were ready to pay for it so we could bring more quickly. This showed their desperation, whereas we had planned to donate to a population in distress.

We had nowhere to turn to for more supply. There was no producer anywhere in the whole nation. The response would be to bring in a 40-tonne load of water purification tablets in a week or two, for people could not keep their hands off the contaminated water unless there was a substitute. A call to Alvin and Amy was all that was needed. They landed in Kinshasa four days after their consignment arrived by air. They wanted to help with the distribution.

We sold out in two days whilst leaving people holding cash. They were grateful for the opportunity to spend less than a 10th of the cost of 1.5-litre of bottled water from the shop to give themselves 1,000 litres of drinking water. They did not mind cleaning, decolouring, disinfecting, and purifying it on their own once a little briefing was provided. On our part, we tripled the revenues on this experiment, therefore having the means to assist further, for we had decided not to earn money from this operation. Provincial health authorities invited us to make the availability of this product permanent in this part of the country. This was because their populations relied on rivers that brought in this type of outburst, among many other diseases, time and time again.

This situation made us to reveal our core business, leading to a rash of viable orders landing in the palms of our hands, to the point that we regretted calling for the trouble we could not handle yet. We had only intended to gauge the locals' interest. Regardless of whether we were ready to establish a drilling presence there or not, the ardent need they faced denied us the right to disregard their cry for our help.

On the list of demands, we counted four medical clinics, seven schools, and over 1,800 homes in this district alone. Some wealthy people and dignitaries, although living in Kinshasa or Matadi, still had beautiful second residences in the villages we were reaching out to. However, they had not worked out how to stop this recurring destruction. Visiting the region frequently, they and their families came loaded with bottled water. So, sadly only them were safe.

Not Through Yet

Thanks to the rich who were mindful of those with less: populations in similar dire conditions to Tshela's throughout the province were beneficiaries of their goodwill. They sponsored a few villages so we could roll out a communal plan when water would become available. It was in one of these locations that we met *Matondo*. He advised us that many survivors had, over the years, relocated to places with relatively better sources of water. But he would not do like them, no matter what.

That night, we received a call from Zola, who did not know we were back in the country. He offered funding for the region. He said he had just had a strong feeling to call me, despite keeping in contact via emails since we handed the management of the drilling business to our local partners. We had returned to our homes in 2013, coming back to the Congo for the last five years sporadically for some pressing matters. Most of these times, we refrained from disturbing him.

We had not understood his insistence to start this new contract where his call found us. This was Matondo's village. Then, in the morning, Amy spotted the likeness between the two men.

"Just look at the shape of his nose," she said. "And the smile!"

"His nose looks the same as mine," I replied, giggling.

"To me, it is the sound of his voice," said Alvin. "Do they share the same family name?"

"Zola *Bawu*," (Love *Them*) I said. "Matondo *Kwa-Nzambi*" (Thank *God*).

But that means nothing in the Congo. It is more than common for none of the siblings to bear what is supposed to be their surname, sometimes sending out a wrong message that they have different fathers. To have fully meaningful names that remind someone of what their families had been through, or to express a wish for the future, is privileged.

Zola came down three days later, providing a lift to Günter and Jan, who had landed the night before. He was keen to see how we were faring with the disinfectant and whether his company could further assist. We were in Matondo's village still, and watched him being welcomed like a celebrity. Young, old, male, and female, all bowed to him. He could not conceal it anymore:

"I am *Kabeya*!"

"And I, *Mulumba*," replied Matondo.

"Basil's?" Günter asked.

"Blimey!" I reacted.

Not only were we the first to find out, but it was also the first time they had again pronounced their real names since making the change, let alone calling each other so, not even in private. Hence their cries and embraces we witnessed. We likewise responded with tears.

They had run and walked 25 kilometres that day, with the certainty that their mother would not survive, to get where they could find a lift to anywhere away from the capital, so they would not be found. They introduced themselves to those manning the station for Matadi departures with these Kongo Central names—*Zola* and *Matondo*. They loaded goods too heavy onto a lorry for a ride on top thereof. The driver cared not that they risked falling off and dying. He said to have washed his hands with the warning to hold fast onboard, insisting he always drove over the limit.

A week as porters at the maritime port of Matadi, sleeping under the stars, one lady would have compassion despite them not being the only kids there. She took them to hers in Tshela because of hearing they had been recently orphaned and this was their first time in their parents' *native* province. She had never had children of her own. But she would die of a heart attack 14 months after taking them in and putting them through school for a year.

By this time, everyone but her extended family had already accepted them as hers. They turned up soon after the burial and sold the property. A will is a waste of time in the Congo. Many had been torn and burnt while the coffin was being lowered, siblings and cousins showing no mercy for the widow and the orphans.

The poor lads turned to delivering water, first in exchange for a room here and there, before starting to get paid and finding the family that housed them longer. This was a little muddy hut they shared with goats, chickens, and ducks, but by far better than sleeping outside or moving daily. By the time school was back, they had enough for uniforms and the first two quarters' fees. But Matondo refused to enrol so he could infallibly support his young brother. He added farming to water drawing and occasionally fishing, to be on the safe side.

When we met him, he was a successful farmer and had rejected offers to go share the life that was now Zola's—something he could not have achieved without this praiseworthy sacrifice.

"It was my obligation to get him through school," he said. "We miss Basil and our parents every day. But who are we to change God's course?"

"Please, do not tell anyone who we are," Zola insisted.

This is the same with many in this book. They refused to be known. They fear, still, for their lives due to the sensitive nature of their accounts. Hence even some locations have been altered, but not the events.

Another surprise, but good news, is Gilbert, whose father we gave work to out east so he could pay for him to go to Uni. He is one of those we would have loved to show off, openly. But he wants his rebel's past concealed, as he is not proud of having killed his own compatriots. He studied mineralogy, but ran for parliament in 2018 and won. He strongly advocates against child-soldier and child-miner recruitment.

9

NEXT

Exit

Despite coming down with no solid project, we had the end in mind:

"*Leave people better than we found them,*" Laura had vowed.

We also had an exit strategy, although not elaborated to the bone:

"*Build, operate, and transfer to the locals,*" I had demanded when I answered Laura's call.

This exit has provided some of us with the grounds to propel to new heights.

After a decade in and out of the Congo, six years of which were kind of permanent there, it was time for Alvin and Amy to go into their second and last retirement. At 70 plus, it surely made sense. They had advised, trained, and helped many. They were grateful for the love received and relatively good health enjoyed throughout their lives, especially during this entire adventure.

It could not be said enough of their sacrifices, yet they made too little reference to such. They had missed weddings, births, graduations, burials, and other important family events, whenever they had to choose between the Congo and a set of flights home for a few days. More than often, they had patiently dealt with some illnesses and bugs, not to mention the weekly in-taking of malaria pills and other tablets people their age are subject to. The culture was not easy to absorb, but they managed to and witnessed lives change. In an effort to blend in with their hosts, a few local words were picked up here and there and used regularly.

"We are taking home more than we are leaving here," was Alvin's address at Ndôto (forever *Basil's Well* to him and Amy) when we were back with a barbecue to bid all farewell.

"Take care of your little ones for me," said his wife.

She was referring to Basil's fate but not saying his name for fear of spoiling the good time everyone was having around the food. With that, she broke because of being prohibited from revealing the guy behind the 30 wells in the vicinity. It took a lot of restricting herself, whereas it should have been great for them to know that the boys were alive, married, and rearing children.

Similarly, Laura considered it a mission accomplished based on what Beth had achieved, what Clara was up to, and Emma's mysterious emergence. She had not had time to visit as she wished long before we got to what we considered to be the end. The weight of the family and businesses on three continents had taken its toll. A career-progressing cardiologist husband had been plausibly unselfish to share her with us this long.

She, however, left with one regret:

"My investment never made it in the Congo as I had wished."

But as far as the rest of us were concerned, we owed her for every grain of success. For as much as our enterprise was hard rowing, she was the reason for our coming this way.

Günter and Jan were somewhat disappointed that their spouses could not relocate. But, their participation added much to our strength. It was, in great part, because of them that we had, directly and indirectly, installed water wells. They knew we could not reach out to everyone despite our good intention, but as Günter said it, we were "leaving a trail that other entrepreneurs could branch out into highways". They still monitored the business from their homes, keeping in contact with our local partners and key employees monthly long after we had called it a day.

Themba had returned home in 2013 to a fatality, leaving us heartbroken. He, his wife, their children, and their own families had not holidayed together during our crazy six years of plenteous sweating. This is because each time we broke up, he could not do more than relax at home; the body refused further travelling due to the hard work undertaken. Now that he was there to stay, they drove to the Cape province and had a good time. On their way back, two of their grandchildren jumped in his car to enjoy their grandparents' collection of tales from life.

Then came a sharp bend on a steep part of the road. An oncoming big coach descending hit them heads-on, sending their almost new vehicle flying in the trees. None of them four survived. The rest of the family's convoy of five cars was a few minutes behind. They stopped at the scene of the accident, disbelieving their own eyes and hearing from passengers on the coach how their driver had been speeding all the way.

We saw Themba everywhere in our minds while in the Congo. The locals loved him because of speaking Lingala fluently within a year of coming over. He felt at home to the point of demanding a Congolese name the moment people started calling him *Zulu*, which he was not comfortable with because he was of the *Ndebele* tribe. Hence, they named him *Elombe* (the *mighty one*, a *warrior*). This was due to his unbending attitude to bring water to the surface once a borehole started, no matter the obstacles. He loved the name, especially that *Themba* means *hope*.

His children returned all his royalties to the Congo to further the business their mum, Fikile, had set up. She had come to live with him in 2011. Her enterprise consisted of *taking in orphans and finding parents to adopt them*; in exchange, she created jobs for these parents. She believed this to be a more inclusive structure for children to grow in than an orphanage. Thus, she deprived society of any chance of labelling these children. Most of her time was spent with these parents and *their* children to ensure things worked like within a normal family setting.

It was out east in the Congo that Fikile started this venture. She joined us when she heard we had nowhere to leave Job and the other kids. Her social work qualifications and experience came in handy. Her being this busy, he got on with drilling wells undistracted by her presence. Inspiration was not needed when she, too, sought to be nicknamed: *Kitoko* (beauty) suited her very beautiful face and charitable heart.

Tino wanted to linger around longer, but Peru was calling to replicate what we did in the Congo. He is waiting for me to go live there with him for at least two years. He went back speaking Lingala, so he pointed out that I will remain indebted to him until I, too, go master Spanish from within Peru, on a project. I cannot wait!

As for me, the Congo is home, no matter where in the world I am. I always return. Half of me is there. This could be seen in how, where I could have retracted, I clocked in 155 flights in the first 18 months of this project, in and out of the country, to meet the demands of my other ventures. One time, I made it to four continents in seven days for meetings I could not miss. However, while away, I was restless until I was back to water drilling. I often felt guilty for leaving those who were supposed to be my guests working, although for a short period each time.

Our little achievement—much is yet to be done—is there to spark an interest in others to come to lend a hand. Where permits would be granted in the future, and provided funding is available, my burning desire is to provide water through hydro-stations in a private-public partnership. This is because drilling everywhere in residential areas is not fully environmentally friendly. This takes courage to admit.

Together

To my fellow Congolese who have benefited, this project has been a reminder of the importance of working together, which our ancestors have long taught us. The world (not only the Congo) needs more investors and leaders to come together to reach out to more people with water. This venture was realised with the locals' desire, belief, time, effort, and money. Hence all credit to them for overcoming their individual ego, even today, paying for what they consume. Taking responsibility has played a big part in bringing clean water to themselves, and it has helped them avoid illnesses and free up their children so they can attend school, and safeguard women.

The possibility of employment that has come to some of them, although very few, cannot be undermined. Likewise, many in Administration have realised how rendering their processes hard to complete holds back advancement. Their red tape had unnecessarily prolonged the duration of this mission, leading a few of my friends in the UK to believe that I had a wife in the Congo. I only managed a smile each time they brought up the subject. Today, I am pleased to reply with what we have achieved by upping sticks in the Congo:

- Six years working under somewhat harsh conditions
- Four more years of visiting now and then to support local partners

- A least 470 communal wells drilled
- A minimum of 164,688,000,000 litres of clean water produced a year
- Catering to 7,520,000 people
- A modest $82,344,000 turnover at the cost of $0.0005 a litre to the consumer
- Permanent and temporary employment for more than 4,500 individuals

Let it be noted that had double this production been all in Kinshasa, the capital would have said goodbye to water penury.

Nonetheless, where each beneficiary family of five had three school-age children and supposed that only one of them furnished their household with water, we would have freed up 1,504,000 children from the labour of carrying water and allowed them to attend school. However, with children more than 20 times this number nationwide still under this yoke, any boasting on our part would be in vain. Hence, since the handover, I have been very preoccupied with finding ways to take this water provision initiative to the next level, that even this manuscript has had to wait to be put together until one phone call in March 2020 changed my priorities.

"If I do not make it, Joe, I trust you to publish!"

It was Laura. Her husband had dialled and put her on loudspeaker. She had been unwell for a couple of weeks with

Covid-19, and it was the closest to home it had struck for me.

"You are going nowhere," I replied.

But Laura passed away the day after in intensive care.

"Sleep tight, my motivator," was the message tagged to the flowers a local florist delivered on my behalf, to be placed on her tomb, the pandemic having not permitted me to travel.

"Your *DNA* is undeniably all over whatever I become tomorrow," Clara said at the restricted burial. She had braved the highway from Montreal to San Francisco—3,000 miles—and back. She was completing her degree in medicine, hence her immense gratitude.

10

AFTERWORD

The work we carried out in the Congo is of utmost importance, which I am proud of. But there are still too many out there in great need of water, let alone clean water. I had promised them that I would speak widely about their situation and highlight what they could achieve with targeted support.

Now, I hope this publication will act as a magnet for investment where individuals would join hands to save lives while not losing their capital. Charity, where water and similar necessities are concerned, has failed to live up to expectations. The world knows it.

Those in dire need of water can pay for it if made available and close to them.

Our experience and research have revealed that a sum of $4,000,000, for instance, would allow any well-intended operator to cater to 5,000 individuals within the first year of getting adequate equipment, tools, and materials on the job. The fifth year would see them serving 2,000,000 people daily and floating the business to empower the locals, with at least $32,000,000 in the bank. At that point, there would be 500 water purification plants in service in the beneficiary region if the project shifts to produce all the gears in-house.

However, whatever one decides on to help alleviate the water calamity, we advise:

Don't donate; invest!

Printed in Great Britain
by Amazon